"一带一路"能源合作年度报告 2021

ANNUAL REPORT ON ENERGY COOPERATION ALONG BELT AND ROAD 2021

中国 - 东南亚
能源合作报告

REPORT ON ENERGY
COOPERATION BETWEEN
CHINA AND SOUTHEAST ASIAN
COUNTRIES

电力规划设计总院 ◎编著

CHINA ELECTRIC POWER PLANNING & ENGINEERING INSTITUTE

人民日报出版社
PEOPLE'S DAILY PRESS

图书在版编目（ＣＩＰ）数据

中国 - 东南亚能源合作报告：汉文、英文 / 电力规划设计总院编著
. —北京：人民日报出版社, 2022.1
ISBN 978-7-5115-7145-8

Ⅰ . ①中… Ⅱ . ①电… Ⅲ . ①能源经济—经济合作—国际合作—研究报告—中国、东南亚国家联盟—汉、英Ⅳ . ① F426.2 ② F450.62

中国版本图书馆 CIP 数据核字 (2021) 第 203979 号

书　　　名：**中国 - 东南亚能源合作报告**
作　　　者：电力规划设计总院

出 版 人：刘华新
责任编辑：周海燕
封面设计：绳婉朦

出版发行：**人民日报**出版社
社　　　址：北京金台西路2号
邮政编码：100733
发行热线：（010）65369527　65369509　65369512　65369846
邮购热线：（010）65369530　65363527
编辑热线：（010）65369518
网　　　址：www.peopledailypress.com
经　　　销：新华书店
印　　　刷：北京领先印刷有限公司
法律顾问：北京科宇律师事务所 010-83622312

开　　本：889mm×1194mm　　1/16
字　　数：390千字
印　　张：19
版次印次：2021年10月第1版　　2021年10月第1次印刷

书　　号：ISBN 978-7-5115-7145-8
定　　价：198.00元

主　　编　　杜忠明

执行主编　　胡　明　　姜士宏　　何　肇　　方晓松

技术顾问　　谢秋野　　孙　锐　　徐小东

编写人员　　王顺超　　王姝力　　赵子坤　　谢逸天　　曹　阳　　王　珺　　张瑞卿

　　　　　　赵金飞　　丁　剑　　包维宁　　徐　悦　　傅天伊　　李　忍　　张鹏飞

　　　　　　龚　媛　　韩艺童　　蔡文畅　　甄自竞　　黑　阳　　何学鑫　　刘　畅

EDITOR IN CHIEF	DU Zhongming		
EXECUTIVE EDITOR	Hu Ming	Jiang Shihong	He Zhao	Fang Xiaosong
TECHNICAL CONSULTANT	Xie Qiuye	Sun Rui	Xu Xiaodong	
CONTRIBUTORS	Wang Shunchao	Wang Shuli	Zhao Zikun	Xie Yitian
	Cao Yang	Wang Jun	Zhang Ruiqing	Zhao Jinfei
	Ding Jian	Bao Weining	Xu Yue	Fu Tianyi
	Li Ren	Zhang Pengfei	Gong Yuan	Han Yitong
	Cai Wenchang	Zhen Zijing	Hei Yang	He Xuexin
	Liu Chang			

前言

　　东南亚国家是中国陆海相连的友好邻邦，也是共建"一带一路"重要合作伙伴。中国 - 东盟建立对话关系 30 年来，双方走出了一条团结奋进、合作共赢之路，经贸合作不断深化，2020 年，东盟成为中国最大贸易伙伴，中国则连续 12 年保持东盟第一大贸易伙伴地位。

　　近年来，东南亚地区经济发展形势向好，能源和电力需求快速增长。同时，在全球碳中和的背景下，中国与东南亚国家均面临能源转型的全新课题，实现更加安全、更加绿色、更加经济、更加包容可及的能源转型是双方的共同目标。中国和东南亚国家在能源领域合作基础良好、优势互补明显，能源转型领域合作正在成为双方经贸和投资合作新的增长极。开展中国 - 东南亚能源合作研究，全面梳理东南亚国家国民经济和能源电力行业概况，准确把握东南亚国家能源发展的潜力和增长点，系统分析双方能源合作的基础和重点领域，有助于双方在能源领域开展更大范围、更高水平、更深层次的合作。

　　《中国 - 东南亚能源合作报告》是电力规划设计总院"一带一路"能源合作年度报告之一，聚焦东南亚地区的能源发展现状与未来趋势，为中国—东南亚双方开展更具针对性的务实合作提供参考。本报告共分为五个章节，主要对东南亚地区基本情况及能源行业发展情况进行了全面梳理，对中国与东南亚国家能源合作现状及未来合作机遇进行了分析预测，对未来中国 - 东南亚能源合作的重点领域提出了下一步行动建议。

　　在此对本报告编写过程中提出宝贵意见的领导和同事表示诚挚的感谢。因经验和时间有限，报告难免有疏漏之处，恳请读者批评指正。

《中国 - 东南亚能源合作报告》编写组

2021年10月

FORWARD

Southeast Asian countries are friendly neighbors of China connected by land and sea, as well as important partners of China along Belt and Road. Over the past 30 years since the establishment of China-ASEAN dialogue relations, the two sides have embarked on a road of unity, progress and win-win cooperation, and economic and trade cooperation has been deepened. In 2020, ASEAN becomes China's largest trading partner, while China maintains ASEAN's largest trading partner status for 12 consecutive years.

In recent years, the economic development situation in Southeast Asia has improved, and the demand for energy and electricity has increased rapidly. At the same time, in the context of global carbon neutrality, China and Southeast Asian countries are facing a new topic of energy transformation. It is the common goal of both sides to achieve a safer, greener, more economic and more inclusive energy transformation. China and Southeast Asian countries have a good foundation for cooperation in the field of energy and obvious complementary advantages. Cooperation in the field of energy transformation is becoming a new growth pole of bilateral economic, trade and investment cooperation. The prospective study of China-Southeast Asia energy cooperation is helpful to comprehensively sort out the overall situation of national economy and energy and power industry in Southeast Asian countries, deeply exam the energy development potential in the region, and systematically analyze the basis and key areas of energy cooperation between the China and Southeast Asia, so as to propose action suggestions for comprehensive and practical cooperation in the energy field between the two sides in the future.

Outlook for China-Southeast Asia Energy Cooperation is one of China Electric Power Planning & Engineering Institute's annual reports on the Belt and Road Initiative energy cooperation, focusing on the current situation and future trend of energy development in Southeast Asia, and providing reference for more targeted and pragmatic cooperation between China and Southeast Asia. This report is divided into five chapters, which mainly combs through the general situation of Southeast Asia and the development of energy industry in the area, analyzes the current situation and makes projections about future cooperation chances in the energy sector between China and Southeast Asian countries, and puts forward suggestions for the next step in the key areas of China-Southeast Asian energy cooperation in the future.

We would like to express our sincere thanks to the leaders and colleagues for their valuable comments and suggestions during the preparation of this report. Due to limited experience and time, it is inevitable that there are deficiencies in the report, therefore we would also be grateful for any feedback readers should wish to provide.

Authors of Report on Energy Cooperation between
China and Southeast Asian Countries

October, 2021

目录

03 中国 - 东南亚国家
能源合作现状

04 东南亚能源
发展展望

中国 - 东南亚国家能源合作行动建议

附录

CONTENTS

Overview of Southeast Asia

Energy Industry Development of Southeast Asia

Report on Energy Cooperation between China and Southeast Asian Countries

03 **Current Situation of Energy Cooperation between China and Southeast Asian Countries**

04 **Energy Development Outlook in Southeast Asia**

Suggestions on Energy Cooperation between China and Southeast Asian Countries

Appendix

01 东南亚国家基本情况

东南亚国家
基本情况

　　东南亚地区是沟通亚洲与大洋洲、印度洋与太平洋的重要枢纽，也是中国在"一带一路"沿线的重要合作伙伴。近年来，东南亚地区经济高速发展，营商环境不断提升，在亚太地区扮演着愈发重要的角色。中国与东南亚地区共同构建了一系列政府间国际合作机制，双方依托各项机制不断拓展合作领域，深化合作内容，在贸易和投资领域均获得长足发展。

1 东南亚地区概况

1.1 国家及地区简介

东南亚（SEA）地区位于亚洲东南部，由中南半岛和马来群岛组成，东濒太平洋，西临印度洋，处于亚洲与大洋洲、太平洋与印度洋的十字路口，包括文莱、柬埔寨、东帝汶、印度尼西亚、老挝、马来西亚、缅甸、菲律宾、新加坡、泰国和越南等十余个国家。东南亚总面积443.56万平方公里。东南亚国家联盟，简称东盟（ASEAN），成立于1967年8月8日，是东南亚地区重要的国家间政治、经济、安全一体化合作组织。东盟以首脑会议和部长会议作为主要决策机构，奉行全体一致原则、不干涉内政原则、y-x原则和协商原则，在有效推动东南亚国家一体化发展的同时彰显了各国追求平等、互相尊重的精神。

表 1.1.1 · 东南亚主要国家基本信息表

国家	加入东盟时间	2020年人口（万）	陆地面积（万平方公里）
菲律宾	1967	10811.7	29.97
柬埔寨	1999	1671.9	18.10
老挝	1997	727.6	23.68
马来西亚	1967	3236.6	33
缅甸	1997	5440.9	67.66
泰国	1967	6962.6	51.3
文莱	1984	43.3	0.58
新加坡	1967	580.4	0.07
印度尼西亚	1967	27062.6	190
越南	1995	9646.2	32.9
合计	—	66072	443.56

数据来源：世界银行，商务部国别指南，本报告研究

2020 年，东南亚国家人口合计约为 6.6 亿，占全球总人口 8.6%，过去 5 年年均增长率为 1.1%，与全球平均水平基本一致（1.1%）。东南亚地区人口结构较为年轻，大部分国家人口中位数年龄在 30 岁及以下，低于全球人口中位数年龄（30.9）。

图 1.1.1 · **东南亚主要国家人口中位数年龄**

数据来源：Worldometers，本报告研究

1.2 宏观经济发展情况

1.2.1 东南亚主要国家 GDP 总量稳定增长

2020 年，东南亚国家 GDP 总量达到 2.96 万亿美元（2010 年不变美元价格），位列全球第五大经济体。2000 年至 2019 年，东南亚主要国家 GDP 总量基本保持稳定增长，GDP 增速基本维持年均 5% 的水平，显著快于全球平均水平（2.5%）。近年来，东南亚地区的经济高速发展主要得益于全球制造业的产业转移效应。东南亚国家总体良好的营商环境和人口红利吸引了大量外资。

长期以来东南亚主要国家以外向型经济为主导，东南亚国家与全球经济环境关联度较高，经济表现容易受到全球宏观经济的影响，总体经济韧性仍有待提高。2008~2009 年全球金融危机期间，国际市场需求的萎缩对东南亚制造业带来显著负面影响。2019 年，中美贸易摩擦升级，全球单边主义和保护主义抬头，大国间的关税博弈对东南亚国家的价值链贸易造成了一定冲击。

2020 年，全球新冠疫情爆发，东南亚国家经济陷入严重衰退，东南亚 GDP 总量同比下降 4.0%。疫情期间，东南亚各国实施严厉防疫措施，国内消费和投资下滑，生产与进出口贸易骤减，服务业亦受重创，东南亚地区产业链和供应链受到新冠疫情剧烈冲击，部分外向型企业面临严重财务困难。

图 1.2.1 · 东南亚主要国家2000—2020年GDP总量及增速

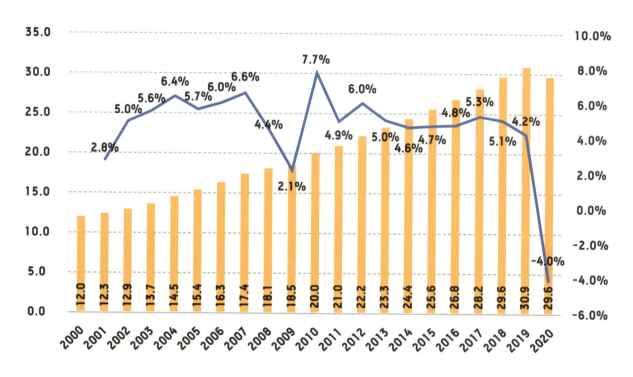

单位：千亿美元（2010年不变美元价格）

数据来源：世界银行，商务部国别指南，本报告研究

　　过去十年间，东南亚国家中经济增速较快的国家有老挝、柬埔寨和越南。其中老挝和柬埔寨主要依赖于农业和自然资源行业的快速发展；越南除农业之外，制造业同样发展迅猛，连续数年实现贸易顺差。菲律宾、缅甸、印度尼西亚和马来西亚经济呈中高速增长态势，其中菲律宾经济增长主要动因有国内基础设施建设、外国直接投资、消费支出、海外劳工和业务流程外包等方面；缅甸以农业和自然资源行业作为主要经济发展驱动点；印度尼西亚和马来西亚经济发展结构以零售业、制造业和种植业为主导。泰国经济发展领域集中于消费品、零售业和制造业，受资源禀赋和技术要素限制，泰国制造业结构调整和技术升级缓慢。

图 1.2.2 · 东南亚国家2010—2020年GDP累计增速对比

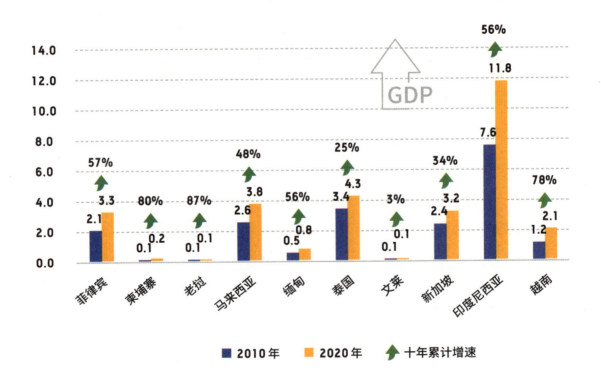

单位：千亿美元（2010年不变美元价格）

数据来源：世界银行，本报告研究

● **东南亚地区多数国家人均 GDP 显著低于全球平均水平**

2020 年，东南亚多数国家人均 GDP 不足 5000 美元，地区整体人均 GDP 约为 4485.2 美元，显著低于世界平均水平（10925.7 美元），其中老挝、柬埔寨、缅甸等国位列联合国发展政策委员会发布的最不发达国家（LDC）名单之中。

图 1.2.3 · 东南亚主要国家2020年人均GDP

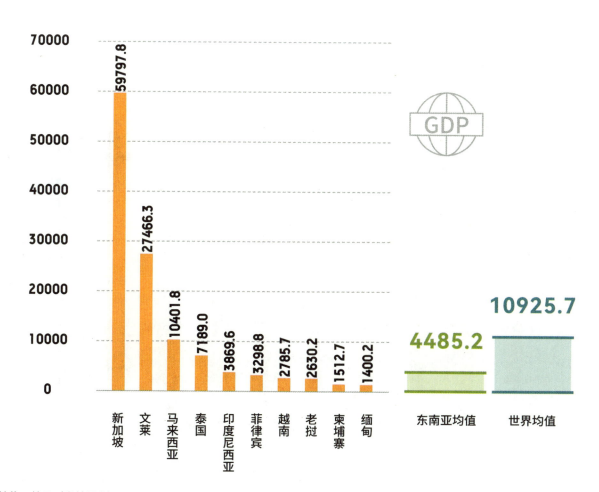

单位：美元（当前汇率）

数据来源：世界银行，本报告研究

1.2.2 东南亚第三产业占 GDP 比重超过一半

　　东南亚各国间的产业结构差异较大，一定程度上体现出国家经济发展水平及发展阶段的不同。其中，新加坡、马来西亚、泰国等国家服务业占比较高；柬埔寨、缅甸等国农业占比较高，均超过 20%；文莱、印尼等国工业占比较高，约为 60%。在全球发展中国家中，东南亚地区发展中国家第三产业占比相对较高，其中菲律宾、马来西亚、泰国等国的零售业是最为重要的经济领域之一。

图 1.2.4 · 东南亚地区各国2020年产业结构

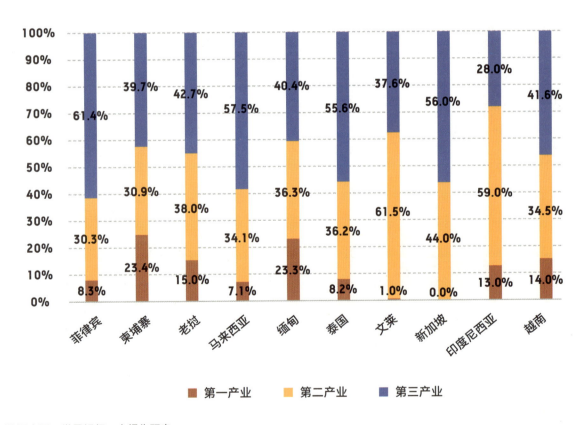

数据来源：世界银行，本报告研究

据近五年东南亚国家整体产业结构演变情况分析，第一产业和第二产业占比呈缓慢下降趋势，第三产业占比逐渐提高，部分国家出现"去工业化"的苗头。为进一步夯实工业根基、缓解产业结构"去工业化"过程，东南亚各国纷纷制定"工业 4.0"发展战略，根据各自的资源禀赋、产业基础和市场需求，以制造业为核心打造重点发展行业，并带动传统产业升级，促进新型产业发展。

2020 年的新冠肺炎疫情严重阻滞了东南亚各国经济转型和产业结构调整的进程，相当一部分基础设施和重点项目被迫停工停产，如泰国"工业 4.0"中的东部经济走廊（EEC）项目投资于 2020 年上半年下滑近 50%。东南亚整体第二、第三产业缩减幅度较大，第一产业占比回升。

图 1.2.5 · 东南亚国家2016—2020整体产业结构演变

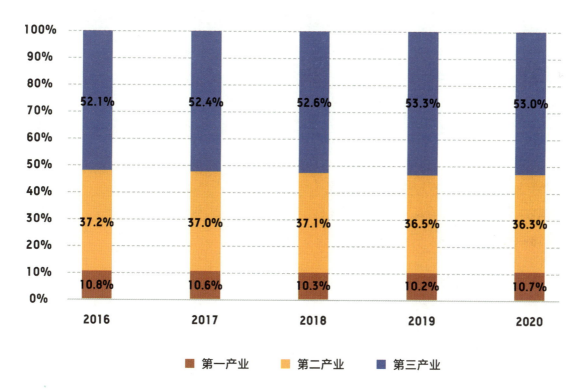

第一产业　　第二产业　　第三产业

数据来源：世界银行，本报告研究

1.2.3 东南亚国家债务情况总体良好

东南亚地区各国债务情况总体良好，其中新加坡作为高度外向型经济体，国债和外债比例很高；其余发展中国家的负债水平一定程度上体现出各国过去十年经济发展速度。以越南为例，因其经济活动规模与频率的增加，经济增速相对较快，负债率增长也较为显著。

表 1.2.1·东南亚主要国家债务水平指标

国家	国债GDP占比（2019）	国债GDP占比（2010）	外债GDP占比（2020）	外债GDP占比（2010）	主权信用评级（2019）
菲律宾	39.1%	50.196%	27.2%	36.872%	Baa2
柬埔寨	29.57%	—	56.9%	31.983%	B2
老挝	64.13%	—	52.6%	41.040%	—
马来西亚	56.32%	49.56%	67.6%	52.868%	A3
缅甸	39.19%	—	—	—	—
泰国	41.47%	26.901%	36.7%	27.1%	Baa1
文莱	2.63%	—	—	—	—
新加坡	109.37%	101.45%	471.3%	417.015%	AAA
印度尼西亚	29.29%	26.166%	39.4%	26.796%	Baa2
越南	57.36%	40.7%	47.1%	—	Ba3

数据来源：世界银行，World Population Review，Ceicdata，商务部国别指南，本报告研究

1.3 营商环境和国家风险

1.3.1 东南亚国家营商环境处于发展中国家相对领先水平

营商环境便利度排名能较为具体地反映目标国家或地区的监管环境是否利于当地公司的启动和运营。据世界银行发布的 2020 年营商环境排名显示，该年度东南亚国家营商环境排名总体良好，多数国家营商环境排名居世界前半。

图 1.3.1 · 东南亚国家世界银行2020年营商环境排名

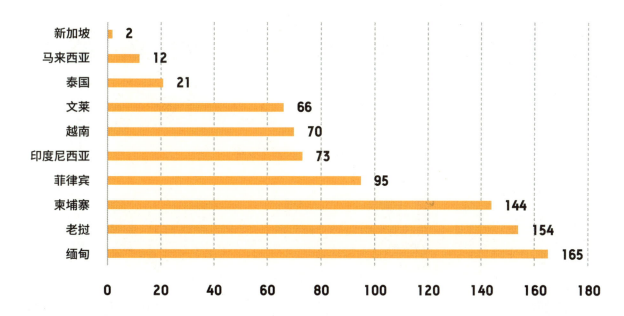

数据来源：世界银行，本报告研究

据 2010 年和 2020 年世界银行发布的营商环境评分分析，东南亚国家过去十年里营商环境整体上了一个大台阶。其中较为突出的国家有文莱、印度尼西亚和越南，评分增长均在 10 分以上。

图 1.3.2 · 东南亚国家2010—2020营商环境评分对比

数据来源：世界银行，本报告研究

面对国内外经济形势的急剧变化，东南亚国家积极改善营商环境，放宽市场准入，调整行政管理机制，出台投资便利化措施。其中，菲律宾政府通过颁布《营商便利和有效政府服务法令》来促进政府办事效率提升；印度尼西亚政府推出了振兴经济配套计划，以改善贸易限制多、土地征用难、行政效率低等现存弊端；越南政府完善其国家"一站式"服务机制，大大提高其公共服务效率。得益于东南亚国家采取的一系列针对营商环境提升的举措，各国在近年世界银行发布的营商环境排名中总体表现逐年提高。

1.3.2 东南亚国家风险评级总体良好，展望基本稳定

在经合组织（OECD）和中国出口信用保险公司分别发布的国家风险评级中，东南亚国家总体评价良好。根据 OECD 的评级，多数国家在 0 — 4 之间，较往届评级基本维持稳定。根据中信保发布的国家风险评级，多数国家处在 3 — 5 级区间，属于政治和经济形势中等至良好，商业环境稳定但需改进，国家风险水平中等至较低的水平，展望均为稳定。

国家风险评级较高的国家主要集中在柬埔寨、老挝和缅甸等国。其中，柬埔寨国家风险主要体现于社会稳定性存在隐患、司法独立性不高、支柱行业竞争力下滑等方面。老挝国家风险主要体现于债务风险水平较高、国际储备规模较小、水电项目潜在外交隐患等方面。缅甸国家风险主要体现在民族和解进程缓慢、经济增长可持续性不足、采矿业投资受环境保护因素制约等方面。

表 1.3.1 · 东南亚主要国家风险评级和展望

国家	OECD 国家风险评级		中国出口信用保险公司 国家风险评级	
	当前评级	上届评级	评级结果	展望
文莱	—	—	3	稳定
柬埔寨	6	6	7	稳定
印度尼西亚	3	3	5	稳定
老挝	7	7	6	稳定
马来西亚	2	2	4	稳定
缅甸	6	7	8	稳定
菲律宾	3	3	5	稳定
新加坡	0	0	1	稳定
泰国	3	3	4	稳定
越南	4	4	6	稳定

数据来源：OECD，中国出口信用保险公司，本报告研究

1.4　中国与东南亚国家合作概况

1.4.1　政府间国际合作机制

● **东亚合作机制（东亚峰会能源部长会议、东盟地区论坛）**

首届东亚峰会于 2005 年 12 月在吉隆坡召开，提出促进东亚能源安全。第二届东亚峰会能源部长会议成立了能源合作工作组。随后的各届东亚峰会能源部长会分别以能源领域不同主题展开磋商。

东盟地区论坛成立自 1994 年，是当前亚太地区最具影响力的多边对话机制，共有含东盟、中、美、俄、日、韩、印度等国在内的 27 个成员国。2008 年 4 月在新加坡举行了东盟地区论坛能源安全会议，各成员国充分交流相关经验。

● **"10+3"合作机制（东盟和中日韩能源部长会议）**

首届东盟和中日韩能源部长会议于 2004 年 6 月在马尼拉举行，并随后每年召开一次能源部长会议。该机制下由能源高官会负责能源合作具体运作，设有能源安全、石油市场、石油储备、天然气、可再生能源与能效等五个论坛。

● **中国一东盟自贸区框架**

得益于中国一东盟自贸区框架搭建，中国与东盟国家经贸合作发展突飞猛进。自贸区建设分为三个阶段，各阶段均对应着不同的经贸合作特点。

第一阶段为 2002 — 2010 年，是中国与东盟自贸区组建阶段，主要签署了一系列自贸区法律文件，如：货物贸易协议、服务贸易协议、投资协议等。第二阶段为 2011 — 2015 年，是自贸区建成阶段，期间中国与东盟国家开放贸易投资市场，促进商品流通，互相成为对方的第一大和第三大贸易伙伴。第三阶段为 2015 至今，是自贸区升级阶段，在原有市场开放的基础上注重商品贸易和投资效率的全方位提升。

● 澜沧江—湄公河合作（LMC）机制

澜沧江—湄公河合作是中国与柬埔寨、老挝、缅甸、泰国、越南共同发起建设的新型次区域合作机制。自 2016 年澜湄合作首次领导人会议以来，六国共同创建了合作机制框架，确定了政治安全、经济和可持续发展、社会人文三大支柱，以及互联互通、产能、跨境经济、水资源、农业和减贫五个优先合作方向。

2020 年 8 月，李克强总理出席澜湄合作第三次领导人视频会议，就加强澜湄合作提出六点倡议：将水资源合作推向新高度，拓展贸易和互联互通合作，深化可持续发展合作，提升公共卫生合作，加强民生领域合作，践行开放包容理念。

● 大湄公河次区域合作（GMS）机制

大湄公河次区域包括柬埔寨、越南、老挝、缅甸、泰国和中国云南省。自 2012 年起，GMS 于交通、信息等领域开展全方位互联互通建设，建立经贸合作区和工业园区推动贸易便利化发展。同时成立 GMS 铁路联盟加快铁路建设，推动泛亚铁路网络形成。2014 年推出的《区域投资框架执行计划》进一步加大了能源、农业等领域的投资。

● 区域全面经济伙伴关系（RCEP）协定

区域全面经济伙伴关系（RCEP）于 2011 年由东盟发起。2020 年 11 月 15 日，第四次 RCEP 领导人会议以视频方式举行，会后东盟 10 国和中国、日本、韩国、澳大利亚、新西兰共 15 个亚太国家正式签署了《区域全面经济伙伴关系协定》。此次 RCEP 协定的服务贸易和投资开放水平高于东盟与中日韩等国各自的"10+1"协定，纳入了高水平的知识产权、电子商务、竞争政策、政府采购等现代化议题，也形成了统一的规则，大大降低运营成本，减少不确定性，发挥区域内经贸规则"整合器"的作用。

同时，RCEP 协定充分照顾不同国家国情，给予最不发达国家特殊与差别待遇，促进本地区的包容均衡发展，使各方都能充分共享 RCEP 成果。

1.4.2 双边贸易

中国与东南亚国家双边贸易可根据贸易规模和贸易平衡两因素大致分为三个阶段。第一阶段是 1995 — 2001 年，在这一阶段，中国与东南亚国家双边贸易起步，进出口规模存在一定增长，中国与东南亚贸易差额出现小幅逆差。第二阶段是 2002 — 2011 年，这一阶段是中国与东南亚国家双边贸易高速发展阶段，双方在此期间共建中国 - 东盟自贸区，双边贸易规模年均增长率达 25% 以上，中国与东南亚国家贸易逆差增加。第三阶段是 2012 年至今，中国与东南亚国家双边贸易放缓，总体规模仍在增加，中国逐渐进入对东南亚贸易顺差阶段。第三阶段的形成主要原因有金融危机后经济放缓带来的影响，以及取消关税等措施对贸易的刺激程度下降。中国和东南亚双方需要寻求进一步深化双边贸易关系的契机。

随着中国与东南亚国家货物贸易的快速发展，双方逐渐将贸易领域拓展到服务行业。2007 年双方基于中国—东盟自由贸易区签署了《服务贸易协议》，推动双边服务贸易自由化。协议签署以来，双方服务贸易进出口规模得以不断增长，互访人次屡创新高。当前，东盟已成为中国五大服务贸易伙伴之一。

1.4.3 投资合作

近年来，中国与东南亚国家间的投资获长足发展。2011 年东南亚成为中国企业海外投资最大市场。2019 年中国对东南亚直接投资流量 130.24 亿美元，年末存量 1098.91 亿美元；2019 年末，中国共在东南亚设立直接投资企业超过 5600 家，雇佣外方员工近 50 万人。

从投资的行业构成情况来看，中国在东南亚投资第一目标行业为制造业，2019 年直接投资流量 56.71 亿美元，同比增长 26.1%，主要目标国为印度尼西亚、泰国、越南、马来西亚及新加坡。第二目标行业是批发和零售业，2019 年投资流量 22.69 亿美元，同比下降 34.7%，主要目标国为新加坡。列第三位的是租赁和商务服务业，共计 11.89 亿美元，主要流向新加坡、老挝和印度尼西亚。电力/热/燃气/水的生产供应业以 8.98 亿美元位居第四，流向国主要有越南、印度尼西亚、柬埔寨和老挝。

图 1.4.1 · 2019年中国对东南亚地区直接投资主要行业

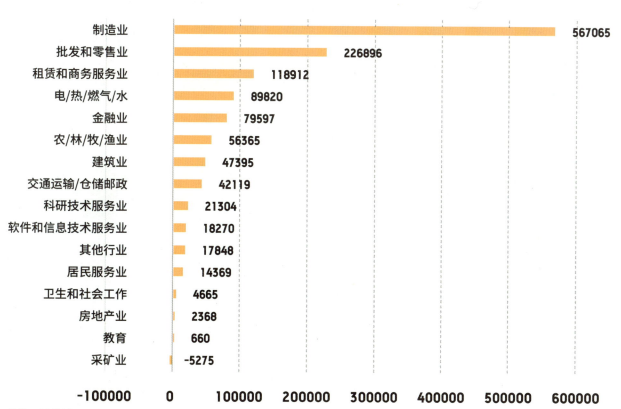

单位：万美元

数据来源：2019年度中国对外直接投资统计公报，本报告研究从投资流向的国家构成来看，新加坡以 48.26 亿美元位居首位，同比下降 24.7%，主要投向批发和零售业、租赁和商务服务业、制造业、金融业等；印度尼西亚和越南分别以 22.23 亿美元（+19.2%）和 16.49 亿美元（+43.3%）居第二、第三位，均以制造业、电力 / 热 / 燃气 / 水的生产供应业为主。

图 1.4.2 · 2019年末中国对东南亚地区直接投资存量情况

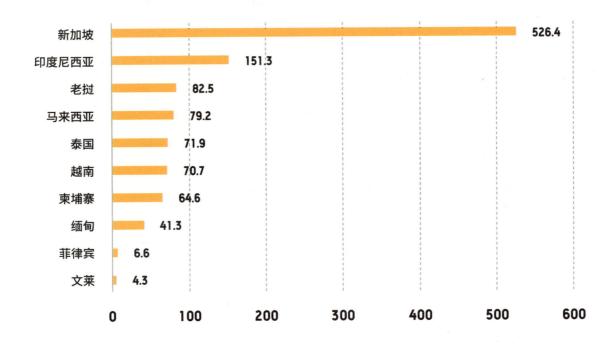

单位：亿美元

数据来源：2019年度中国对外直接投资统计公报，本报告研究东南亚地区市场对华投资总体也呈现高速增长态势。2018 年东盟国家在华新设外商投资企业 1709 家，同比增长 35.5%；实际投资金额达 57.2 亿美元，同比增长 12.6%。

东南亚国家中，新加坡 2018 年在华新设外商投资企业 998 家，实际投资金额达到 52.1 亿美元，投资规模位居首位。马来西亚以新设外资 454 家，实际投资 2.1 亿美元 的规模居于次席。越南和菲律宾对华投资在 2018 年实现大幅增长。

图 1.4.3 · 2018年东南亚地区国家在华投资统计

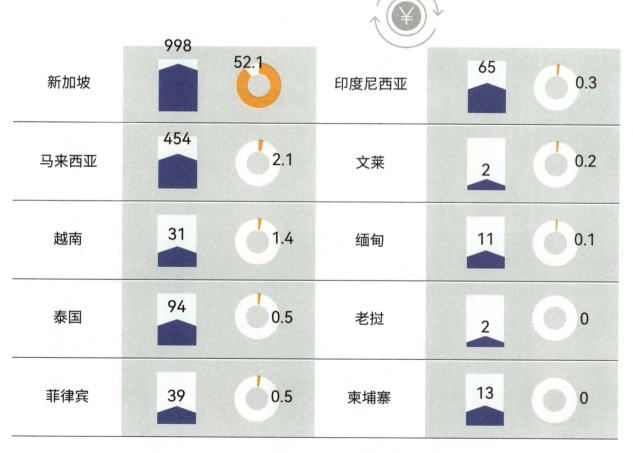

■ 新设企业数　■ 实际投资额

单位：亿美元

数据来源：2019中国外商投资报告，本报告研究

02 东南亚国家能源行业发展情况

东南亚国家能源行业发展情况

　　东南亚地区具有一定的油气资源，可再生能源资源禀赋较好。近年来，该地区能源生产及消费正处于总量持续增长、结构不断调整的过程，能源自给率相对较高。电力需求维持高速增长态势，可再生能源增速较快，有望取代气电成为装机总量最大的电源品种。部分地区已开展电力互联互通建设，但总体仍处在相对初期的阶段，电力互联发展潜力较大。

2.1 能源资源

2.1.1 化石能源

● **东南亚地区多数国家煤炭资源较为匮乏**

东南亚地区煤炭资源储量 421 亿吨，约占亚太地区煤炭储量总额的 9%，占全球煤炭储量总额的 4%，多数国家煤炭资源相对匮乏，煤炭消费主要依赖进口。东南亚地区的煤炭资源主要集中在印尼、越南等国家，其中印尼煤炭储量最为丰富，约占东南亚地区煤炭总量的 80% 以上，其煤炭资源主要分布在苏门答腊和加里曼丹两岛。

图 2.1.1-1 · 东南亚国家煤炭储量

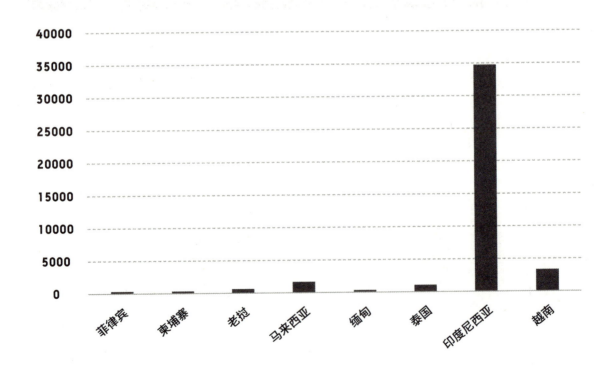

单位：百万吨（mt）

数据来源：国际能源署，英国石油公司，本报告研究

东南亚地区具有一定油气资源储量，但产能呈现萎缩趋势

　　东南亚地区石油资源储量 15 亿吨，约占亚太地区石油储量总额的 24%，占全球石油储量总额的 1%。东南亚地区石油资源主要集中在越南、马来西亚、印尼、文莱等国家。其中越南石油储量最为丰富，约占东南亚地区石油总量的 40%，其石油资源主要分布在湄公河三角洲盆地、南昆山盆地等地区，但越南石油开采成本普遍较高，石油产量并不大。马来西亚石油储量约占东南亚地区总量的 27%，是东南亚地区第二大石油生产国，其石油资源主要集中在马来半岛的东海岸、沙捞越和沙巴地带。印尼石油资源较为丰富，且开采成本具有一定竞争力，是东南亚最大的石油生产国。近年来，由于油田老化、投资力度减小、国际油价下跌等原因，东南亚地区石油产量总体呈逐年下降的趋势。

图 2.1.1-2 · 东南亚国家石油储量

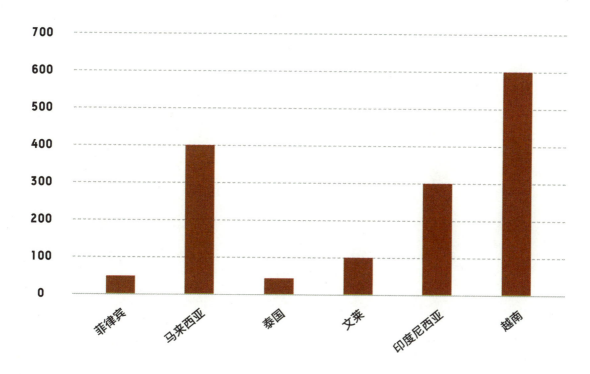

单位：百万吨（mt）

数据来源：国际能源署，英国石油公司，本报告研究

东南亚地区天然气资源储量 3.6 万亿立方米，约占亚太地区天然储量总额的 21%，占全球天然气储量总额的 2%，天然气储量丰富，但各国储量及分布差异较大，主要集中在印尼、马来西亚、越南等国家。其中印尼天然气资源储量最为丰富，占东南亚地区天然气储量的 40% 左右，是东南亚最大的天然气生产国。然而，其天然气产量并不稳定，受北美非常规天然气开采的冲击，近十年来印尼天然气的生产量呈下降趋势。马来西亚的天然气储量仅次于印尼，约占东南亚地区总量的 25%，主要分布在西部沿海和东部沿海地区，近年来天然气产量呈上升趋势。

图 2.1.1-3 · 东南亚国家天然气储量

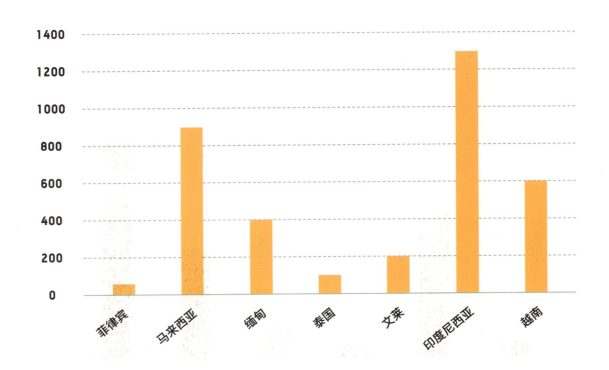

单位：十亿立方米（bcm）
数据来源：国际能源署，英国石油公司，本报告研究

2.1.2 可再生能源

● **东南亚地区水能资源禀赋较好**

以油气和煤炭为代表的化石能源是东南亚地区电力发展的主要来源，除此之外，东南亚地区水能资源丰富，水电技术可开发量超过 150 吉瓦，是东南亚地区重要的清洁能源来源，主要分布在缅甸、印尼、越南、老挝等国家。其中缅甸水能资源丰富，技术可开发量超过 46 吉瓦，约占东南亚地区水电可开发总量的 30%，主要集中在伊洛瓦底江、钦敦江、萨尔温江三大水系，目前水能开发利用率仅有约 7%。印尼的水电开发潜力较大，但由于资源较为分散、开发成本较高等原因，目前开发程度较低，水能开发利用率不足 10%。此外，越南、老挝等国家水能资源也具有较大的开发潜力。

图 2.1.2-1 · 东南亚国家水电技术可开发量

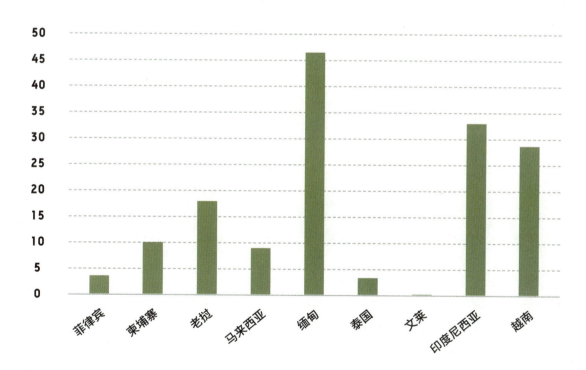

单位：吉瓦（GW）
数据来源：Hydropower & Dams World Atlas 2020, 各国规划，本报告研究

● **东南亚多数地区为风能资源次优地区**

东南亚具有一定的风能资源，风电开发潜力超过 1 太瓦，主要集中在中南半岛的越南、泰国、老挝等国家。其中越南风能资源最为丰富，风电开发潜力约占东南亚地区的一半以上。越南海岸线长度超过 3000 公里，沿海地区风能资源丰富，部分岛屿平均风速达到 8 米 / 秒，目前开发利用程度较低，未来具有较大的开发潜力。此外，泰国的东部和西部地区、老挝的中部省份等区域，具有一定的风能潜能。

图 **2.1.2-2 · 东南亚国家风能开发潜力**

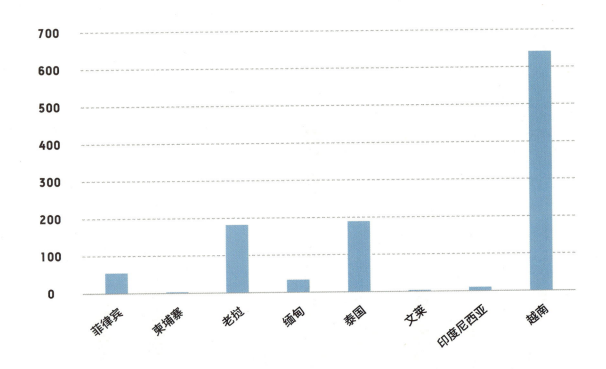

单位：吉瓦（GW）
数据来源：《Wind Future in Asia Report》，各国规划，本报告研究

● 光伏开发潜力巨大

东南亚地区处在赤道附近，太阳能资源丰富，日照时间较长，年利用小时数在
1400 小时左右，辐射强度较大，光伏技术可开发量接近 10 太瓦，主要分布在缅甸、柬
埔寨、泰国、印尼、越南等国家。目前，除越南开展了一定规模的光伏电站，其他国家
光伏资源开发利用程度较低，未来具有较大的发展潜力。

图 2.1.2-3 · 东南亚国家光伏发电利用小时数

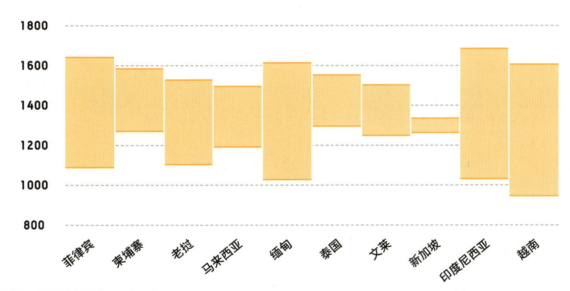

单位：利用小时数/年
数据来源：SOLARGIS，本报告研究

图 2.1.2-4 · 东南亚国家光伏技术可开发量

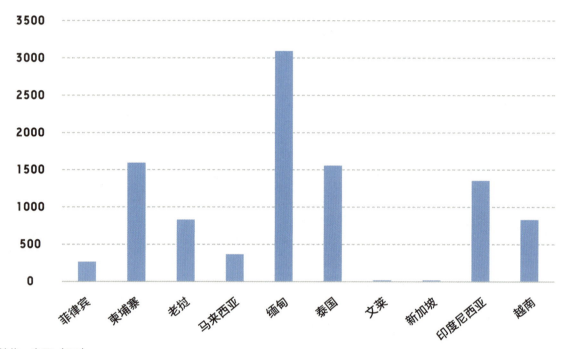

单位：吉瓦（GW）

数据来源：《东盟国家光伏规模化发展创新模式研究》，东盟能源中心，水电水利规划设计总院

生物质能源发展潜力较大

东南亚多数国家农业较为发达，同时拥有广袤的森林资源，农产品和木制品产量较高，生物质资源丰富，在全球生物质能源领域具有重要战略地位，生物质理论可开发量超过 400 吉瓦，其中越南、印尼、马来西亚、泰国、缅甸等国开发潜力较大。据统计，东南亚地区每年来自农林部门的生物质原料超过 5 亿吨，其中最具潜力的生物质原料包括稻壳、甘蔗渣、油棕残留物和木材等，每年产生的生物质残留量超过 2 亿吨。

2.2 能源消费

2.2.1 能源消费总量

● **能源消费总量呈稳定增长态势**

2020 年，东南亚地区能源消费总量 6.6 亿吨标油。2000 年至 2019 年，得益于该地区诸多发展中国家的人口红利、全球制造业转移及各国对改善营商环境做出的努力，东南亚地区总体经济增长势头强劲，并带动能源消费总量以年均 2.9% 的幅度增长。2020 年，受到全球新冠疫情爆发的影响，东南亚地区经济出现较为严重的衰退，能源消费总量随之出现较大程度下降，同比下降 7.9%。

图 **2.2.1-1** · **2000—2020年东南亚地区能源消费总量及增速**

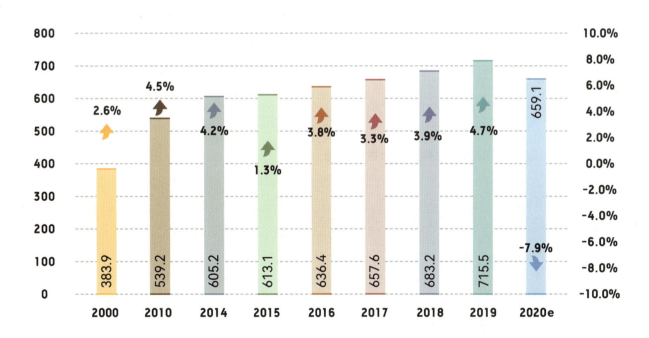

单位：百万吨标油（mtoe）
数据来源：国际能源署，英国石油公司，本报告研究

● 人均能源消费量总体偏低

2020 年，东南亚地区人均能源消费量为 0.99 吨标油／人，低于全球人均能源消费水平（1.45 吨标油／人）。由于各国经济发展水平、产业结构和能源资源禀赋的不同，人均能源消费量存在一定差异，其中文莱和新加坡人均能源消费量较高，均超过 5 吨标油／人；柬埔寨、缅甸、菲律宾人均能源消费量较低，均不足 0.5 吨标油／人。

图 2.2.1-2 · **2020年东南亚国家能源消费总量**

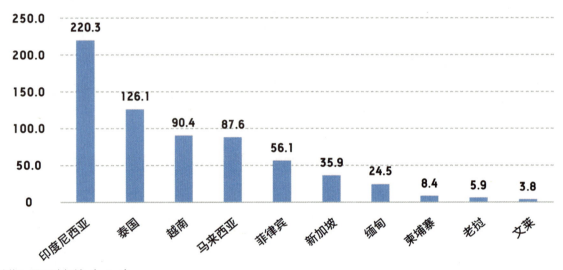

单位：百万吨标油（mtoe）
数据来源：国际能源署，英国石油公司，本报告研究

图 2.2.1-3 · **2020年东南亚国家能源消费人均量**

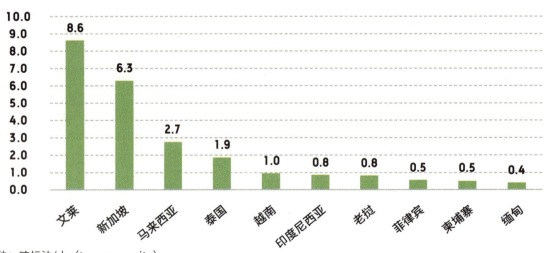

单位：吨标油/人（toe per capita）
数据来源：国际能源署，英国石油公司，本报告研究

2.2.2 能源消费结构

● **可再生能源超过煤炭成为第二大能源消费品类**

2020 年，东南亚地区可再生能源消费总量为 2 亿吨标油，占比 27.9%；煤炭消费量 1.7 亿吨标油，占比 24.2%；石油消费量 2.1 亿吨标油，占比 29.8%；天然气消费量 1.3 亿吨标油，占比 18.1%。2000 至 2020 年，由于燃煤发电的带动作用，东南亚地区煤炭消费占比提升了近 16 个百分点；石油占比显著降低，下降幅度超过 10 个百分点，但仍然是最大的能源消费品类；2018 年前，东南亚地区能源消费增量主要来源于化石能源，2018 年后随着风电、光伏的大规模发展，可再生能源消费占比呈现上升趋势，目前可再生能源消费占比已经超过煤炭，成为第二大能源消费品类。

图 2.2.2-1·2000—2020年东南亚地区能源消费品种结构

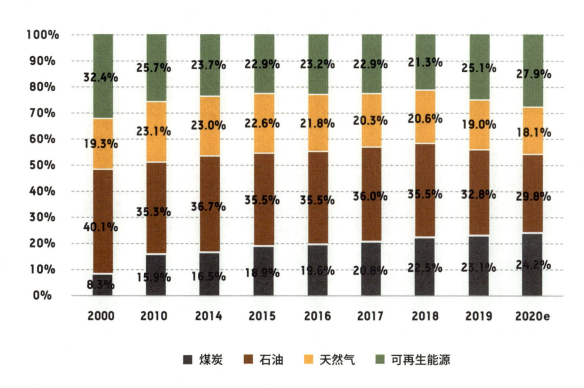

数据来源：国际能源署，英国石油公司，本报告研究

2.2.3 碳排放情况

● **碳排放量呈上升趋势，但人均碳排放量不高**

2019 年，东南亚地区 CO_2 排放量接近 17 亿吨，约占亚洲地区 CO_2 排放总量的 8%，约占全球 CO_2 排放总量的 5%。2015-2019 年，东南亚地区 CO_2 排放量呈上升趋势，年均增速约为 4%、累积增幅约为 17%。这是由于东南亚地区能源需求增长主要依赖化石燃料，自 2000 年以来 90% 的能源需求增长来自煤炭、石油、天然气等，在化石能源消费量增长的驱动下，CO_2 排放量持续增长。分国别来看，印尼、泰国、马来西亚、越南等国 CO_2 排放量在区域内占比较高，占区域排放总量的比重均达到 15% 以上；老挝、柬埔寨、越南等国增长较快，年均增速约为 10%；新加坡承诺将在 21 世纪下半叶尽快实现净零排放，近年来 CO_2 排放量大幅下降，年均降速超过 10%。

图 2.2.3-1·东南亚国家CO_2排放量

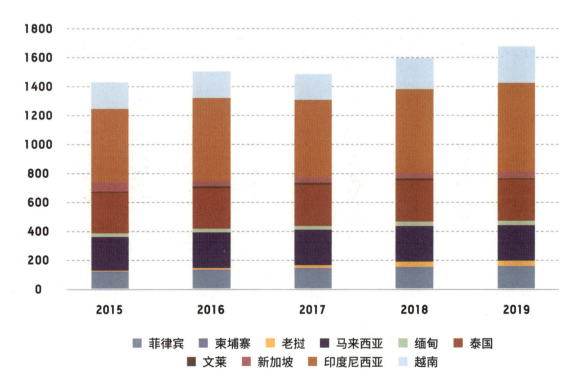

单位：百万吨
数据来源：Our World in Data，本报告研究

2019 年，东南亚地区人均 CO_2 排放量为 2.53 吨 / 人，显著低于全球平均值，约是亚洲地区人均 CO_2 排放总量的 57%、全球人均 CO_2 排放总量的 54%。其中，文莱人均 CO_2 排放量最高，其次是马来西亚、新加坡，其余国家人均 CO_2 排放量均在 5 吨 / 人以下，这与各国人口数量、电力可及性、经济发展水平和产业结构等因素密切相关。

图 2.2.3-2 · 2019年东南亚国家人均CO₂排放量

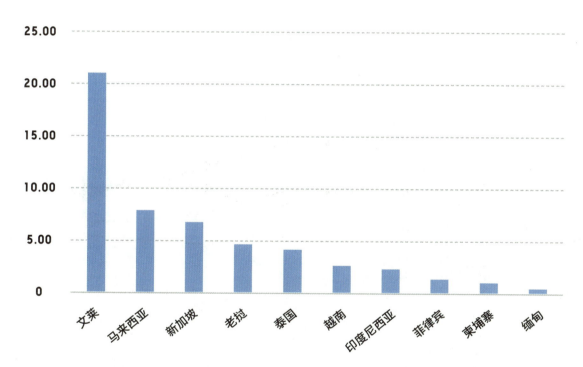

单位：吨/人
数据来源：Our World in Data，本报告研究

2019 年，东南亚地区碳排放强度为 2.12 吨 / 百美元，低于全球平均水平，约为全球平均碳排放强度的 72%。2000 — 2019 年，东南亚地区碳排放强度呈先降后升的趋势，整体来看基本保持不变。分国别来看，2000 — 2019 年，老挝、柬埔寨、越南、文莱的碳排放强度呈上升趋势，其余国家均有所下降，这与各国经济发展阶段和发展特征、能源效率等因素有关。

图 2.2.3-3 · 东南亚国家碳排放强度

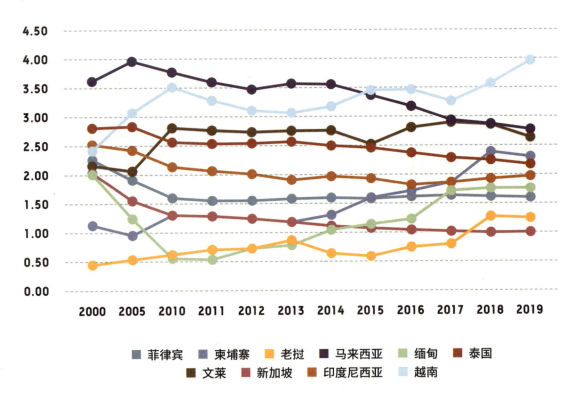

单位：吨/百美元

数据来源：knoema，本报告研究

2.2.4 终端能源消费

● **工业和交通领域驱动终端能源消费稳步增长**

2020 年，东南亚地区终端能源消费总量为 4.5 亿吨标油，同比降低 7.8%。2000 至 2019 年终端能源消费总量平均年增长率为 3.1%。分领域来看，工业领域终端能源消费为 1.5 亿吨标油，占比为 33.2%；交通领域终端能源消费为 1.3 亿吨标油，占比为 29.8%；居民终端能源消费 0.7 亿吨标油，占比为 16.5%；服务业终端能源消费 0.3 亿吨标油，占比为 6.1%。2000 年以来，东南亚地区交通领域终端能源消费占比提升明显，居民终端能源消费占比显著下降，降幅约为 17 个百分点。

图 2.2.4-1 · 2000—2020年东南亚地区终端能源消费总量及增速

单位：百万吨标油（mtoe）

数据来源：国际能源署，国际可再生能源署，本报告研究

图 2.2.4-2 · 2000—2020年东南亚地区终端能源消费结构

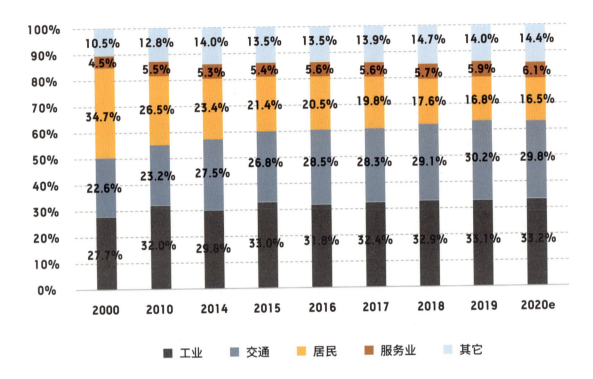

数据来源：国际能源署，英国石油公司，本报告研究

2.2.5 主要能源价格

● **石油产品销售价格**

　　东南亚地区石油产品主要分汽油和柴油两类，二者分别有各自的销售价格，多数国家汽油价格要高于柴油价格。2021年，东南亚地区大多数国家石油产品销售价格低于全球平均水平（同期全球平均汽油销售价格为 1.19 美元 / 升；柴油销售价格为 1.06 美元 / 升）。

图 2.2.5-1 · **2021年东南亚国家石油产品售价**

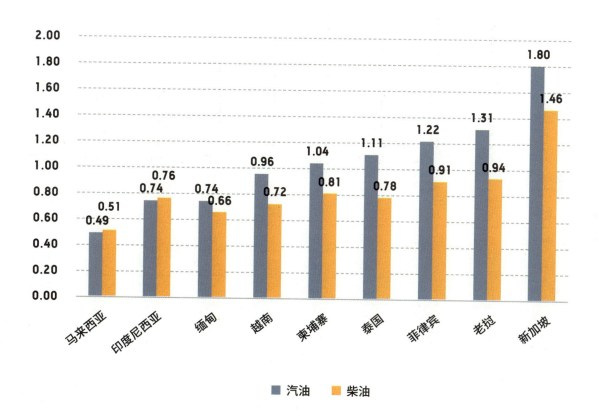

单位：美元/升（US$/L）
数据来源：GlobalPetrolPrices，本报告研究

近 10 年来，东南亚地区大多数国家石油产品售价于 2013 年达到峰值后开始逐渐下跌，于 2016 — 2017 年左右重新开始呈现上涨趋势。

图 2.2.5-2 · 2011—2019年东南亚国家汽油售价

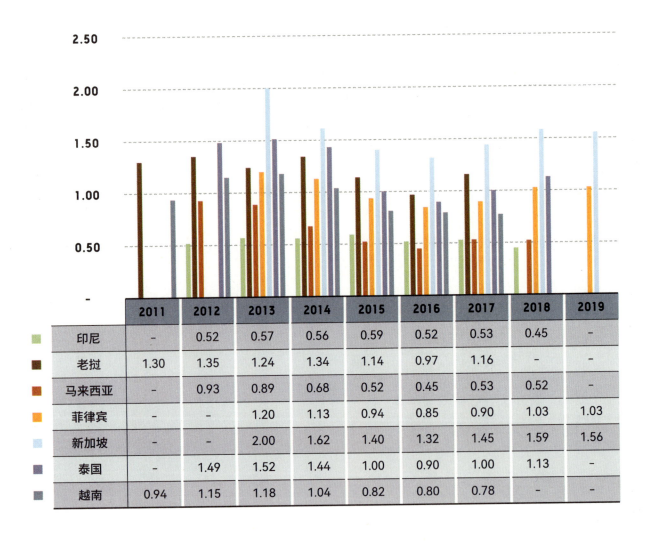

	2011	2012	2013	2014	2015	2016	2017	2018	2019
印尼	-	0.52	0.57	0.56	0.59	0.52	0.53	0.45	-
老挝	1.30	1.35	1.24	1.34	1.14	0.97	1.16	-	-
马来西亚	-	0.93	0.89	0.68	0.52	0.45	0.53	0.52	-
菲律宾	-	-	1.20	1.13	0.94	0.85	0.90	1.03	1.03
新加坡	-	-	2.00	1.62	1.40	1.32	1.45	1.59	1.56
泰国	-	1.49	1.52	1.44	1.00	0.90	1.00	1.13	-
越南	0.94	1.15	1.18	1.04	0.82	0.80	0.78	-	-

单位：美元/升（US$/L）
数据来源：Enerdata，本报告研究

图 2.2.5-3 · 2011—2019年东南亚国家柴油售价

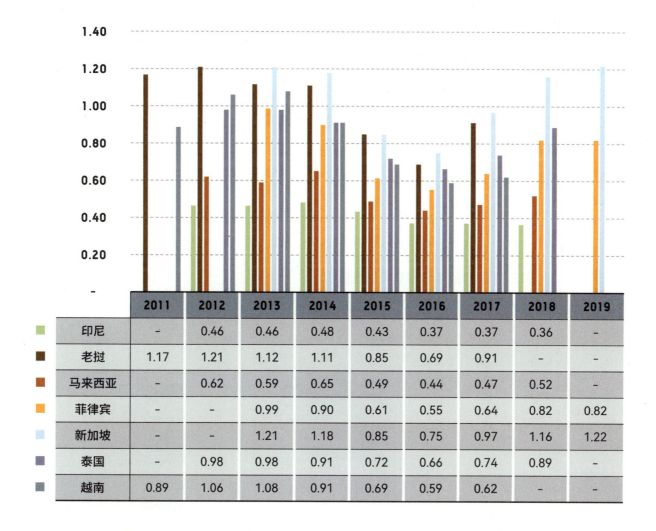

	2011	2012	2013	2014	2015	2016	2017	2018	2019
印尼	-	0.46	0.46	0.48	0.43	0.37	0.37	0.36	-
老挝	1.17	1.21	1.12	1.11	0.85	0.69	0.91	-	-
马来西亚	-	0.62	0.59	0.65	0.49	0.44	0.47	0.52	-
菲律宾	-	-	0.99	0.90	0.61	0.55	0.64	0.82	0.82
新加坡	-	-	1.21	1.18	0.85	0.75	0.97	1.16	1.22
泰国	-	0.98	0.98	0.91	0.72	0.66	0.74	0.89	-
越南	0.89	1.06	1.08	0.91	0.69	0.59	0.62	-	-

单位：美元/升（US$/L）
数据来源：Enerdata，本报告研究

● **天然气销售价格**

　　东南亚地区天然气销售价格主要分民用和商用两类。总体来看，民用天然气价格要显著高于商用价格。东南亚地区主要天然气消费国家中，2021年新加坡天然气销售侧民用气价为13.6美分/千瓦时（等效热值），商用气价为12.4美分/千瓦时（等效热值），均高于全球平均天然气销售价格（民用4.6美分/千瓦时，商用5.3美分/千瓦时）；自2013年以来，新加坡天然气售价呈先增后减态势，2015 — 2016年售价达近年最低值。马来西亚天然气销售侧民用气价为2.0美分/千瓦时（等效热值），商用气价为2.6美分/千瓦时（等效热值），均低于全球平均天然气销售价格。

图 2.2.5-4 · 2021年东南亚部分国家天然气售价

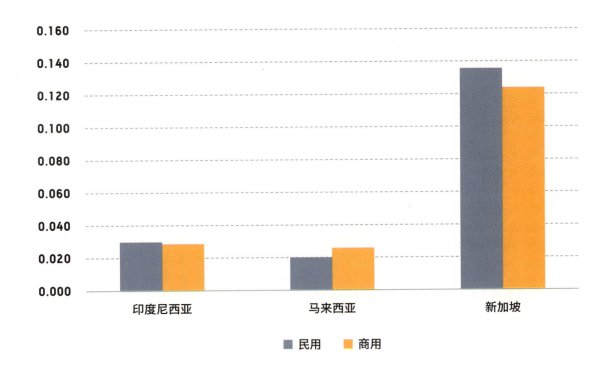

单位：美分/千瓦时 等效热值（US$c /kWh GCV）
数据来源：Enerdata，本报告研究

2.3 能源供给

2.3.1 能源生产总量

● **能源生产总量呈上升趋势，且国别集中度较高**

2020 年，东南亚地区能源生产总量为 7.9 亿吨标油，同比减少 3.4%。2010 至 2019 年间，东南亚地区能源生产总体呈上升趋势，其中 2015 年受全球油价大幅下跌影响，该地区能源生产量较上一年小幅下降，并在随后数年中不断回升。2020 年，受到全球新冠疫情影响，东南亚地区能源生产总量回落。

图 2.3.1-1 · 2000—2020年东南亚地区能源生产总量及增速

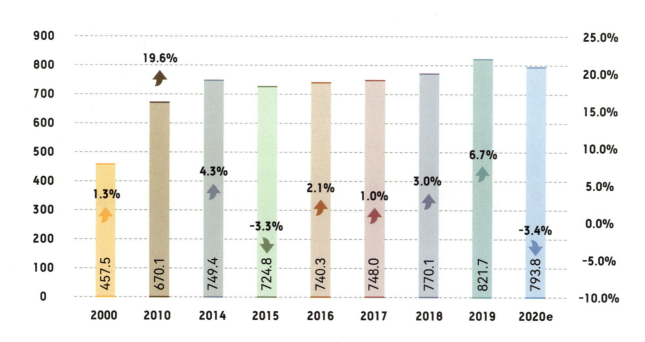

单位：百万吨标油（mtoe）
数据来源：国际能源署，国际可再生能源署，本报告研究

分国别来看，印度尼西亚是东南亚地区能源生产大国，2020 年印度尼西亚能源生产总量为 4.5 亿吨标油，占东南亚地区总量一半以上。此外，越南和马来西亚等国家能源生产量较高。受能源资源禀赋所限，新加坡等国家能源生产总量远不及能源消费量。总体来看，由于东南亚各国资源和行业发展水平不同，其能源生产总量及结构存在较大差异。

图 2.3.1-2 · 2020年东南亚各国能源生产总量

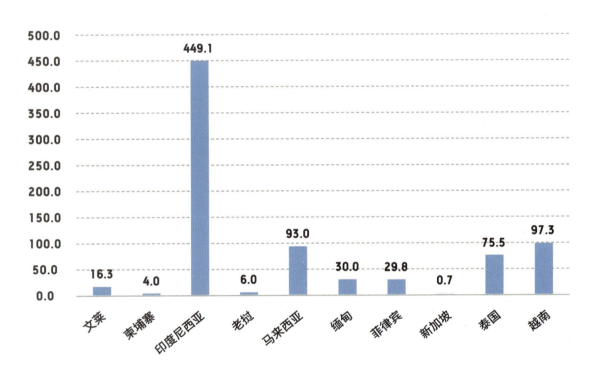

单位：百万吨标油（mtoe）
数据来源：国际能源署，国际可再生能源署，本报告研究

2.3.2 能源生产结构

　　2020 年，东南亚国家可再生能源生产总量为 1.93 亿吨标油，占比为 24.3%；煤炭生产量为 3.36 亿吨标油，占比为 42.4%；石油生产量为 0.97 亿吨标油，占比为 12.2%；天然气生产量为 1.68 亿吨，占比为 21.1%。2015-2020 年，化石能源占比总体呈下降趋势，石油和天然气占比均下降了 4.4 个百分点；可再生能源占比得到显著增长，涨幅为 4.8 个百分点。

图 2.3.2-1 · 2015—2020年东南亚地区能源生产结构

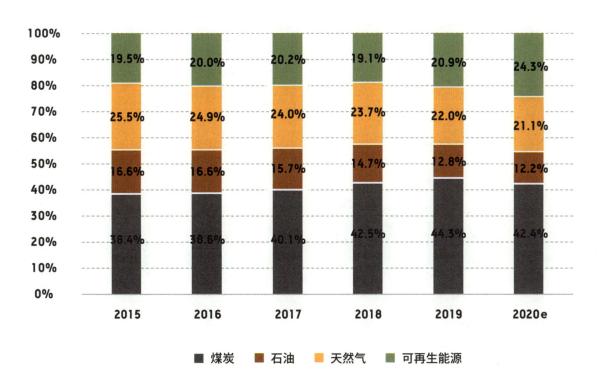

数据来源：国际能源署，英国石油公司，国际可再生能源署，本报告研究

2.3.3 能源自给率

● **能源自给率相对较高，但油气仍有较高的对外依存度**

整体来看，东南亚地区能源自给率水平相对较高，2020 年平均自给率达到 120%。分国别来看，东南亚地区各国能源自给率总体良好，大部分国家自给率高于 100%。其中，文莱、印度尼西亚等国能源自给率较高，能源出口量较大；柬埔寨、菲律宾、泰国等能源自给率相对较低。

图 2.3.3-1 · 2020年东南亚国家能源自给率

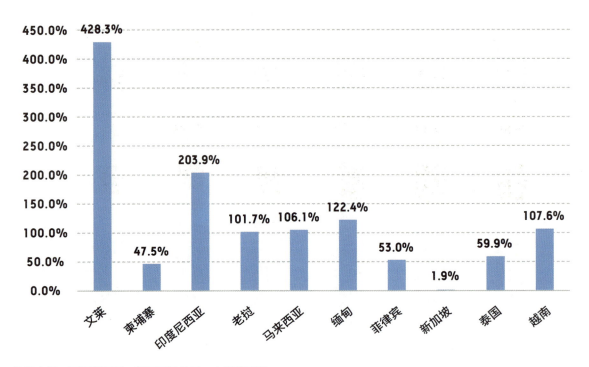

数据来源：国际能源署，英国石油公司，本报告研究

2.4 电力消费

2.4.1 电力消费增长较快，但人均用电量仍然很低

自 2000 年以来，东南亚经济社会的持续稳定发展，随着区域内电气化水平的提高，电力需求不断提升。除去特殊年份，东南亚地区电力消费年均增速维持在 5% 以上。2015 — 2020 年电力消费累计增幅约 34.8%，显著高于亚洲平均水平（24.8%）和全球平均水平（10.1%）。

图 2.4.1-1 · 2000—2020年东南亚地区电力消费总量及增速

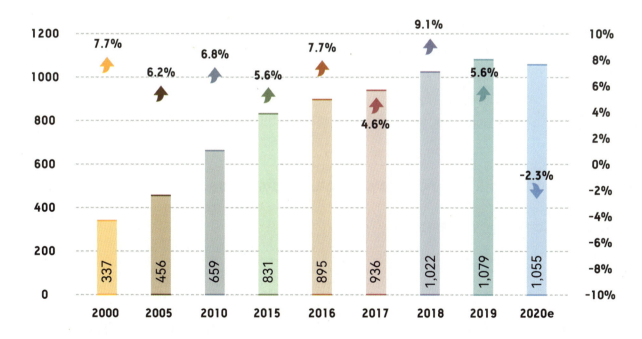

单位：太瓦时（TWh）
数据来源：国际能源署，Enerdata，本报告研究

　　由于东南亚国家经济发展水平和发展阶段仍有较大区别，各国间电力消费增速也有明显差异。2015-2020 年，柬埔寨和越南电力消费增幅超过 70%，远高于东南亚其他国家。从电力消费累积增量来看，越南、印度尼西亚、菲律宾的电力消费绝对值增长最大，分别达到 111.4 太瓦时、53.9 太瓦时、17.1 太瓦时，是东南亚地区电力增长的主要驱动力。

图 2.4.1-2 · 2015—2020东南亚国家电力消费增幅

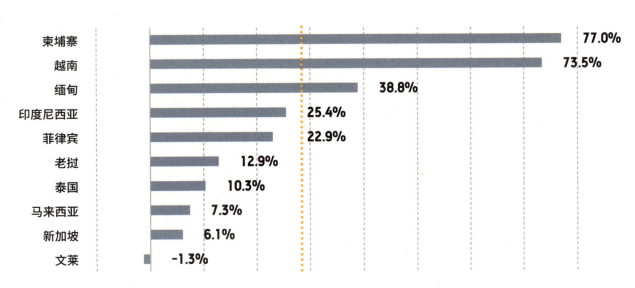

数据来源：国际能源署，Enerdata，本报告研究

　　从国别来看，印度尼西亚、越南是东南亚地区电力消费大国，2020 年电力消费总量分别占整个东南亚地区的 25.2% 和 24.9%。此外，泰国、马来西亚和菲律宾也是东南亚地区电力消费总量较高的国家。从人均用电量来看，2020 年东南亚地区人均用电量为 1581 千瓦时，与亚洲平均水平（4300 千瓦时 / 人）相比差距明显。新加坡、文莱人均用电量超过 8000 千瓦时，马来西亚、泰国、越南达到 2500 千瓦时以上，其他国家人均用电量均低于 1000 千瓦时。

图 2.4.1-3 · 2020年东南亚国家电力消费总量

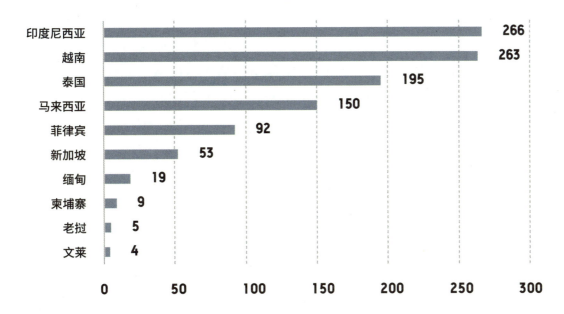

单位：太瓦时（TWh）
数据来源：国际能源署，Enerdata，CEIC，本报告研究

图 2.4.1-4 · 2020年东南亚国家人均用电量

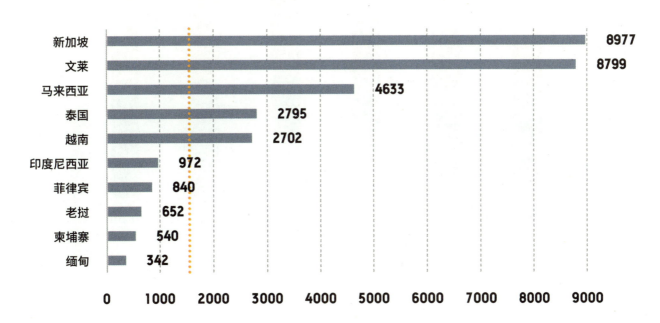

单位：千瓦时（kWh）
数据来源：国际能源署，Enerdata，CEIC，本报告研究

2.4.2 各行业终端电力消费占比保持稳定

2020 年，东南亚地区工业领域电力消费 452.5 太瓦时，占终端电力消费总量的 42.0%；居民领域电力消费 332.2 太瓦时，占比 31.5%；服务业领域电力消费 229.9 太瓦时，占比 21.8%。近年来，东南亚地区各行业终端电力消费结构基本保持不变，工业仍是终端电力消费的主要领域。2015-2020 年，东南亚地区工业领域电力消费占比小幅提高，上升了 0.5 个百分点；居民领域电力消费占比总体保持平稳；服务业领域电力消费占比降低了 1.9 个百分点。随着电气化进程加速，东南亚地区各行业电气化程度越来越高，国民经济的发展为电力需求的增长带来较大空间，工业仍将是东南亚地区电力需求增长的主要驱动力。

图 2.4.2-1 · 2015—2020年东南亚地区终端电力消费结构

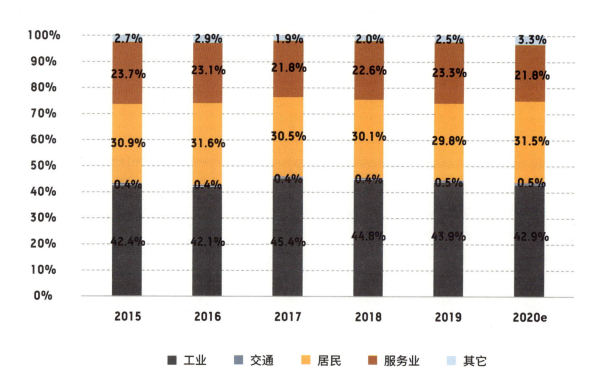

数据来源：国际能源署，各国能源部门数据，本报告研究

2.4.3 部分国家仍有大量无电人口

近年来，东南亚地区电力覆盖率整体有所提升，虽然区域通电率达到96%，但目前仍有近2700万无电人口，主要集中在缅甸、菲律宾、印度尼西亚、柬埔寨。其中，缅甸是东南亚地区通电率最低的国家，通电率仅为68.4%，目前仍有超过1700万人无法用电，主要集中在偏远农村地区。菲律宾、印度尼西亚、柬埔寨近年来电力覆盖率明显提升，但各国偏远地区仍有超过100万人无法用电。老挝近年来通过电网扩建，已实现了电力全境覆盖。

图 2.4.3-1 · 2019年东南亚国家通电率

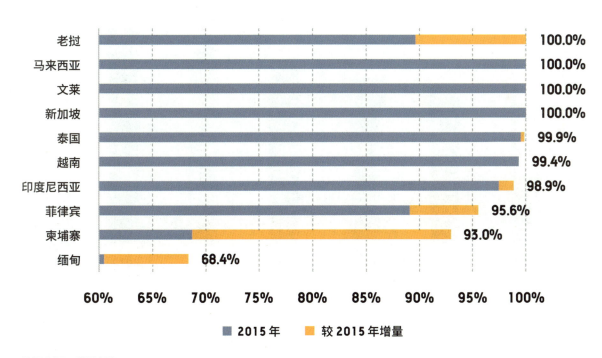

数据来源：世界银行

2.5 电力供应

2.5.1 电力装机增速较快，但人均装机仍明显偏低

2020 年东南亚地区电力装机总量为 292 吉瓦，较上年同比增长 7.2%，较 2015 年装机累计增幅达到 50.3%，电力装机保持高速增长。近年来，东南亚地区整体工业化和电气化发展迅速，为了满足日益增长的用电需求，东南亚地区电力装机规模迅速扩大。

图 2.5.1-1 · 2015—2020年东南亚地区电力装机总量及增速

单位：吉瓦（GW）

数据来源：国际能源署，国际可再生能源署，各国能源部门数据，本报告研究

从人均装机水平来看，东南亚地区人均发电装机容量仅为 440 瓦，不足世界人均装机水平（930 瓦）的一半。由于东南亚国家电气化水平及人口规模差异较大，各国人均装机水平差距明显。文莱、新加坡经济发达、人口规模小，人均电力装机超过 2 千瓦；印度尼西亚、菲律宾、柬埔寨、缅甸人均电力装机不足 300 瓦，电力装机水平有待提高。

图 2.5.1-2 · 2020年东南亚国家人均发电装机容量

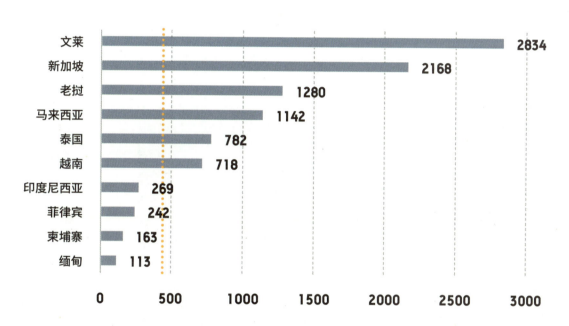

单位：瓦/人（W/人）
数据来源：国际能源署，国际可再生能源署，各国能源部门数据，本报告研究

从国别来看，东南亚国家电力装机的增长水平，能够反映出近期各国电力发展的情况。近年来，越南电力行业保持加速发展，大力吸引投资，五年内电力装机增加4.13吉瓦，装机规模扩大1.5倍，成为东南亚地区电力装机累计增量最大、增速最高的国家。此外，电力装机增长水平较为突出的国家还有印度尼西亚（2.24吉瓦，44%）和泰国（1.58吉瓦，41%）。

图 2.5.1-3 · 2020年东南亚国家电力装机累计增量及增速

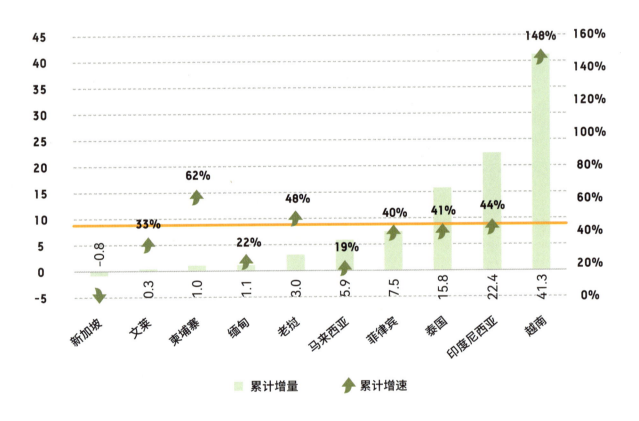

单位：吉瓦（GW）
数据来源：国际能源署，国际可再生能源署，各国能源部门数据，本报告研究

2.5.2 气电仍是东南亚最大电源品种

2020年，东南亚地区电力装机结构仍以火电为主，其中气电和煤电占电力装机总量超过60%。近年来，煤电占比有所上升，气电占比有所下降，但气电仍然是装机最大的电源品种。可再生能源装机占比稳步提升，水电是最主要的可再生能源品种，水电装机占电力装机总量的比重约为20%。东南亚地区还未建成核电机组。

图 2.5.2-1 · 2015—2020年东南亚地区电力装机结构

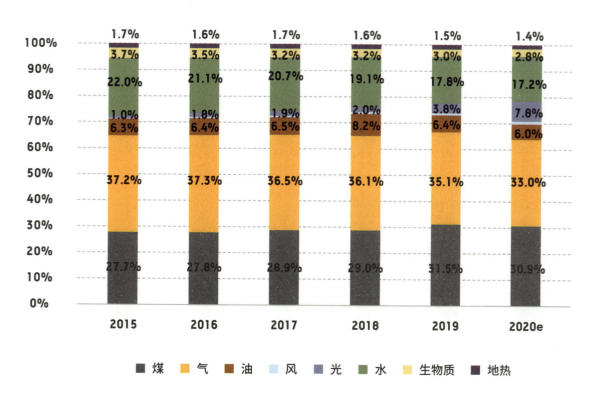

数据来源：国际能源署，国际可再生能源署，各国能源部门数据，本报告研究

　　2020年，东南亚地区非化石能源装机占比达到30.2%，略低于全球平均水平（33%）。从国别来看，东南亚国家非化石能源装机水平与各国能源结构、资源禀赋及开发政策高度相关。印度尼西亚拥有丰富的水能、太阳能和地热资源，鼓励大力开发非化石能源，是东南亚地区目前非化石能源装机总量最高的国家，非化石能源装机超过10.55吉瓦，占区域非化石能源装机总量的22.6%。此外，区域内非化石能源装机容量较高的国家还有马来西亚、老挝、菲律宾、越南，占区域非化石能源装机比重均在10%以上，非化石能源装机容量超过500兆瓦。

图 2.5.2-2 · 2020年东南亚各国非化石能源装机占比

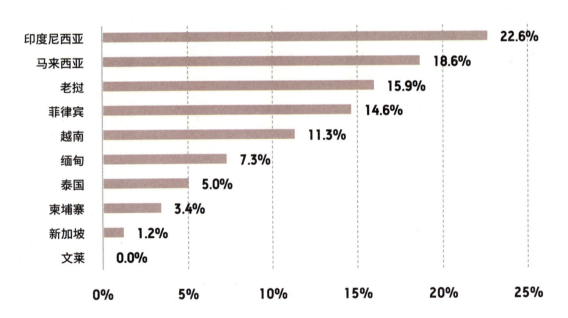

数据来源：国际能源署，国际可再生能源署，各国能源部门数据，本报告研究

2.5.3 多数煤电机组为近 10 年投运

　　东南亚地区电力发展起步较晚，机组年龄整体较小，57% 的煤电机组于近 10 年内投产运行，约 21% 的煤电机组年龄在 20 年以上。印度尼西亚、越南作为东南亚煤电大国，其近 10 年内的新建机组分别占到了各自煤电装机总量的 64% 和 80%。此外，老挝、柬埔寨、文莱的煤电机组均为 10 年内新建机组。

图 2.5.3-1 · 东南亚国家煤电机组年龄

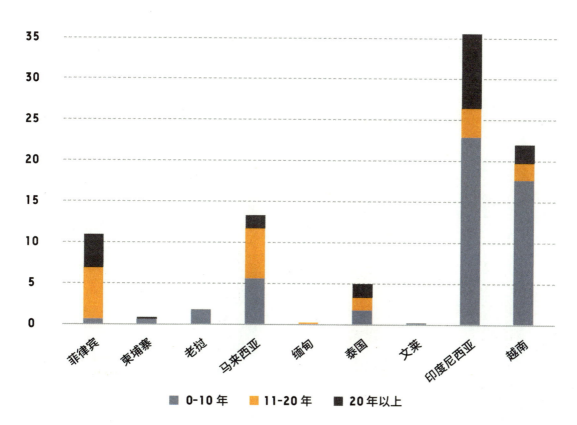

单位：吉瓦（GW）

数据来源：各国能源部门统计数据、Enerdata、EndCoal

气电是东南亚目前最主要的电源，区域内气电机组年龄总体较小，34% 的气电机组于近 10 年内投运，30% 的气电机组运行超过 20 年。未来，部分气电机组升级改造和更新换代需求将逐渐提升。东南亚地区每年约 60% 的天然气用于电力供应。泰国、印度尼西亚、马来西亚、新加坡作为区域内气电装机大国，气电装机规模均在 10 吉瓦以上。其中，印度尼西亚、马来西亚依靠丰富的天然气资源，近年来不断扩大气电装机，气电将仍占据其电源主体地位。此外，泰国、新加坡近年来持续提升天然气进口量，支持本国气电的大规模发展。

图 2.5.3-2 · 东南亚地区气电机组年龄分布

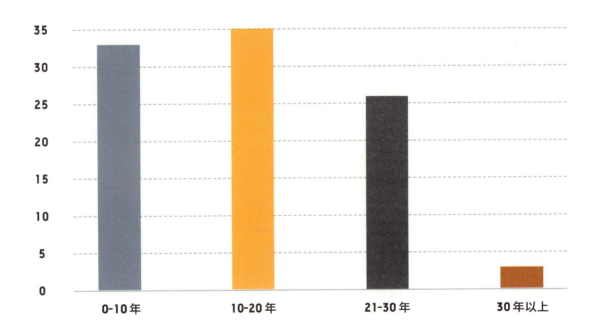

单位：吉瓦（GW）

数据来源：《Energy Technology Perspectives 2020》，国际能源署

2.6 电力输送

2.6.1 电网跨国互联规模较小

东南亚地区的电力互联互通主要集中在中南半岛地区，中南半岛区域内电力跨境交易主要集中在泰国、老挝、柬埔寨、缅甸、越南以及中国之间。由于各国间电力发展水平差距较大，以及菲律宾、印度尼西亚等独立岛屿国家电网延伸困难，电网互联成本较高，目前在区域内还未形成一体化的电网项目。

东南亚国家输电线路总长约 241732 公里，其中 400 千伏及以上输电线路长度为 25805 公里，占比 11%；275 — 220 千伏输电线路长度为 72113 公里，占比 30%；138 — 115 千伏 94796 公里，占比 39%；70 — 22 千伏输电线路长度 49283 公里，占比 20%。

表 2.6.1-1 · 东南亚国家电网长度及电压等级

国家	简称	线路长度 单位：km	500—400 千伏占比 (%)	275—220 千伏占比 (%)	138—115 千伏占比 (%)	70—22 千伏占比 (%)
菲律宾	PH	20079	-	11	7	82
柬埔寨	KH	11301	6	60	34	-
老挝	LA	11595	4	4	89	3
马来西亚	MY	31621	8	42	49	1
缅甸	MM	13631	-	45	17	38
泰国	TH	37456	19	42	39	-
文莱	BN	-	-	-	-	100
新加坡	SG	26458	3	17	-	81
印度尼西亚	ID	61591	9	6	76	9
越南	VN	28000	31	69	-	-

数据来源：各国能源部门数据

2.6.2 跨境电力交易总量仍然不高

　　东南亚地区的跨国电力交易以区域内为主，区域外主要通过大湄公河次区域互联电网从中国进口电力。2019 年东南亚地区跨国电力交易总规模超过 62 太瓦时，约占全区域当年电力总消费的 6%。2015 — 2018 年，东南亚进口和出口电量总体保持平稳增长，2019 年呈现小幅回落。其中泰国、老挝是东南亚地区主要的电力交易国，其进出口电量分别占到全区域电力交易总量的 45% 和 37%。

图 2.6.2-1 · 2015—2019年东南亚国家进出口电量

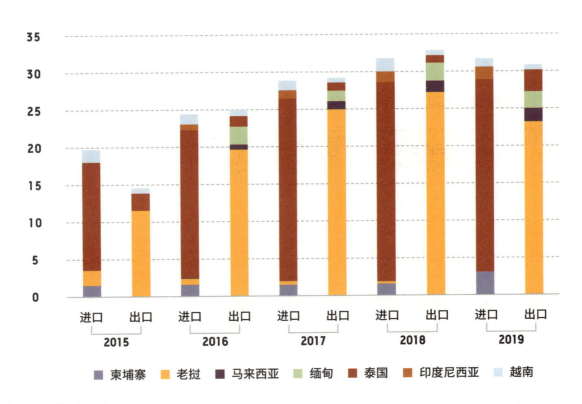

单位：太瓦时（TWh）
数据来源：国际能源署，各国能源部门数据

从国别来看，老挝是东南亚地区最大的电力出口国，主要向泰国、柬埔寨、越南、缅甸输送电力，总出口规模（以货币计）占到区域内的75%；泰国是东南亚地区最大的电力进口国，总进口规模（以货币计）占到区域内的80%；柬埔寨、印度尼西亚是东南亚地区的电力净进口国。区域外跨境电力交易方面，主要是越南、老挝通过大湄公河次区域互联电网从中国进口电力。

表 2.6.2-1 · 东南亚国家2020年电力进出口交易额

	电力交易 国别	进口额 （百万美元）	出口额 （百万美元）	电力交易总额 （百万美元）
柬埔寨	老挝	98.3	–	98.3
	泰国	76.9	–	76.9
	越南	104.1	–	104.1
老挝	中国	5.6	–	5.6
	柬埔寨	–	35.5	35.5
	马来西亚	–	1.0	1.0
	缅甸	–	11.6	11.6
	泰国	75.3	758.4	833.7
	越南	1.1	25.4	26.5
马来西亚	泰国	1.1	0.2	1.3
	印度尼西亚	–	122.1	122.1
泰国	柬埔寨	–	107.2	107.2
	老挝	1761.7	93.2	1854.9
	马来西亚	0.2	1.0	1.2
	缅甸	–	13.3	13.3
印度尼西亚	马来西亚	120.0	–	120.0
越南	中国	107.9	–	107.9
	柬埔寨	–	197.5	197.5
	老挝	65.3	2.7	67.9
合计		2352.2	1168.9	3521.1

数据来源：ASEANStats DataPortal

2.7 电力价格

2.7.1 工业销售电价呈现上涨趋势

东南亚各国工业电价在 7 美分 / 千瓦时 — 17 美分 / 千瓦时之间，总体略低于全球平均水平（12.3 美分 / 千瓦时）。各国间工业电价差异较大，与各国产业结构、工业领域电气化水平以及电价政策等因素相关。其中，新加坡、柬埔寨工业电价水平较高，2020 年工业电价超过 14 美分 / 千瓦时。近年来，东南亚地区工业电价整体呈上涨趋势。

图 2.7.1-1 · 2020年东南亚各国工业销售电价

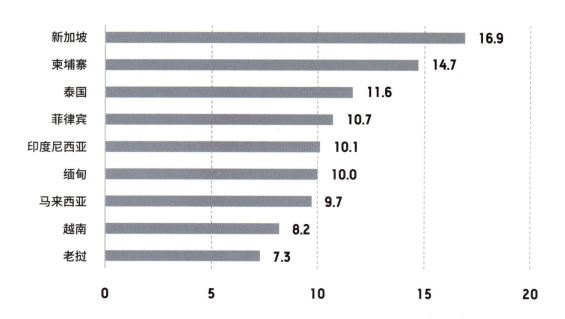

单位：美分/千瓦时（US$c/kWh）
数据来源：GlobalPetrolPrices, Enerdata

表 2.7.1-1 · 东南亚各国2015—2020年工业销售电价

国家	简称	2015	2016	2017	2018	2019	2020
菲律宾	PH	-	-	-	11.7	-	10.7
柬埔寨	KH	-	-	-	-	14.7	14.7
老挝	LA	7.7	7.9	7.9	-	-	7.3
马来西亚	MY	7.8	7.4	7.8	8.6	-	9.7
缅甸	MM	-	-	-	-	-	10.0
泰国	TH	9.7	8.8	9.1	9.8	-	11.6
文莱	BN	-	-	-	-	-	-
新加坡	SG	15.2	12.1	13.7	16.0	16.4	16.9
印度尼西亚	ID	8.6	7.9	8.2	7.8	-	10.1
越南	VN	6.6	6.5	6.5	7.8	-	8.2

单位：美分/千瓦时（US$c/kWh）
数据来源：GlobalPetrolPrices, Enerdata
*暂无文莱电价数据

2.7.2 居民电价总体低于工业电价

受交叉电价补贴、电价捆绑等因素影响，东南亚地区居民销售电价总体低于工业电价，大多数国家居民电价低于全球平均水平（13.8 美分 / 千瓦时）。各国居民电价差异较大，其中，菲律宾、柬埔寨居民电价水平较高，2020 年居民电价超过 15 美分 / 千瓦时；越南、印度尼西亚、马来西亚、老挝、缅甸居民电价在 8 美分 / 千瓦时以下。近年来，东南亚地区居民电价整体呈现下降趋势。

图 2.7.2-1 · 2020年东南亚各国居民销售电价

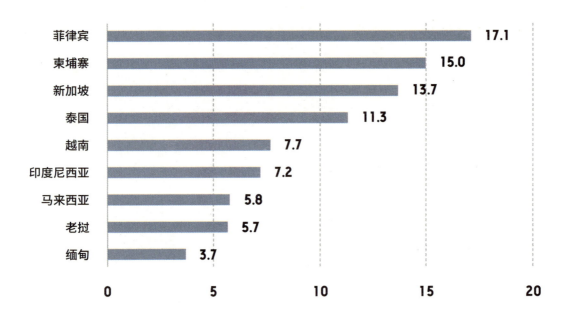

单位：美分/千瓦时（US$c/kWh）
数据来源：GlobalPetrolPrices, Enerdata
*暂无文莱电价数据

表 **2.7.2-1** · 东南亚国家2015—2020年居民销售电价

国家	简称	2015	2016	2017	2018	2019	2020
菲律宾	PH	20.3	17.6	16.8	16.7	15.7	17.1
柬埔寨	KH	-	-	-	-	-	15.0
老挝	LA	7.1	7.2	7.2	-	-	5.7
马来西亚	MY	7.7	7.3	6.8	7.4	-	5.8
缅甸	MM	-	-	-	-	-	3.7
泰国	TH	12.0	10.9	11.2	11.0	-	11.3
文莱	BN	-	-	-	-	-	-
新加坡	SG	16.9	14.6	16.0	18.1	18.5	13.7
印度尼西亚	ID	6.3	6.4	7.9	10.3	-	7.2
越南	VN	8.2	7.5	7.6	-	-	7.7

单位：美分/千瓦时（US$c/kWh）
数据来源：GlobalPetrolPrices, Enerdata
*暂无文莱电价数据

2.8 可再生能源电力

2.8.1 可再生能源保持快速发展态势

近年来，东南亚可再生能源装机规模不断扩大，2020 年可再生能源装机总量达到 87.97 吉瓦，较 2015 年累计增加了 31.9 吉瓦，累计增幅达到 56.9%。东南亚地区拥有丰富的水能资源，日益增长的用电需求以及较好的投资开发模式，使水电成为最具吸引力的清洁能源之一，水电仍然是区域内最主要的可再生电力。近年来，光伏装机快速增长，逐渐成为东南亚可再生能源装机增长的主要驱动力。此外，东南亚拥有丰富的生物质能源，也是重要的可再生能源资源。同时，菲律宾、印度尼西亚地热资源丰厚，拥有巨大的地热发电潜力。

图 2.8.1-1 · 2015-2020年东南亚地区可再生能源装机结构

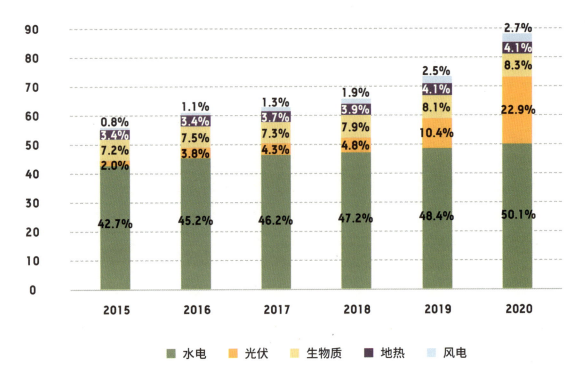

单位：吉瓦（WG）

数据来源：国际可再生能源署

2.8.2 光伏和风电装机呈现加速增长的态势

近年来，东南亚地区光伏和风电装机呈现加速增长态势，年均增速分别超过60%和25%。2020年光伏和风电装机分别占区域可再生能源装机总量的26%和3%。其中，光伏装机近三年迅速增长，2020年装机达到22.85吉瓦，较上年扩容1.2倍，较2015年扩大了11.5倍。同时，近年来风电装机规模也在不断扩大，2020年装机容量超过2.7吉瓦，较2015年装机规模扩大了2.4倍。

图 2.8.2-1 · 2015—2020年东南亚光伏装机总量及增速

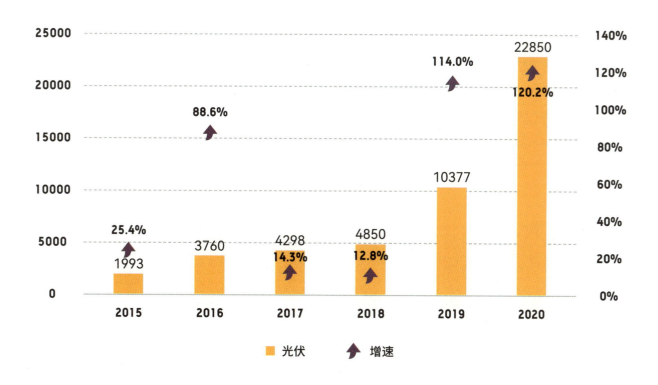

图 2.8.2-2 · 2015—2020年东南亚风电装机总量及增速

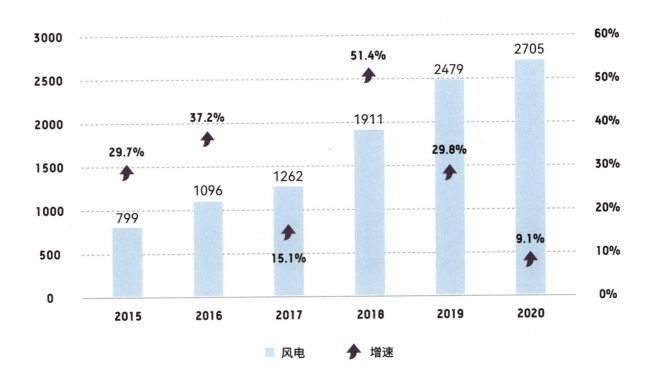

单位：兆瓦（MW）

数据来源：国际可再生能源署，本报告研究

2.8.3 光伏和风电装机分布较为集中

　　从国别来看，东南亚地区光伏和风电装机分布较为集中，其中光伏主要集中在越南（72%）和泰国（13%）；风电主要分布在泰国（56%）、越南（22%）和印度尼西亚（16%）。2015 — 2020 年，东南亚地区光伏装机增量最大的国家是越南（16499MW），泰国（1563MW）、马来西亚（1264MW）、菲律宾（875MW）也较为突出；风电装机增量最大的为泰国（1273MW），越南（464MW）、印度尼西亚（153MW）装机增长也较为明显。

图 2.8.3-1 · 2015—2020年东南亚国家光伏和风电装机增量

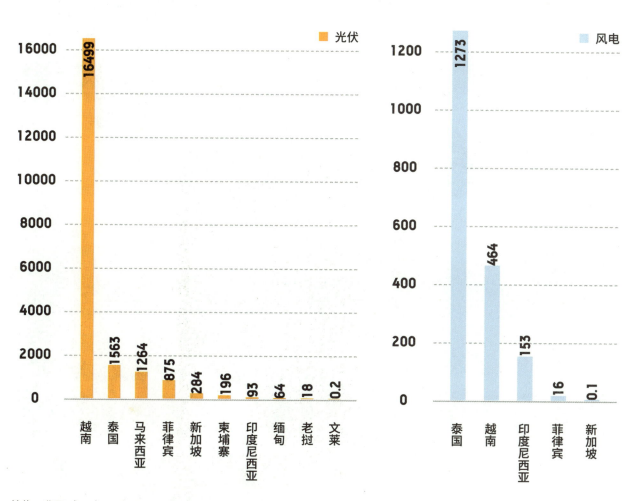

单位：兆瓦（MW）

数据来源：国际可再生能源署，本报告研究

03 中国与东南亚国家能源合作现状

03

中国与东南亚国家
能源合作现状

　　东南亚是我国能源和电力企业"走出去"的重要地区，中国与东南亚国家在能源领域合作成果丰硕。双方石油、天然气、煤炭贸易十分活跃，有效保障了各国能源安全。双方企业在水电、新能源、火电、电网等领域开展了大量项目投资、项目设计、项目工程服务合作，有效改善了当地电力供应、增进了当地人民福祉。

3.1 能源贸易合作

3.1.1 中国与东南亚国家石油贸易总体呈现稳步增长态势

中国与东南亚国家长期保持着密切的石油贸易合作，2015 — 2019 年，中国与东南亚石油贸易额总体呈现增长趋势，年均增长率为 3.2%。2020 年，受新冠疫情影响，国际油价持续下跌，中国与东南亚国家石油贸易较 2019 年下降 33.8%，贸易总额仅为 154 亿美元，该贸易额占中国与全球石油贸易总额的 7.1%（2162 亿美元），占东南亚与全球石油贸易总额的 8.7%（1776 亿美元）。

图 3.1.1-1·2015—2020年中国与东南亚国家石油贸易总额

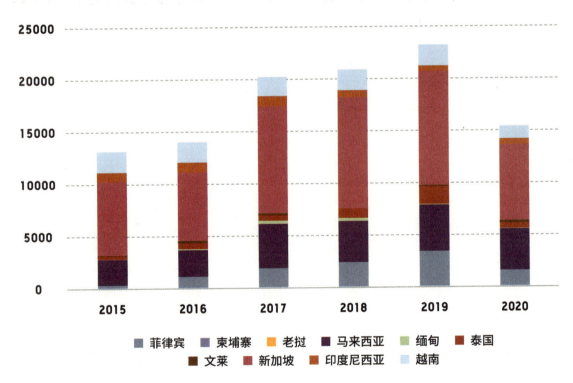

单位：百万美元

数据来源：ASEAN Stats Data Portal

从国别来看，新加坡和马来西亚与中国的石油贸易额较大。其中，由于新加坡是世界重要的炼油中心、石油贸易枢纽，另一方面，中航油、中石油先后于 2004 年和 2009 年分别收购了新加坡石油公司 20.6% 和 45.5% 的股份，以上因素为中国与新加坡开展石油贸易合作积累了有利条件，中新两国间石油贸易额常年维持在较高水平，2020 年达到 75 亿美元。马来西亚作为东南亚第二大石油生产国，长期向中国出口原油。近年来，中国对马来西亚成品油出口额也在不断增长，中马两国间石油进出口贸易逐渐趋于平衡。此外，中国与缅甸通过中缅油气管道长期保持着较高的石油贸易活跃度。截至 2020 年 5 月，经中缅油气管道缅甸累计向中国输送原油 3000 万吨。中缅油气管道是中国实现石油运输渠道多元化的里程碑，有效缓解了中国对马六甲海峡的依赖程度，进一步增强了石油供应保障。

图 3.1.1-2 · 2020年中国与东南亚国家石油进出口贸易额

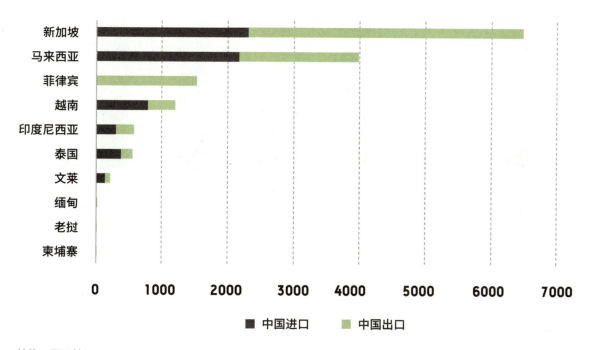

■ 中国进口　■ 中国出口

单位：百万美元

数据来源：ASEAN Stats Data Portal

3.1.2 中国从东南亚国家天然气进口量持续上升

东南亚是中国进口天然气的主要区域之一，近年来中国与东南亚国家天然气贸易额呈波动态势。2020 年，受新冠疫情影响，中国与东南亚国家天然气贸易较 2019 年下降 25.5%，贸易总额仅为 53 亿美元，该贸易额占中国与全球天然气贸易总额（349 亿美元）的 15.2%，占东南亚与全球天然气贸易总额（324 亿美元）的 16.4%。

图 3.1.2-1 · 2015—2020年中国与东南亚国家天然气贸易总额

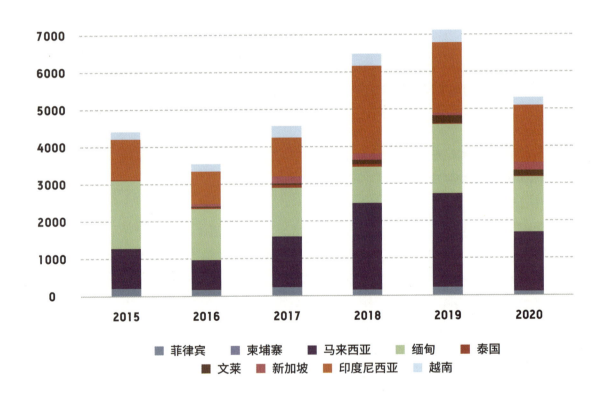

单位：百万美元
数据来源：ASEAN Stats Data Portal

从国别来看，天然气进口源来自马来西亚、印度尼西亚和缅甸三国。其中，马来西亚、印度尼西亚向中国出口液化天然气，缅甸则通过中缅油气向中国出口管输天然气。近年来，中国从马来西亚、印度尼西亚、缅甸三国的天然气进口量总体呈上升趋势，2015 — 2020 年天然气进口量年均增长率为 9.4%。2020 年，中国从上述三国进口天然气 1418 万吨，以进口液化天然气为主，占总进口量的 78.6%。

图 3.1.2-2 · 2015—2020年中国在东南亚天然气进口量

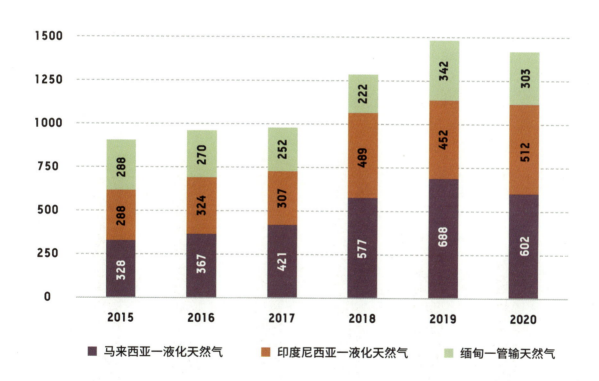

单位：万吨
数据来源：中国海关

3.1.3 东南亚是我国最重要的煤炭进口来源地

中国与东南亚地区的煤炭贸易以中国从东南亚进口为主。2020 年中国与东南亚地区煤炭贸易额约为 78 亿美元。根据我国海关总署统计，我国有近一半的煤炭进口来自东南亚国家。

从国别来看，印度尼西亚是中国煤炭进口的主要来源地，中国每年从印度尼西亚煤炭进口量占中国从东南亚煤炭进口总量的 70% 左右。

图 **3.1.3-1** · **2015—2020年中国与东南亚国家煤炭贸易总额**

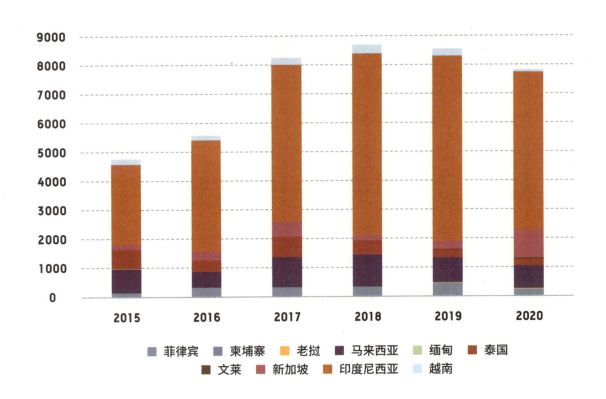

单位：百万美元

数据来源：ASEAN Stats Data Portal

图 3.1.3-2 · 2020年中国与东南亚国家煤炭进出口贸易额

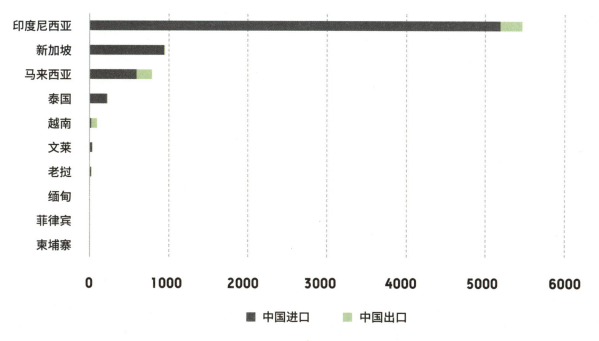

单位：百万美元
数据来源：ASEAN Stats Data Portal

3.2 电力领域投资合作

3.2.1 可再生能源投资合作以水电为主

中国在东南亚国家的可再生能源投资合作主要集中于水电领域，涉及少数太阳能、生物质发电项目。从国别来看，可再生能源项目投资主要分布在柬埔寨、老挝、马来西亚、缅甸、泰国、印度尼西亚和越南等国。

表 3.2.1 · 中国—东南亚国家可再生能源主要投资合作项目

序号	国别	项目名称	装机(MW)	中方投资企业	投资模式
1	柬埔寨	甘再水电站	193.2	中国电建	BOT
2	柬埔寨	斯登沃代水电项目	120	大唐集团	BOT
3	柬埔寨	额勒赛下游水电站	338	中国华电	BOT
4	柬埔寨	桑河二级水电站	400	中国华能	BOT
5	柬埔寨	上达岱水电站	150	中国重机	BOT
6	老挝	南俄5号水电站	120	中国电建	BOT
7	老挝	南塔河1号水电站	168	南方电网	BOT
8	老挝	南欧江梯级水电站项目	1272	中国电建	BOT
9	老挝	湄公河北本水电项目	912	大唐集团	BOT
10	老挝	湄公河萨拉康水电项目	660	大唐集团	BOT
11	老挝	色拉龙一级水电站项目	70	云南能投	BOT
12	老挝	Nam Ngum 1号水面漂浮光伏发电项目	1200	杭州赛芳科技	—
13	马来西亚	吉打太阳能电站	50	中广核集团	—
14	缅甸	瑞丽江一级水电站	600	中国华能	BOT
15	缅甸	伊江公司小其培电站	99	国家电投	BOT
16	缅甸	太平江水电项目	240	大唐集团	BOT
17	印度尼西亚	巴丹图鲁水电站项目	510	浙富控股	股权并购
18	越南	小中河水电站	220	南方电网	BOT
19	越南	河内垃圾焚烧发电项目	75	中国天楹	—

根据公开信息整理

在投资建设东南亚水电项目时，中资企业主要采取的模式为绿地投资，投资的水电项目装机规模大多在 100 兆瓦以上。从国别来看，中国在柬埔寨、老挝、缅甸等国的水电投资较多。

在东南亚非水可再生能源项目开发方面，目前中国参与投资建设的项目数量依然较少。然而，东南亚国家能源低碳转型发展的态势强劲，采用清洁低碳、智慧高效的能源供应方式解决能源可及性问题成为各国共识。东南亚国家已相继制定非水可再生能源发展规划，并颁布一系列能源转型政策，未来东南亚非水可再生能源市场前景广阔，这将为中国与东南亚国家开展更深层次的可再生能源合作提供了大量机会。

3.2.2 火电投资以大容量高参数煤电为主

中国投资东南亚国家的火电项目以大容量高参数煤电为主。从投资模式来看，中国与东南亚国家投资合作的煤电项目以绿地投资为主，涉及少数股权并购。从国别来看，火电项目投资主要分布在柬埔寨、印度尼西亚、越南等国。

近年来，中资企业在东南亚国家投资的煤电项目累计装机超过 10 吉瓦，约占东南亚地区煤电装机总量的 10%。其中包括印度尼西亚爪哇 7 号燃煤电厂、印度尼西亚玻雅坑口燃煤电站、越南海阳燃煤电站等吉瓦级煤电项目。中资企业投资建设的火电机组均大都采用了先进环保的清洁煤电技术，年利用小时数普遍较高，为进一步提升当地电力系统的安全稳定性作出了重要贡献。

表 3.2.2 · 中国一东南亚国家火电投资合作项目

序号	国别	项目名称	装机(MW)	中方投资企业	投资模式
1	柬埔寨	西哈努克港燃煤电站	700	中国华电	BOT
2	印度尼西亚	巴淡燃煤电站	130	中国华电	BOT
3	印度尼西亚	莨苏穆印煤电项目	300	国家能源集团	BOO
4	印度尼西亚	玻雅坑口燃煤电站	1320	中国华电	BOOT
5	印度尼西亚	巴厘岛燃煤电站	426	中国华电	BOOT
6	印度尼西亚	南苏1号独立燃煤发电厂	700	国家能源集团	BOO
7	印度尼西亚	爪哇7号燃煤电厂	2100	国家能源集团	BOO
8	印度尼西亚	明古鲁燃煤电站项目	200	中国电建	BOOT
9	印度尼西亚	万丹火电项目	670	国投集团	股权并购
10	印度尼西亚	米拉务燃煤发电项目	450	大唐集团	BOOT
11	印度尼西亚	占碑2号超临界燃煤机组	700	中国华电	—
12	越南	海阳燃煤电站	1200	中国能建	BOT
13	越南	永新燃煤电厂一期	620	南方电网 中电国际	BOT
14	越南	沿海二期燃煤电站项目	1320	中国华电	BOT

根据公开信息整理

3.2.3 电网投资力度加大，股权收购类项目增多

近年来，中国参与东南亚国家的电网投资力度加大。从投资模式来看，中国与东南亚国家投资合作的电网项目以收购为主。从国别来看，电网项目投资主要分布在菲律宾、柬埔寨、老挝、马来西亚、新加坡和印度尼西亚等国。

表 3.2.3 · 中国—东南亚国家电网投资合作项目

序号	国别	项目名称	中方投资企业	投资模式
1	菲律宾	菲律宾国家电网（NGCP）特许经营权	国家电网	股权并购
2	柬埔寨	金边—马德望294km 230kV输变电项目	大唐集团	BOT
3	老挝	组建老挝国家输电网公司（EDL-T）	南方电网	—
4	印度尼西亚	275kV变电站及输电工程项目	大唐集团	BOT
5	印度尼西亚	占碑2号煤电联营项目118km 500kV输电线路	中国华电	—

根据公开信息整理

3.3 电力项目工程建设合作

3.3.1 规划设计咨询工作成效显著

近年来，中国与东南亚国家在能源规划设计咨询方面的合作成果十分显著。

在规划咨询方面，中国先后为越南、菲律宾、老挝、缅甸等国家开展了能源电力合作规划研究，不但有效促进了东道国能源电力产业的有序健康发展，同时也为双方共同开展务实项目合作奠定了良好基础。其中，《老挝电力规划研究》是中国政府首次协助"一带一路"国家编制国家级电力规划，并获得老挝政府高度评价，规划的编制更是推动《关于建立电力合作战略伙伴关系的谅解备忘录》的签署，具有里程碑意义。

在项目设计咨询方面，中国设计单位充分发挥全产业链优势，为东南亚国家大量的火电、水电、新能源、电网项目提供了评估评审、勘察设计、工程建设及管理、运行维护和投资运营、技术服务、装备制造、建筑材料等系列服务，有效带动了中国技术、标准、装备、服务"走出去"。

表 3.3.1·中国—东南亚国家级电力规划设计咨询项目

序号	国别	项目名称	承担单位	时间
1	缅甸	中缅电力合作规划	水电水利规划设计总院	2015
2	越南	中越能源合作规划研究	电力规划设计总院	2016
3	菲律宾	中菲能源合作规划研究	电力规划设计总院	2017
4	老挝	老挝电力规划研究	电力规划设计总院	2018
5	缅甸	缅甸全国可持续水电开发的水资源总体规划	水电水利规划设计总院	2019

根据公开信息整理

3.3.2 东南亚是中国海外电力项目工程建设的主要市场

近年来，东南亚逐渐成长为中资企业提供海外能源项目工程建设服务的主要市场。

在电源项目工程服务方面，截至目前中资企业在东南亚国家提供的电源项目工程服务的装机规模近 30 吉瓦，其中可再生能源项目超过 13 吉瓦。中资企业提供的电源项目工程建设服务主要集中在印度尼西亚、越南、菲律宾、老挝等国家。

图 3.3.2-1 · 2016—2021年上半年中国与东南亚国家工程建设合作情况

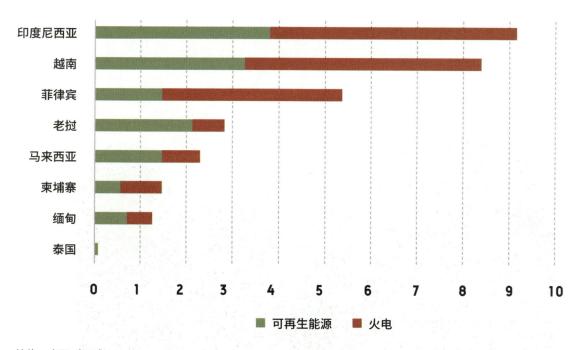

单位：吉瓦（GW）
数据来源：根据政府及企业公开信息整理

在可再生能源项目工程服务方面，中资企业在东南亚国家的可再生能源项目工程服务从早期的以水电项目为主，已向光伏、风电以及生物质发电等新能源领域不断扩展。中资企业近年在东南亚地区参与建设的新能源项目已超过 5 吉瓦，为合作国打造了一批大型新能源发电的示范项目。其中，越南是中国在东南亚地区光伏和风电项目工程建设合作规模最大的市场。由中国电建在越南承建的油汀 500 兆瓦光伏发电项目，是东南亚地区目前规模最大的单体光伏电站，也是全球最大的半浸没区光伏项目。

在火电项目工程服务方面，除煤电项目外，中资企业在东南亚还承建了一批大型气电项目。在电网项目工程服务方面，中资企业在中南半岛国家、菲律宾、马来西亚承建了多项电网基础设施及输电线路建设工程，有效提高了东南亚国家电力传输能力，进一步提高了当地的电网安全稳定性。例如，由国家电网承建的缅甸北克钦邦与 230 千伏主干网联通输变电项目，年输电能力 300 兆瓦，满足缅甸 500 万家庭用电需求，帮助缅甸架起了"北电南送"电力通道，也进一步加快了中国与缅甸及其周边国家基础设施互联互通步伐；由中国重机承建的柬埔寨农村电网扩建工程，覆盖柬埔寨 13 个省份的农村电网，有效解决农村用电问题，显著提升了柬埔寨电网覆盖率。

3.4 电力互联互通合作

3.4.1 中国已与部分东南亚国家实现电力互联

　　近年来，东南亚国家经济发展迅速，各国电力市场需求旺盛，各国希望通过加强电力互联互通，实现资源优化配置、保障电力可靠供应的意愿越发强烈，这为加快中国与东南亚国家的电力互联互通工作提供了重要的机遇窗口。截至目前，中国通过 14 回110 千伏及以上输电线路，与缅甸、越南、老挝三国实现了电力互联，进一步提升了三国的电力供应保障能力，有效解决了部分偏远地区无电人口的用电问题。

表 3.4.1 · 中国—东南亚国家电力互联情况

国别	联网线路
中缅	1回500千伏线路
	2回220千伏线路
	3回110千伏线路
	8回35千伏线路
	36回10千伏线路
中越	3回220千伏线路
	4回110千伏线路
中老	1回115千伏线路
	3回35千伏线路

数据来源：《中国电力发展报告2020》，电力规划设计总院

2004 年，中国与越南首个电网互联项目，云南河口至越南老街 110 千伏联网工程投运，标志着中国第一次大规模向境外送电的开始。截至目前，中国与越南主要通过 3 回 220 千伏线路实现互联，由中国向越南出口电量。

2001 年，中国与老挝实现电网互联，先后通过 10 千伏、35 千伏、115 千伏线路从云南向老挝北部进行供电，使老挝北部农村及偏远地区实现了电力联通。2017 年 11 月，习近平主席与老挝国家主席本扬共同见证签署了《关于建立电力合作战略伙伴关系的谅解备忘录》。2018 年 8 月，南方电网公司与老挝计划投资部签署《关于开发建设老挝国家输电网可行性研究谅解备忘录》。2021 年 3 月，由中国南网公司与老挝国家电力公司共同出资组建的老挝国家输电网公司（EDL－T），正式与老挝政府签署特许经营权协议，标志着中老两国在输电领域开展互利共赢合作迈出了实质性步伐。

2014 年底，中国与缅甸电网互联项目，缅方首次提出从中国云南建设 500 千伏输电线路向缅甸仰光地区送电。2017 年，由南方电网公司和国家电网公司组成的项目中方工作组正式成立。2020 年 1 月，在中缅两国领导人共同见证下，南方电网公司与缅甸电力与能源部签署了《关于开展中缅联网项目可行性研究的备忘录》，缅方授权中方工作组负责开展中缅联网项目可行性研究。中缅联网项目建成后，将有助于缓解缅甸用电紧张状况，改善民生用电，助力缅甸社会经济发展。

3.4.2 电力贸易规模仍然较小

中国通过联网线路与越南、老挝和缅甸三国开展电力贸易合作，目前电力贸易规模总体较小，年交易电量总体保持在 4 太瓦时左右，年交易额保持在 1 亿美元左右。2020 年，中国分别向越南、缅甸和老挝出口电量 1.94 太瓦时、544 吉瓦时、90 吉瓦时，同时从缅甸进口电量 1.54 太瓦时，年度交易额共计 1.14 亿美元。

表 3.4.2 · 2020年中国与东南亚国家电力交易量

国家	中国出口电量（吉瓦时）	中国进口电量（吉瓦时）
缅甸	544	1539
越南	1940	—
老挝	90	—

数据来源：《中国电力发展报告2020》，电力规划设计总院

3.5 国际交流合作

3.5.1 依托能源领域多双边合作平台积极开展国际交流合作

依托各类多双边制度框架和合作机制下的国际会议及论坛，中国与东南亚国家在能源领域长期保持着密切友好的国际交流合作。

表 3.5.1 · 中国—东南亚国家主要国际交流平台

	交流平台
多边	中国一东盟（10+1）领导人会议
	澜沧江一湄公河（LMC）合作领导人会议
	大湄公河次区域（GMS）经济合作领导人会议
	东亚峰会能源部长会议
	东盟与中日韩（10+3）能源部长会议
	东盟与中日韩（10+3）清洁能源圆桌对话会
	东亚峰会清洁能源论坛
	东亚峰会新能源论坛
	中国一东盟电力合作与发展论坛
	亚太经合组织（APEC）能源工作组会议
双边	中老能源合作工作组会议
	中泰能源工作组会议
	中缅电力合作委员会会议
	中菲油气合作政府间联合指导委员会会议

能源合作是中国一东盟（10+1）领导人会议、澜沧江一湄公河（LMC）合作领导人会议、大湄公河次区域（GMS）经济合作领导人会议等各国元首和政府首脑高级别会议的重要议题。2020 年 11 月，李克强总理在第 23 次中国一东盟领导人会议中提出：中方欢迎各方签署《区域全面经济伙伴关系协定》，落实好《中国－东盟自贸协定》及升级《议定书》，继续深化共建"一带一路"倡议同东盟发展规划对接，支持东盟基础设施、能源资源等领域重大项目建设，为地区经贸往来提供支撑。

在多边能源合作方面

东亚峰会能源部长会议、东盟与中日韩（10+3）能源部长会议、东盟与中日韩清洁能源圆桌对话会等高端对话平台为中国与东南亚国家开展能源合作搭建了重要的国际合作通道。同时，东亚峰会清洁能源论坛、东亚峰会新能源论坛、中国一东盟电力合作与发展论坛、亚太经合组织（APEC）能源工作组会议等国际论坛及会议，也为中国与东南亚国家在能源电力领域的信息互通和交流合作搭建了高效的互动平台。2021 年 9 月，中国一东盟电力合作与发展论坛在广西南宁举行，中国国家能源局局长章建华表示，电力作为能源技术的核心是中国与东盟各国合作的重要领域。

在双边能源合作方面

中老能源合作工作组会议、中泰能源工作组会议、中缅电力合作委员会会议、中菲油气合作政府间联合指导委员会会议等系列双边会议为双方在能源电力领域开展务实合作创造了深入交流的良好平台。2017 年 10 月，中国国家能源局与老挝能源和矿产部在广州共同主持召开了中国一老挝能源合作工作组第一次会议，中老双方就中方协助老方编制电力规划、加强中老联网并向第三国送电、两国企业合作开展老挝输电网投资、建设和运营以及两国电力互送等事宜进行了深入交流，并达成了广泛共识。

3.5.2 能力建设是中国协助东南亚国家加强能源软实力建设的重要方式

能力建设是中国协助东南亚国家加强自身软实力建设的重要方式，通过人员培训、项目考察、交流研讨会、最佳实践分享等能力建设活动，中国与东南亚国家就能源电力合作交流进行广泛沟通，为东南亚国家培养打造一支专业化、本土化的能源人才队伍提供了有效平台，也为中国与东南亚开展更广泛、更深层次的能源合作奠定了坚实基础。

2019 年，中国电力规划设计总院受中国国家能源局委托，组织开展澜沧江—湄公河电力互联互通合作项目，先后在中国举办了三期电力互联互通合作培训班及两次研讨会。来自澜湄六国能源电力主管部门、电力企业、国际组织的代表参加了培训、考察及研讨活动，就电力互联互通方面的技术、标准、政策及相关法律等进行了深入研讨，并围绕各国电力行业的实践经验成果以及区域电力互联互通的实现路径和前沿技术展开了深入交流。项目累计培训了百余名澜湄国家电力专业技术人员，为澜湄国家提升电力技术管理水平，推动区域电力互联互通设施建设，带动澜湄地区电力持续发展做出了积极贡献。

2017 年，中国水电水利规划设计总院联合东盟能源中心启动了中国一东盟清洁能源合作旗舰项目——中国一东盟清洁能源能力建设计划。2018 年和 2019 年，项目先后围绕"多能互补"和"抽水蓄能"领域举办了两期培训；2020 年，项目以"提升东盟光伏应用占比路径"为主题，开展了水光互补、水上光伏等先进光伏应用形式在东盟区域应用的预热和探讨；2021 年 7 月，项目围绕"推动东盟风电规模化发展"主题，召开了预热会，展望了东盟国家风电开发的潜力。项目旨在推动区域清洁能源可持续发展，分享清洁能源发展政策规划和技术应用等经验，推进相关领域的核心人才交流建设，针对抽水蓄能、风电、太阳能、核电、传统水电五大专题领域，计划 10 年为东盟国家培养百位政策技术骨干。

04 东南亚能源发展展望

东南亚能源
发展展望

　　东南亚地区能源消费预计将继续保持较快增长态势，能源转型的步伐也将显著加快。可再生能源在 2030 年前有望成为东南亚最大的能源消费品种，可再生能源装机比重将在 2030 年达到一半左右，大部分地区光伏和风电在部分地区在 2030 年前将实现平价化。在全球碳中和进程的影响下，东南亚化石能源结构也将发生大幅调整，煤炭和石油消费预计在 2025 — 2030 年之间达峰。煤电装机仍将有小幅增加，但火电装机的增量主要为气电，天然气消费也将受到气电发展的带动而保持平稳增长的态势。

4.1　场景设定

　　在综合考虑人口增长、经济发展、政策完善、技术进步等因素的基础上，本研究面向 2040 年设计了三种情景，分别为延续情景、转型情景、加速转型情景。其中，延续情景是以当前政策措施基本保持不变、技术创新稳步推进为基础而预测的未来能源发展形势；转型情景是以实现联合国可持续发展目标以及巴黎协定的能源及气候变化相关内容为导向，能源转型政策得到实施、技术创新步伐加快为基础而预测的未来能源发展形势；加速转型情景是以尽快实现联合国可持续发展目标以及巴黎协定为目标，大幅度调整各国既有的能源政策、大量的创新技术得到规模化应用为基础而预测的未来能源发展形势。

4.2 东南亚地区能源发展展望

4.2.1 经济将继续保持快速增长态势

东南亚是全球经济增长最为活跃的地区之一，随着疫情后经济逐渐复苏，东南亚地区内需将持续增长，基础设施建设加速推进，工业化水平和城市化率逐步提高，预计未来经济将保持快速增长的态势，是全球经济增长的重要引擎之一。到 2030 年，东南亚地区 GDP 总量将接近 4.5 万亿美元，2021 — 2030 年年均增速超过 4%。到 2040 年，东南亚地区 GDP 总量将超过 6 万亿美元，2030 — 2040 年年均增速超过 3%。

图 **4.2.1-1 · 2000—2040年东南亚地区GDP总量**

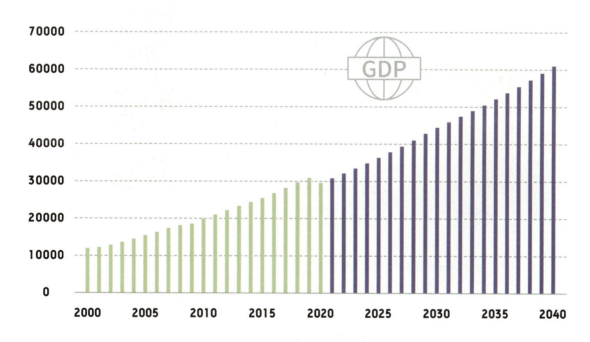

单位：亿美元

数据来源：世界银行，国际货币基金组织，本报告研究

　　从人均 GDP 来看，到 2030 年，东南亚地区人均 GDP 得到显著提高，预计将达到 6000 美元 / 人以上，较 2020 年增幅接近 40%，然而仍远低于当前全球平均水平（约 1.1 万美元 / 人），经济发展存在巨大的潜力，未来具有较大的提升空间。到 2040 年，东南亚地区人均 GDP 将接近 8000 美元 / 人，较 2020 年增幅接近 80%。

图 4.2.1-2 · 2020—2040年东南亚地区人均GDP

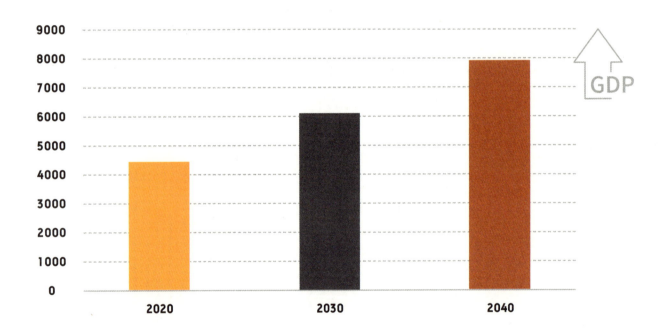

单位：美元/人

数据来源：联合国人口司，国际货币基金组织，本报告研究

4.2.2 能源需求将稳步提升

　　受经济快速发展、工业化进程加速、城市化率提升等多种因素的影响,未来东南亚地区能源需求将呈现稳步增长态势,成为全球能源需求增长的重要驱动因素。在延续情景下,东南亚地区能源需求增长较快,2030 年能源需求总量超过 9 亿吨标油,较 2020 年增幅超过 30%,2021 — 2030 年年均增速接近 3%,2040 年能源需求总量超过 11 亿吨标油;在转型情景下,能源利用效率持续提升,节能减排力度加大,技术创新能力提升,能源转型的潜力释放,能源需求增长放缓,2030 年能源需求总量接近 9 亿吨标油,较 2020 年增幅超过 25%,2021 — 2030 年年均增速超过 2%,2040 年能源需求总量超过 10 亿吨标油;在加速转型情景下,能源利用效率得到进一步提升,电气化水平不断提高,新兴技术得到广泛应用,能源消费呈现低速增长,2030 年能源需求总量超过 8 亿吨标油,较 2020 年增幅约 16%,2021 — 2030 年年均增速约 1.5%,2040 年能源需求总量超过 9 亿吨标油。

图 4.2.2-1·2000—2040年东南亚地区能源需求预测

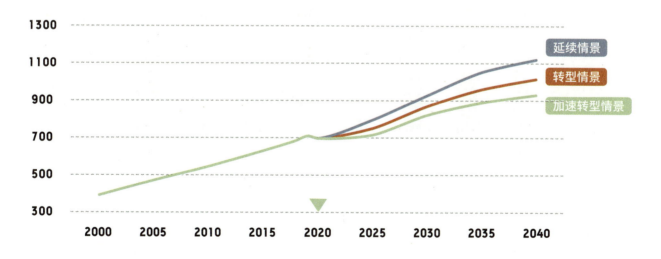

单位:百万吨标油

数据来源:国际能源署,BP,本报告研究

从能源消费结构来看，在转型情景下，从 2020 年起东南亚地区煤炭消费占比持续下降，2030 年预计降至 20%，2040 年预计降至 14%；随着交通电气化程度的提升，石油消费占比自 2015 年以后呈现下降趋势，2030 年降至 27%，2040 年降至 21%；天然气消费占比先升后降，2030 年约为 19%，2040 年降至 17%；可再生能源消费比重快速上升，2030 年占比达到 34%，2040 年占比达到 48%，成为东南亚地区能源消费的主要来源。

图 4.2.2-3 · 2000—2040年东南亚地区能源消费结构

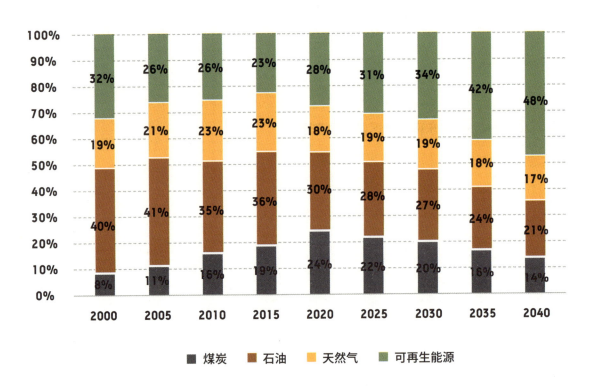

数据来源：国际能源署，本报告研究

4.2.3 煤炭需求量有望于 2025 年达峰

   东南亚地区是全球电力需求增长最快的地区之一，受经济发展水平限制，多国在发展电力时都倾向选择价格低廉的煤电，截至 2020 年仍有近 20 吉瓦的煤电正在建设中，其中大部分位于印尼、越南和菲律宾等国。

   在全球能源转型的背景下，菲律宾等多个东南亚国家已宣布停止新建煤电。受煤电存量及经济发展影响，短期内煤炭仍将是东南亚地区能源消费的主力，长期来看煤炭需求将持续下降。在转型情景下，预计东南亚地区煤炭消费量将在 2025 年左右达峰，达峰值接近 2 亿吨标油，2030 年煤炭消费占比降至 20%，较 2020 年下降约 4 个百分点。2040 年煤炭消费量将降至 1.4 亿吨标油左右。

图 4.2.3-1 · 2000—2040年东南亚地区煤炭需求预测

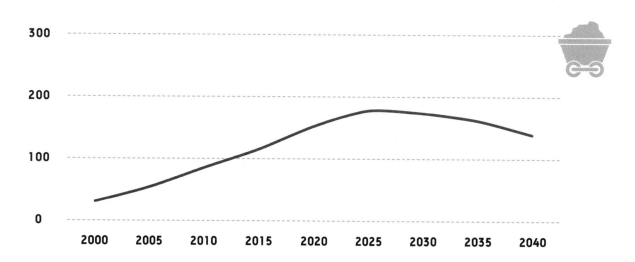

单位：百万吨标油
数据来源：国际能源署，BP，本报告研究

4.2.4 石油消费比重持续下行，天然气需求快速增长

东南亚地区油气资源较为丰富，是东南亚各国能源消费的重要来源。近年来，受油田老化、投资力度减少、国际油价下跌等因素影响，石油产量呈下降趋势，目前石油自给率仅为 50%，主要从中东地区进口，未来对进口石油的依赖程度将不断提升。在转型情景下，东南亚地区石油消费呈现缓慢增长态势，预计石油需求量将在 2030 年左右达峰，达峰值约为 2.4 亿吨标油，达峰后将缓慢下降；2040 年石油需求总量将降至 2.2 亿吨标油左右。燃油效率的提升及交通电气化水平的提高，是影响东南亚地区石油消费的主要因素。

图 4.2.4-1·2000—2040年东南亚地区石油需求预测

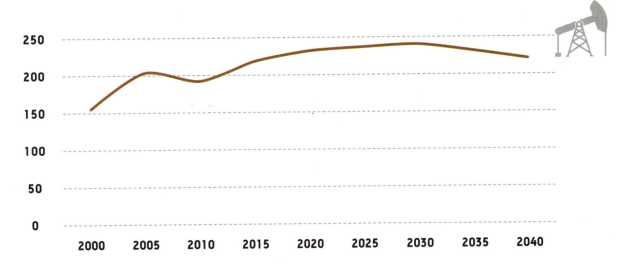

单位：百万吨标油

数据来源：国际能源署，BP，本报告研究

东南亚地区天然气资源较为丰富，自给率超过 120%，以出口为主。近年来，东南亚地区天然气产量较为波动，此外受北美非常规天然气开采的冲击，天然气供应量呈下降趋势。未来东南亚地区将从天然气净出口转变为净进口地区，尤其对进口液化天然气的依赖程度将不断提升。

在转型情景下，由于煤炭消费占比下降，天然气消费将不断提升，其中电力板块的天然气消费增速较快，以弥补煤电机组停建带来的电力缺口。2030 年东南亚地区天然气消费量约 1.7 亿吨标油，2040 年东南亚地区天然气消费量接近 1.8 亿吨标油。

图 4.2.4-2 · 2000—2040年东南亚地区天然气需求预测

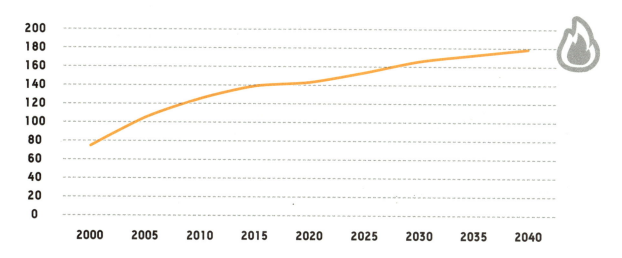

单位：百万吨标油
数据来源：国际能源署，BP，本报告研究

天然气是东南亚地区能源转型的重要选项，未来东南亚地区对进口天然气的依赖程度将不断加强。中国是区域内的天然气进口大国，立足天然气消费国的整体利益，中国可与东南亚地区共同探索搭建区域天然气合作机制，加强区域内油气贸易中心的合作，推动区域油气管道的互联互通，促进天然气进口和贸易的多元化。

为了提高油气互联程度以及传输效率，油气开发、管网建设等基础设施领域是东南亚许多国家的发展重点。中国在油气开采和管网建设方面技术领先，掌握了世界先进的超深井钻井技术，随钻测井一体化技术应用效果显著，油气储运建设技术实现跨越式发展，可与东南亚国家在油气基础设施建设领域开展合作。

4.2.5 可再生能源需求量将大幅提升

东南亚地区水能、太阳能、生物质能等可再生能源资源丰富，在全球能源转型的背景下，各国将大力发展可再生能源，多数国家实施了上网电价、项目拍卖等政策措施来鼓励可再生能源发展。基于各国的可再生能源发展目标，在转型情景下，预计 2030 年东南亚地区可再生能源需求总量约 2.9 亿吨标油，较 2020 年增幅超过 40%，2021 — 2030 年年均增速约为 4%。其中，水能、太阳能等可再生能源需求增长主要用于发电，生物质燃料将主要用于生物质制气、取暖和炊事等。2030 年后，可再生能源需求将快速增长，预计 2040 年东南亚地区可再生能源需求总量将接近 5 亿吨标油，2030 — 2040 年年均增速约 5%。

图 **4.2.5-1** · **2000—2040年东南亚地区可再生能源需求预测**

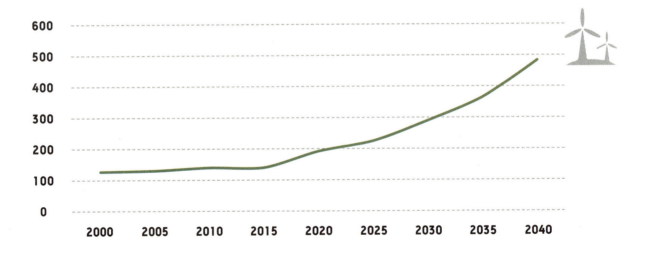

单位：百万吨标油
数据来源：国际能源署，BP，本报告研究

4.3 东南亚地区电力发展展望

4.3.1 电力需求增长势头强劲

随着疫情后经济复苏和电气化率提升，东南亚地区电力消费将保持较快增长，增速仍将处于全球较高水平。在延续情景下，2030年电力需求总量将达到1800太瓦时，2021－2030年年均增速超过5%，2040年电力需求总量将超过2700太瓦时；在转型情景下，2030年电力需求总量接近1700太瓦时，2021－2030年年均增速接近5%，2040年电力需求总量达到2400太瓦时；在加速转型情景下，2030年电力需求总量约为1600太瓦时，2021－2030年年均增速超过4%，2040年电力需求总量约为2200太瓦时。

图 4.3.1-1 · 2000—2040年东南亚地区电力需求

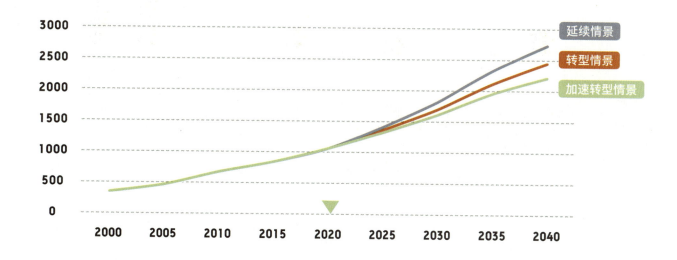

单位：太瓦时（TWh）
数据来源：本报告研究

分国别来看,在转型情景下,越南和印尼是 2021 — 2040 年区域内电力需求增长绝对量最高的国家,分别达到 541 太瓦时和 453 太瓦时,成为区域内电力需求增长的重要来源。此外泰国、菲律宾、马来西亚等国电力需求增长量较大,达到 68 太瓦时以上。经济发展水平和工业化程度的提高是东南亚地区电力需求增长的主要引擎。

图 4.3.1-2 · 2021—2040年东南亚国家电力需求增量

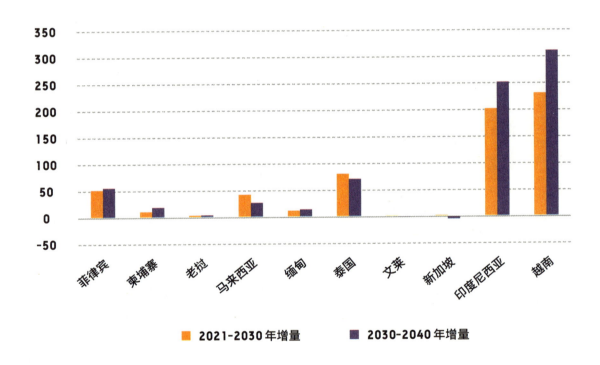

单位:太瓦时(TWh)

数据来源:本报告研究

4.3.2 电力基础设施建设潜力较大

　　随着东南亚各国电力负荷增长，未来该地区电力基础设施建设需求巨大。在延续情景下，东南亚地区 2030 年电力装机总量约 400 吉瓦，2021 — 2030 年年均增速达到 3%，预计 2040 年电力装机总量将超过 560 吉瓦；在转型情景下，2030 年电力装机总量超过 460 吉瓦，2021 — 2030 年年均增速达到 5%，2040 年电力装机总量超过 640 吉瓦；在加速转型情景下，2030 年电力装机总量接近 550 吉瓦，2021 — 2030 年年均增速达到 6%，2040 年电力装机总量超过 700 吉瓦。

图 4.3.2-1 · 2010—2040年东南亚地区电力装机总量

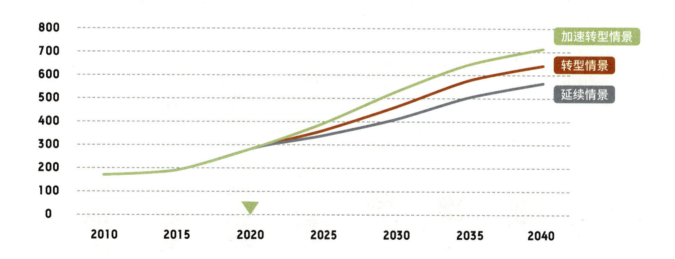

单位：吉瓦（GW）
数据来源：国际能源署，本报告研究

4.3.3 电源装机结构将加速清洁低碳化

随着碳中和进程的推进，东南亚地区新建煤电将大幅减少，短期来看气电将迅速发展以对煤电机组进行部分替代，长期来看可再生能源发电装机将实现大规模发展，成为东南亚地区的最主要的电源装机品种。在转型情景下，由于高污染物和 CO_2 排放，煤电装机将进行大规模改造，2030 年煤电装机量基本保持不变，占比下降至 19%；油电装机量不断下降，2030 年占比降至 4% 左右；气电装机量将稳步增长，但占比呈下降趋势，2030 年气电装机占比约为 29%；以风电、光伏、水电、生物质为主的可再生能源装机实现迅速发展，2030 年装机占比增至 49%，成为东南亚地区最主要的发电装机类型。

图 4.3.3-1 · 2010—2040年东南亚地区电源装机结构

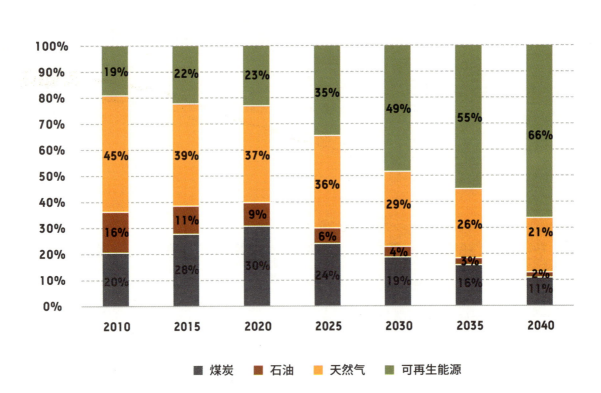

数据来源：本报告研究

● 煤电

目前，东南亚地区的电力装机仍以化石电源为主。在转型情景下，随着新建煤电的大幅减少，2030年东南亚地区煤电装机量将比当前略有上升，新增部分主要为目前在建的煤电项目；2040年煤电装机将逐步下降，现有煤电装机将进行大规模的高效和灵活性改造，同时利用现有煤电设备进行生物质掺烧，以减少煤电机组的碳排放。

图 4.3.3-2 · 2020—2040年东南亚地区煤电装机

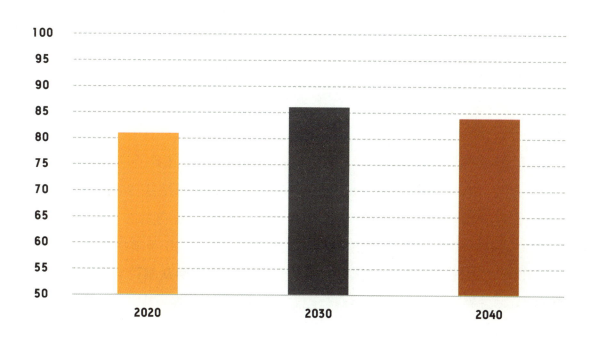

单位：吉瓦（GW）

数据来源：本报告研究

到 2030 年，化石能源发电机组仍占东南亚地区电力装机总量的一半以上，在运火电机组需要进行清洁化和节能改造，以减少污染物排放，提高能源利用效率。同时，东南亚地区的火电机组需要具备更高的灵活性，以满足系统调节的需求，适应大规模的可再生能源接入电力系统。

中国已建成世界上规模最大的清洁高效煤电系统，煤电超低排放机组累计达 9.5 亿千瓦，排放标准世界领先，中国企业在煤电机组超低排放和节能改造方面积累了丰富的经验，可以参与东南亚地区火电机组的升级改造。此外，中国在提升火电机组灵活性方面有着全面的技术优势，已经完成了近 1 亿千瓦煤电机组的灵活性改造，在推动火电机组和可再生能源融合发展方面也积累了大量的实践经验，可与东南亚地区发电企业加强合作。

● 气电

天然气是东南亚地区实现能源转型的重要路径之一。为减少 CO_2 和污染物排放，同时弥补煤电停建带来的电力缺口，东南亚地区气电装机量将实现持续增长，成为东南亚地区最主要的化石能源电源。到 2030 年，气电装机将达到 150 吉瓦左右，较 2020 年增幅超过 50%；到 2040 年，气电装机将达到 190 吉瓦，较 2020 年增幅超过 90%。气电将成为 2040 年前唯一持续增长的化石电源，同时气电将逐渐从基荷电源向灵活调峰电源的角色转换，未来气电将主要作为调节电源，为建设高比例可再生能源的电力系统提供支撑。

图 4.3.3-3 · 2020—2040年东南亚地区气电装机

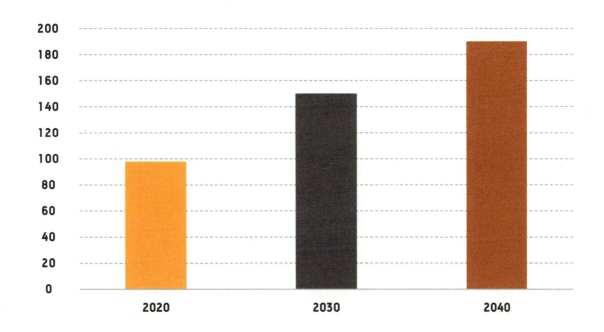

单位：吉瓦（GW）
数据来源：本报告研究

　　作为较为清洁的化石燃料，天然气将在东南亚地区能源转型过程中发挥阶段性的替代作用。天然气发电具有环境保护性能好、优化能源结构、保障电网安全稳定等优点，未来将成为东南亚地区发展的热点领域之一，目前拟新建气电容量已超过90吉瓦。同时，天然气电站将更多地发挥灵活调峰的作用，实现与可再生能源的统筹发展。

　　目前，中国气电装机规模已超过1亿千瓦，较好地支撑了我国电力工业的发展，在气电项目建设、燃机装备、灵活性改造等方面具有较好的技术和经验优势，实现了多项燃气轮机核心关键技术的突破。未来，中国可与东南亚国家在天然气发电项目的投资、建设、技术研发、灵活性改造等领域开展合作，大力推动东南亚地区气电项目的开发。

● **光伏电站**

平准化度电成本（Levelized Cost of Energy，LCOE），是对项目生命周期内的成本和发电量进行平准化后计算得到的发电成本，即生命周期内的成本现值 / 生命周期内发电量现值，在计算成本时考虑资金的时间价值、固定资产折旧、税收等因素的影响。

东南亚地区光伏资源较为丰富，随着技术的进步，光伏发电的成本优势将逐渐凸显。根据测算，2020 年东南亚地区光伏度电成本在 9 美分 / 千瓦时上下，部分光资源较好的地区，光伏度电成本约 7 美分 / 千瓦时。预计到 2030 年，东南亚地区光伏度电成本将下降到 5 美分 / 千瓦时左右，部分光资源较好的地区，光伏度电成本将降至 4 美分 / 千瓦时以下，光伏发电价格将更加具有竞争力。

图 4.3.3-4 · 2020年东南亚各国光伏平准化度电成本

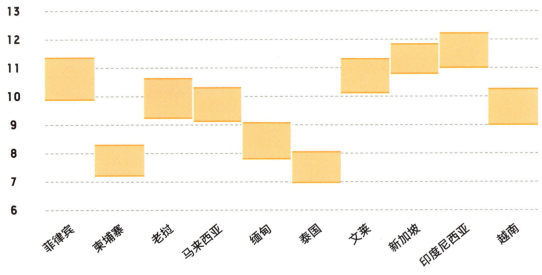

单位：美分/千瓦时
数据来源：本报告研究

图 4.3.3-5 · 2030年东南亚各国光伏平准化度电成本

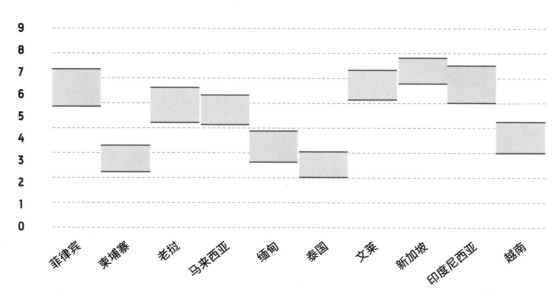

单位：美分/千瓦时

数据来源：本报告研究

综合考虑东南亚地区光伏资源禀赋、经济发展水平、电力需求、电价竞争力等因素，预计到2030年，东南亚地区新增光伏装机约70吉瓦，2030年光伏装机总量超过90吉瓦；2030-2040年新增光伏装机约160吉瓦，2040年光伏装机总量超过230吉瓦。其中，印尼、越南、泰国、菲律宾等国光伏装机增量较大。

图 **4.3.3-6** · **2021—2040年东南亚各国光伏发电装机预测**

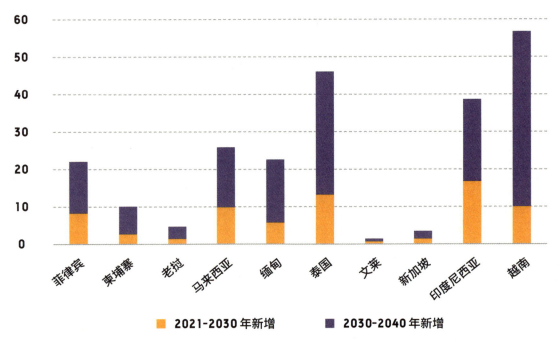

■ **2021-2030 年新增**　　■ **2030-2040 年新增**

单位：吉瓦（GW）
数据来源：本报告研究

　　东南亚地区光伏资源较为丰富，具有开发光伏电站的巨大潜力，随着光伏发电的成本优势逐渐显现，未来东南亚地区光伏开发将大有可为。中国是全球光伏电站投资最大的国家，可参与东南亚地区光伏发电项目的投资建设，为东南亚地区光伏资源的开发利用提供资金、技术等方面的支持。同时，中国也是全球重要的光伏装备生产基地，在集中式光伏电站和分布式光伏电站等领域具有先进的技术和装备优势，可为东南亚地区光伏发展提供装备和技术服务。对于光伏发展速度较快的国家，中国的光伏制造企业也可以在当地投资建厂，服务本地的同时辐射周边区域。

风电

东南亚地区具有一定的风能资源。根据测算，2020 年东南亚地区风电平准化度电成本在 12 美分 / 千瓦时左右，其中风能资源较为丰富的中南半岛地区，风电平准化度电成本可以达到 10 美分 / 千瓦时左右。预计到 2030 年，东南亚地区风电度电成本将下降到 7 美分 / 千瓦时左右，中南半岛地区风电度电成本将降至 5 美分 / 千瓦时左右。

图 4.3.3-7 · 2020年东南亚各国风电平准化度电成本

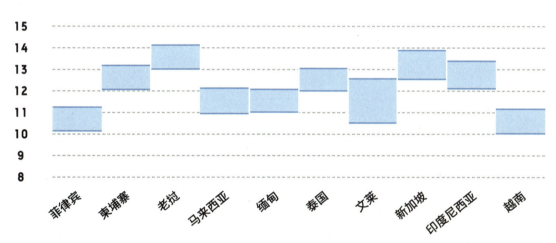

单位：美分/千瓦时
数据来源：本报告研究

图 4.3.3-8 · 2030年东南亚各国风电平准化度电成本

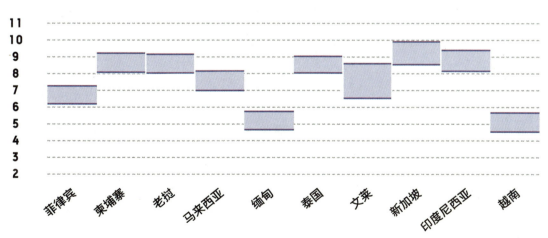

单位：美分/千瓦时
数据来源：本报告研究

综合考虑东南亚地区风能资源禀赋、经济发展水平、电力需求、电价竞争力等因素，预计到 2030 年，东南亚地区新增风电装机约 40 吉瓦，2030 年风电装机总量约 43 吉瓦；2030 — 2040 年新增风电装机约 80 吉瓦，2040 年风电装机总量超过 120 吉瓦。其中，越南、泰国、菲律宾等国风电装机增量较大。

图 **4.3.3-9** · 2021—2040年东南亚各国风电装机预测

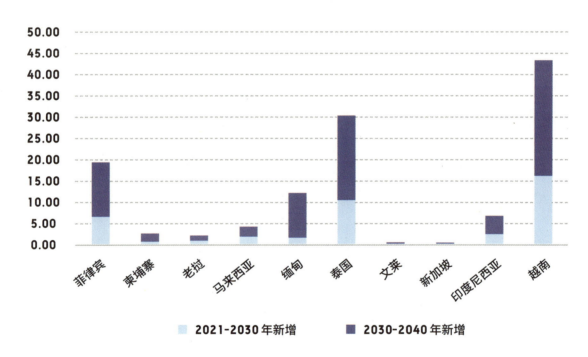

■ 2021-2030 年新增　　■ 2030-2040 年新增

单位：吉瓦（GW）
数据来源：本报告研究

东南亚地区具有一定的风能资源，其中绝大多数为低风速资源，与中国东部和中部的低风速区域类似，具有一定的低风速电站开发潜力。中国在低风速风电开发方面具有先进技术和丰富经验，建立了完善的低风速装备生产线，中方企业可与东南亚地区在陆上低风速风电场的投资、建设、装备制造等领域开展合作。

● 水电

水电是东南亚地区目前最大的可再生能源发电类型，同时待开发的水电资源较为丰富，主要集中在缅甸、印尼、越南、老挝等国家。预计到 2030 年，东南亚地区水电装机新增将接近 40 吉瓦，2030 年水电装机总量接近 90 吉瓦；2030 — 2040 年新增水电装机约为 45 吉瓦，2040 年水电装机总量约为 135 吉瓦。

图 4.3.3-10 · 2021—2040年东南亚各国水电装机预测

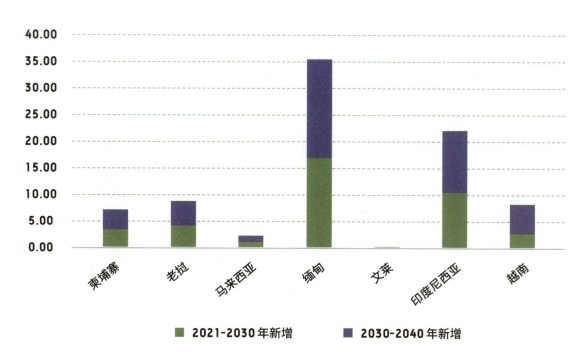

单位：吉瓦（GW）
数据来源：本报告研究

水电是东南亚地区装机总量最大的可再生能源发电品种，该地区水电资源禀赋较好，未来具有巨大的发展潜力。中国在大型水电工程项目建设及流域水电管理运行方面具有显著优势，同时成套设备制造能力持续提升，技术创新能力不断提高，水电行业勘测、设计、施工、运行管理水平均居世界前列，在处理水电开发与生态环境保护、水库移民安置之间的协调关系方面积累了丰富的经验，可与东南亚国家在水电项目开发、工程建设和设备制造等方面开展合作。

● 抽水蓄能电站

东南亚地区水能资源丰富，具有开发抽水蓄能电站的巨大潜力。作为当前技术最为成熟、经济性最优、最具大规模开发条件的清洁性调节电源，抽水蓄能电站可与风电、太阳能发电、火电等形成有效互补。在可再生能源大规模发展的背景下，抽水蓄能将在东南亚地区发挥重要作用。目前，菲律宾和泰国已经具有一定规模的抽水蓄能电站，装机总量接近 2 吉瓦。未来，东南亚地区规划中和已公布的抽水蓄能电站装机接近 7 吉瓦，主要分布在越南、印尼、老挝等国家。

图 4.3.3-11 · 2021—2040年东南亚各国抽水蓄能装机预测

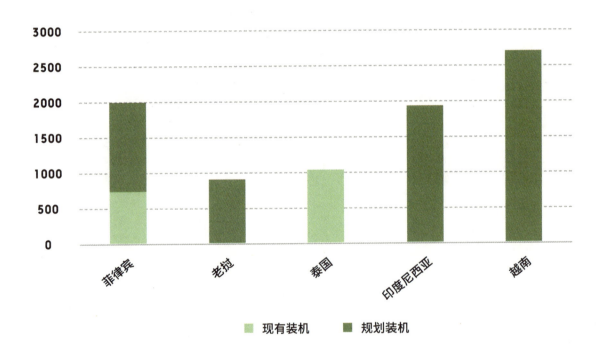

单位：吉瓦（GW）
数据来源：International hydropower association，本报告研究

目前，抽水蓄能电站仍是全球范围内最为成熟和经济的大规模储能方式，未来在东南亚地区具有良好的发展前景。中国是抽水蓄能电站装机规模最大的国家，在抽水蓄能领域具备先进的技术优势和丰富的实践经验。双方可积极开展抽水蓄能电站的规划研究等工作，并根据需要推动工程项目开发和建设方面的合作。

新型电储能

　　储能是实现能源绿色低碳转型的重要装备基础和关键支撑技术。目前，东南亚地区电网互联程度较低，随着间歇性可再生能源电力的市场份额不断增长，储能将在保障电力系统稳定性中发挥重要作用。菲律宾和印度尼西亚岛屿众多、人口分散，台风等自然灾害发生频繁导致了偏远岛屿供电困难，无法与电力公司主网相连，具有部署储能装置的巨大潜力。泰国和越南的负荷中心与资源中心分布不一致，负荷中心与资源中心的电网连接较为薄弱，对现有电网以及新能源发电配套储能装置将有助于实现新能源的大规模开发与利用。通过新型电储能装置的部署，可以有效提升东南亚地区电力支撑水平，减少新能源间歇性、波动性对电力系统带来的冲击。预计到2030年，东南亚地区电储能新增容量将超过10吉瓦，2030-2040年新增电储能容量约20吉瓦。其中印尼、菲律宾、马来西亚等海岛国家电储能发展潜力较大，以满足偏远岛屿的用电需求；同时越南电网结构较为狭长，储能装置的部署可有效避免潮流大范围转移造成的系统稳定性问题。

图 4.3.3-12 · 2021—2040年东南亚地区电储能装机

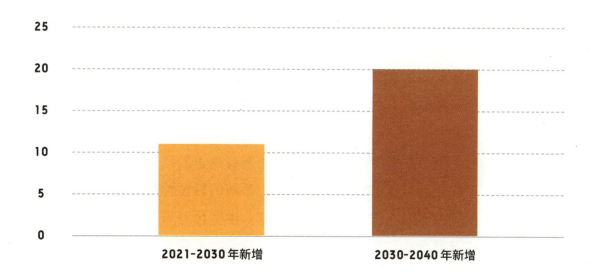

单位：吉瓦（GW）

数据来源：本报告研究

　　中国在新型储能领域具有较强的技术实力，在从材料制备到系统集成的全产业链方面具有显著优势，未来将继续大力推动储能高质量规模化发展。中国企业可参与东南亚地区储能项目的投资与建设，并与东南亚相关国家围绕储能产业链上下游开展深度合作。

4.3.4 电网基础设施建设空间较大

● **骨干电网**

东南亚地区电网基础设施相对薄弱，设备老化现象严重，目前部分国家尚未建立完整的骨干电网，仍有大量农村地区没有实现联网，无电人口数量超过 4000 万，电力可及水平亟待提高。此外，东南亚地区各国能源资源分布不均，电力生产和负荷中心距离较远，加强区域内电力互联互通、统筹区域能源电力资源将有助于区域内资源的优化配置。目前东南亚地区的电力互联互通主要集中在中南半岛地区，受菲律宾、印尼等独立岛屿国家电网延伸困难影响，区域内电力互联互通程度有待加强。

东南亚地区制定了东盟共同电网（APG）发展规划，通过相邻国家间的输电网连接各国的独立电力系统，逐步扩展到次区域，最终实现一体化的东南亚电网系统，具体实施方案为推进 16 个、共 45 条双边电力联网项目的建设。在转型情景下，到 2030 年，东南亚地区新增跨境电力互联容量约 20 吉瓦。

新能源具有波动性、随机性、间歇性等特征，与火电、水电等传统电源存在显著差异，新能源规模化发展势必在各个维度重塑电力系统。随着东南亚地区新能源的大规模发展，电力系统安全稳定运行面临新的风险和不确定性，保障电力供应的难度大幅增加，电力系统调节能力和灵活性亟待提升。

中国在高比例新能源电力系统的建设和运行方面具有先进的技术优势，在大规模新能源接入电力系统领域积累了丰富的经验，对于电力系统的转型路径有着全面的认识，从发电侧、电网侧、用电侧等联合推动绿色电力发展。中国企业可与东南亚地区在高比例新能源电力系统领域开展合作，与东南亚国家共同推动技术研发、项目开发与建设、装备制造、能力建设等方面的相关工作。

● 智能电网

东南亚地区各国电网基础设施发展水平差距较大，多数国家电网运行水平较为落后，电网基础设施改造和升级的需求较为强烈。新加坡和马来西亚电网智能化程度相对较高，其中新加坡电网是世界上最稳定的国家电网之一，自 2009 年智慧能源系统项目启动后，新加坡电网智能化程度再次升级；马来西亚以智能电网技术为核心，构建了低碳、智能的电力系统，实现了城市的现代化能源转型。

未来，随着可再生能源的规模化发展，东南亚地区将有高比例的可再生能源接入电力系统，这要求配套电网具有更高的调度自动化水平和更强的稳定运行能力。分布式能源的快速发展也需要更加高效的配电网技术，建设一个面向分布式发电、交互式供电的分散智能电网。在此背景下，智能电网技术在东南亚地区应用前景良好，东南亚地区将成为智能电网新兴市场中最具有投资潜力的区域之一。到 2030 年，东南地区在智能电网基础设施领域的投资约达到 100 亿美元，其中印尼、马来西亚、泰国、新加坡、菲律宾及越南的智能电网市场发展潜力较大。

05 中国 - 东南亚国家能源合作行动建议

中国 - 东南亚国家
能源合作行动建议

　　东南亚地区已经快速成长为全球最重要的能源消费市场和生产基地，未来能源发展前景十分广阔。为进一步保持和扩大中国 - 东南亚国家能源合作的良好局面，建议双方围绕高比例可再生能源电力系统、绿色能源全产业链、电力互联互通、天然气需求侧合作、能源技术创新、标准互认、人员沟通和技术援助等领域开展更多务实合作，实现共同发展、共同繁荣。

5.1 加强高比例可再生能源电力系统领域多双边务实合作

随着全球能源低碳转型进程的持续加快，许多东南亚国家也制定了宏伟的可再生能源发展规划，风电和光伏可再生能源迎来发展机遇期。可再生能源大规模的并网，将会对各国电力系统带来深远影响，电力系统的安全稳定、供需平衡和高效运行都面临新的挑战，部分国家已经出现了弃风、弃光等问题。

为此，建议推动各方能源转型路径的深度对接，从技术标准、市场机制、运行方式等各方面对电力系统进行统筹优化，在多双边合作机制下启动专项联合工作组，推动各方在电力系统灵活性提升、电网安全稳定性提升等领域加强合作，提升电力系统的可再生能源消纳能力，助力各国电力行业高质量转型发展。

5.2 开展绿色能源全产业链合作

在后疫情时代，很多东南亚国家已将绿色能源发展作为经济复苏的重要动力，但多数国家在绿色能源发展方面缺少经验，绿色能源产业链尚不健全。

建议双方加强在绿色能源项目投资、产能合作、工程建设等绿色产业链上下游的全方位合作，提升能源绿色发展的基础能力；发挥绿色能源对上下游产业的带动作用，促进各国工业化水平提升与经济发展；加强绿色能源开发利用以提高能源可及性，推动实现人人享有可负担、可靠、可持续的现代能源服务，促进绿色能源在消除贫困、增加就业、改善民生中发挥更大的作用。

5.3　大力推动区域电力互联互通

　　随着全球能源低碳转型发展成为各国共识，清洁能源资源丰富的东南亚国家在因地制宜地加快发展水能、风能、太阳能等可再生能源发电，这为电力互联互通提供了天然驱动力。同时，区域全面经济伙伴关系协定（RCEP）的签署，加快了区域经济一体化发展，这也为区域电力一体化提供了强大支撑。

　　建议双方在 RCEP 联合委员会、联合国亚太经社会（UNESCAP）互联互通专家工作组、大湄公河次区域（GMS）机制电力贸易协调委员会或其附属机构、澜沧江湄公河合作（LMC）机制下，加强对电力互联互通相关问题的探讨，共同制定行动路线图，推动电力互联互通网架建设，带动更多项目落地，实现电力全产业链联动发展。同时加强跨境电力贸易机制、跨境电力交易中心建设方案、跨境电力调度和交易模式等方面的研究，推动区域电力一体化进程。

5.4　全面加强区域天然气需求侧合作

全球煤电发展进一步受限，东南亚国家能源转型面临多重选择，天然气如何选择和利用对于东南亚国家能源转型具体实施路径的影响较大。

建议双方可立足天然气消费国的整体利益，在国际场合共同打出强化天然气需求侧合作的联合倡议，探索搭建区域天然气合作部长级机制，加强区域内油气贸易中心的合作，推动双方在天然气合作方面形成合力，不断提高天然气定价方面的话语权。

5.5　加强能源技术创新合作和成果转化

绿色能源新技术和信息新技术的快速发展和规模化应用，为开展更多样、更灵活的绿色能源合作奠定了坚实基础。

建议双方继续深化绿色能源技术创新合作，持续推动绿色能源技术成本下降，全面提升区域绿色能源上网竞争力；共同设立联合实验室和研究中心，在氢能、储能、综合能源、智慧能源等能源新技术方面共同开展合作研究，培育双方能源合作的新动能；重视能源创新技术的跨国转化和应用，推动一批具有引领作用的技术创新示范项目，让绿色能源技术进步的红利惠及更多国家。

5.6　推进技术标准对接和装备认证互信

东南亚国家与中国标准体系存在一定差异，造成项目建设成本提高、质量控制难度变大等问题，给双方开展更高效便捷的能源合作带来一定挑战。

建议双方举办标准化工作交流研讨会，梳理各国标准体系的共性问题及标准缺失情况，加强双方能源项目建设及设备制造相关标准的互相了解，推动双方在电力产品质量、技术国际认证交流合作，推进双方装备认真互信; 共同成立中国 - 东南亚国家标准化联盟，促进区域标准化合作发展，探索合作开展当地技术标准编制，共同参与国际标准的更新和制定。

5.7 加强人员沟通和技术援助

高效的人员沟通和技术援助是双方开展可持续、高质量能源合作的重要基础。

建议双方依托"一带一路"能源合作部长研修班、领军人才培养项目、中国—东盟清洁能源培训项目、澜湄电力互联互通能力建设项目等活动，加强人才培训与交流，促进各国间的互学互鉴，加强双方绿色能源领域人才的全方位储备；同时根据各国需要，组织开展绿色能源领域技术援助，包括协助开展规划编制、派驻专家、技术服务、专项咨询等，为各国绿色能源领域的快速发展提供技术支撑。

06 附录

附录

———

附录 A 东南亚国家能源基础数据

表 A-1 · 2000—2020年东南亚地区分品种能源消费总量

	2000	2010	2014	2015	2016	2017	2018	2019	2020e
煤炭	31.9	85.7	100.1	116.1	124.4	136.5	153.7	165.4	159.5
石油	153.8	190.1	222.2	217.9	225.9	237.0	242.8	234.6	196.2
天然气	74.0	124.6	139.3	138.5	138.5	133.4	140.9	135.7	119.6
可再生能源	124.3	138.8	143.7	140.5	147.5	150.7	145.7	179.8	183.8

单位：百万吨标油

数据来源：国际能源署，英国石油公司，本报告研究

表 A-2 · 2000—2020年东南亚地区分部门终端能源消费总量

	2000	2010	2014	2015	2016	2017	2018	2019	2020e
工业	75.8	122.0	126.4	141.5	138.4	148.7	152.9	161.2	149.1
交通	61.7	88.5	116.9	114.8	124.4	129.7	135.3	147.0	133.8
居民	95.0	101.1	99.5	91.9	89.6	91.0	81.7	81.8	74.1
服务业	12.4	20.8	22.4	23.1	24.6	25.8	26.5	28.7	27.4
其它	28.7	49.0	59.3	58.0	58.9	63.7	68.3	68.2	64.7

单位：百万吨标油

数据来源：国际能源署，国际可再生能源署，本报告研究

表 A-3·2015—2020年东南亚地区分品种能源生产总量

	2015	2016	2017	2018	2019	2020e
煤炭	278.0	285.5	299.9	327.2	364.3	336.2
石油	120.6	122.6	117.6	113.2	105.4	96.7
天然气	185.0	184.2	179.2	182.4	180.5	167.7
可再生能源	141.2	148.0	151.3	147.3	171.6	193.2

单位：百万吨标油

数据来源：国际能源署，英国石油公司，国际可再生能源署，本报告研究

表 A-4 · 东南亚国家CO₂排放量

	2015	2016	2017	2018	2019
菲律宾	112.1	122.2	134.5	138.9	144.3
柬埔寨	8.5	9.7	11.2	15.5	16.0
老挝	8.8	14.3	17.9	32.3	32.8
马来西亚	233.3	246.7	248.9	249.1	250.1
缅甸	22.1	25.5	23.7	26.1	26.2
泰国	283.3	281.7	286.3	292.5	288.3
文莱	7.0	7.5	9.6	9.6	9.1
新加坡	62.1	40.3	39 .1	38.3	38.9
印度尼西亚	507.0	568.2	531.0	576.6	617.5
越南	184.4	185.4	182.6	211.8	247.7

单位：百万吨

数据来源：Our World in Data，本报告研究

表 A-5 · 东南亚国家碳排放强度

	2000	2005	2010	2011	2012	2013	2014	2015	2016	2017	2018	2019
菲律宾	2.2	1.9	1.6	1.5	1.5	1.5	1.5	1.6	1.6	1.6	1.6	1.6
柬埔寨	1.1	1.0	1.3	1.3	1.2	1.2	1.3	1.6	1.7	1.8	2.4	2.3
老挝	0.4	0.5	0.6	0.7	0.7	0.8	0.6	0.6	0.7	0.8	1.2	1.2
马来西亚	3.6	3.9	3.7	3.6	3.4	3.5	3.5	3.4	3.2	2.9	2.9	2.8
缅甸	2.0	1.2	0.5	0.5	0.7	0.8	1.0	1.1	1.2	1.7	1.7	1.7
泰国	2.8	2.8	2.5	2.5	2.5	2.6	2.5	2.5	2.4	2.3	2.2	2.1
文莱	2.1	2.0	2.8	2.8	2.7	2.7	2.7	2.5	2.8	2.9	2.8	2.6
新加坡	2.0	1.5	1.3	1.3	1.2	1.2	1.1	1.0	1.0	1.0	1.0	1.0
印度尼西亚	2.5	2.4	2.1	2.0	2.0	1.9	1.9	1.9	1.8	1.8	1.9	2.0
越南	2.4	3.0	3.5	3.3	3.1	3.1	3.2	3.4	3.5	3.2	3.6	3.9

单位：吨/百美元
数据来源：knoema，本报告研究

附录 B 东南亚国家电力基础数据

表 B-1 · 2015—2020年东南亚国家电力消费总量

国家	简称	2015	2016	2017	2018	2019e	2020e
菲律宾	PH	74.9	82.5	86.1	90.2	95.9	92.0
柬埔寨	KH	5.1	6.2	7.2	8.7	9.1	9.0
老挝	LA	4.2	5.0	4.4	5.0	5.0	4.7
马来西亚	MY	139.8	145.2	152.0	157.2	160.0	149.9
缅甸	MM	13.4	13.1	18.2	18.8	19.5	18.6
泰国	TH	176.9	193.8	193.1	195.1	201.3	195.1
文莱	BN	3.9	3.0	3.7	3.8	3.9	3.8
新加坡	SG	49.5	50.7	51.7	52.6	53.8	52.5
印度尼西亚	ID	211.9	225.9	234.5	263.3	275.2	265.8
越南	VN	151.6	169.6	185.4	227.2	255.4	263.0
合计	-	895.0	936.3	1021.9	1079.2	1054.7	659.3

单位：太瓦时（TWh）
数据来源：国际能源署，Enerdata，CEIC，本报告研究

表 B-2 · 2015—2020年东南亚国家电力装机总量

国家	简称	2015	2016	2017	2018	2019e	2020e
菲律宾	PH	18726	21474	22809	23918	25630	26182
柬埔寨	KH	1682	1712	1919	2228	2458	2729
老挝	LA	6276	6735	6946	7196	8023	9316
马来西亚	MY	31069	33668	34182	34389	36310	36962
缅甸	MM	5036	5242	5778	5787	6097	6165
泰国	TH	38648	44996	45807	53037	54326	54460
文莱	BN	922	922	922	922	1227	1227
新加坡	SG	13395	13445	13618	13653	12563	12582
印度尼西亚	ID	50400	55000	58400	62700	69600	72800
越南	VN	27982	30744	33156	42965	55940	69300
合计	-	194136	213939	223536	246794	272174	291724

单位：兆瓦（MW）

数据来源：国际能源署，国际可再生能源署，各国能源部门数据，本报告研究

表 B-3·2015—2020年东南亚国家煤电装机

国家	简称	2015	2016	2017	2018	2019e	2020e
菲律宾	PH	5893	7419	8049	8844	10417	10944
柬埔寨	KH	403	429	564	551	709	859
老挝	LA	1878	1878	1878	1878	1878	1878
马来西亚	MY	8546	9546	10546	10546	13284	13284
缅甸	MM	120	120	160	160	160	160
泰国	TH	6710	6980	6980	4216	5021	5021
文莱	BN	0	0	0	0	220	220
新加坡	SG	0	0	0	0	0	0
印度尼西亚	ID	26775	28259	29943	30723	33764	35605
越南	VN	3415	4899	6583	14725	20250	22091
合计	-	53740	59530	64703	71644	85703	90062

单位：兆瓦（MW）

数据来源：国际能源署，各国能源部门数据；EndCoal，本报告研究

表 B-4 · 2015—2020年东南亚国家气电装机

国家	简称	2015	2016	2017	2018	2019e	2020e
菲律宾	PH	2862	3431	3447	3453	3453	3453
柬埔寨	KH	0	0	0	0	0	0
老挝	LA	0	0	0	0	0	0
马来西亚	MY	13506	14075	14897	14897	14403	14403
缅甸	MM	1695	1824	2175	2178	2448	2496
泰国	TH	22941	27678	27678	33201	33201	33201
文莱	BN	909	909	909	909	994	994
新加坡	SG	10587	10582	10736	10719	10708	10670
印度尼西亚	ID	12545	14156	14495	16302	20537	21600
越南	VN	7144	7144	7144	7363	9803	9395
合计	-	72188	79799	81480	89022	95547	96212

单位：兆瓦（MW）

数据来源：国际能源署，各国能源部门数据，本报告研究

表 B-5 · 2015—2020年东南亚国家光伏装机

国家	简称	2015	2016	2017	2018	2019e	2020e
菲律宾	PH	173	784	908	914	973	1048
柬埔寨	KH	12	18	29	29	99	208
老挝	LA	3	4	22	22	22	22
马来西亚	MY	229	279	370	536	882	1493
缅甸	MM	21	32	44	48	88	84
泰国	TH	1425	2451	2702	2967	2988	2988
文莱	BN	1	1	1	1	1	1
新加坡	SG	46	97	116	160	272	329
印度尼西亚	ID	79	88	98	69	155	172
越南	VN	5	5	8	105	4898	16504
合计	-	1993	3760	4298	4850	10377	22850

单位：兆瓦（MW）

数据来源：国际可再生能源署，本报告研究

表 B-6 · 2015—2020年东南亚国家风电装机

国家	简称	2015	2016	2017	2018	2019e	2020e
菲律宾	PH	427	427	427	427	443	443
柬埔寨	KH	0	0	0	0	0	0
老挝	LA	0	0	0	0	0	0
马来西亚	MY	0	0	0	0	0	0
缅甸	MM	0	0	0	0	0	0
泰国	TH	234	507	628	1103	1507	1507
文莱	BN	0	0	0	0	0	0
新加坡	SG	0	0	0	0	0	0
印度尼西亚	ID	1	1	1	144	154	154
越南	VN	136	160	205	237	375	600
合计	-	799	1096	1262	1911	2479	2705

单位：兆瓦（MW）
数据来源：国际可再生能源署，本报告研究

表 B-7 · 2015—2020年东南亚国家水电装机

国家	简称	2015	2016	2017	2018	2019e	2020e
菲律宾	PH	3613	3623	3632	3719	3761	3761
柬埔寨	KH	930	930	980	1330	1330	1330
老挝	LA	4355	4813	5006	5256	6083	7376
马来西亚	MY	5742	6121	6145	6165	6245	6275
缅甸	MM	3198	3264	3304	3304	3304	3304
泰国	TH	3639	3649	3649	3667	3667	3667
文莱	BN	0	0	0	0	0	0
新加坡	SG	0	0	0	0	0	0
印度尼西亚	ID	5322	5666	5703	5772	5976	6210
越南	VN	15905	17131	17809	17989	18069	18165
合计	-	42703	45197	46228	47203	48436	50088

单位：兆瓦（MW）
数据来源：国际可再生能源署，本报告研究

表 B-8·2015—2020年东南亚国家生物质装机

国家	简称	2015	2016	2017	2018	2019e	2020e
菲律宾	PH	233	259	276	341	393	368
柬埔寨	KH	32	30	50	51	51	51
老挝	LA	40	40	40	40	40	40
马来西亚	MY	1580	1558	818	839	919	931
缅甸	MM	2	2	5	5	5	5
泰国	TH	3231	3395	3824	4196	4255	4389
文莱	BN	0	0	0	0	0	0
新加坡	SG	205	210	211	219	219	219
印度尼西亚	ID	1734	1775	1849	1875	1884	1887
越南	VN	161	188	192	380	380	380
合计	-	7218	7456	7264	7946	8145	8270

单位：兆瓦（MW）

数据来源：国际可再生能源署，本报告研究

附录 C 中国与东南亚国家工程建设合作项目

表 C-1 · 中国与东南亚国家可再生能源工程项目建设合作

序号	国别	项目名称	装机(MW)	签约时间	中方总包企业
1	菲律宾	班邦水电项目	8.1	2017	中国电建
2	菲律宾	宿务那牙光伏项目	60	2017	中国能建
3	菲律宾	北伊罗柯斯省风光一体化项目	232	2017	恒顺众昇
4	菲律宾	南普兰吉（Pulangi）水电站	250	2019	中国能建
5	菲律宾	Pasuquin风电厂	132	2020	中资中程
6	菲律宾	Burgos光伏电站	100	2020	中资中程
7	菲律宾	Mapanuepe抽水蓄能电站	500	2020	中国能建
8	菲律宾	凯旁安水电站	60	2021	中国能建
9	菲律宾	GBP光伏电站项目	115	2021	中国能建
10	菲律宾	巴拉望生物质电站	15	2021	中国能建
11	柬埔寨	EPC光伏项目	200	2017	亨通光电
12	柬埔寨	暹粒自备光伏发电站项目	300	2017	中国电建
13	柬埔寨	磅清扬光伏发电项目	60	2021	国机集团
14	老挝	芭莱水电站	770	2017	中国电建
15	老挝	南公1水电站项目	160	2017	中国水利水电
16	老挝	南空3号水电项目	54	2017	中国能建
17	老挝	东萨宏水电站项目	260	2018	中国电建
18	老挝	南莫2水电项目	120	2018	东方电气
19	老挝	怀拉涅河水电站项目	60	2018	中国水利水电
20	老挝	南屯1水电站	474	2019	中国电建
21	老挝	波里坎塞光伏项目	230	2019	国机集团
22	马来西亚	巴莱（Baleh）水电站	1285	2017	中国电建
23	马来西亚	霹雳州大型光伏电站项目	62	2018	国机集团
24	马来西亚	柔佛州大型地面光伏项目	25	2020	国家电投
25	马来西亚	雪兰莪州水面漂浮光伏项目	10	2020	国家电投
26	马来西亚	登嘉楼地面光伏项目	5	2020	国家电投
27	马来西亚	吉兰丹州水电项目	84	2021	中国能建

序号	国别	项目名称	装机(MW)	签约时间	中方总包企业
28	缅甸	瑞丽江二级水电站项目	520	2016	中国电建
29	缅甸	钦邦水电项目	150	2019	中国电建
30	缅甸	拉帕拉光伏电站	40	2021	中国能建
31	泰国	Sarahnlom风电项目	67.5	2016	中国电建
32	泰国	孔敬府光热光伏混合电站	90	2020	中国能建
33	印度尼西亚	亚奇省一揽子水电项目	1000	2017	昌兴国际
34	印度尼西亚	连锁式生物质发电站	150	2017	中国建材
35	印度尼西亚	泰普一级水电站	443	2018	中国电建
36	印度尼西亚	卡扬一级水电站	900	2019	中国电建
37	印度尼西亚	门达朗水电站项目	100	2020	中国能建
38	印度尼西亚	DATA DIAN水电项目	1200	2020	中国能建
39	越南	永河水电站	21	2016	中国能建
40	越南	芳梅风电项目	30	2017	中国电建
41	越南	油汀光伏项目	500	2018	中国电建
42	越南	Dau Tieng 1 &2 光伏发电项目	420	2018	中国电建
43	越南	庆和Long Son光伏发电项目	170	2018	中国电建
44	越南	冰洋光伏电站	40	2018	中国电建
45	越南	格桔光伏项目	62	2019	国机集团
46	越南	金兰光伏电站	64	2019	国机集团
47	越南	Saomai二期1光伏电站	106	2020	国机集团
48	越南	禄宁光伏发电项目	550	2020	中国电建
49	越南	富美光伏发电项目	330	2020	中国电建
50	越南	薄寮三期风电项目	141	2020	中国电建
51	越南	平大海上风电项目	310	2020	中国电建
52	越南	宁顺风电项目	117	2020	中国能建
53	越南	昆嵩风电厂	50	2021	中国能建
54	越南	金瓯海上风电项目	350	2021	中国电建

根据公开信息整理

表 C-2 · 中国与东南亚国家火电工程项目建设合作

序号	国别	项目名称	装机(MW)	签约时间	中方总包企业
1	菲律宾	马斯巴特燃煤电厂	15	2017	中国能建
2	菲律宾	迪格宁（GNPD）超临界燃煤电站项目	1320	2017	中国交建
3	菲律宾	Palauig LNG联合循环电站	1100	2017	中国能建
4	柬埔寨	干拉省烈威艾县重油/天然气双燃料电站项目	200	2019	中国能建
5	柬埔寨	国公省燃煤发电厂项目	700	2020	中钢集团
6	老挝	色贡煤电一体化项目	700	2016	国机集团
7	马来西亚	凯德隆联合循环燃气电站	826	2016	中国电建
8	缅甸	孟邦直通燃机电厂	119	2016	中国能建
9	缅甸	仰光THAKETA燃气-蒸汽联合循环电厂	110	2016	中国电建
10	缅甸	皎漂燃气-蒸汽联合循环电站	135	2018	中国电建
11	缅甸	阿弄（Ahlone）燃机电厂	183	2019	中国能建
12	印度尼西亚	坦竣清洁煤电站项目	1320	2016	哈电集团
13	印度尼西亚	明古鲁燃煤电站	200	2016	中国电建
14	印度尼西亚	芝拉扎三期燃煤发电厂	1000	2016	中国能建
15	印度尼西亚	加里曼丹Kalbar-1燃煤发电项目	200	2017	中国电建
16	印度尼西亚	帕卢市火电开发项目	700	2017	泰富重装
17	印度尼西亚	哥伦打洛SULBAGUT-1燃煤电站	100	2018	中国电建
18	印度尼西亚	北苏三（Sulut-3）燃煤电站	100	2018	中国电建
19	印度尼西亚	南苏拉威西省班塔恩燃煤电站	600	2019	中国能建
20	印度尼西亚	廖内双燃料内燃机电厂	200	2019	中国能建
21	印度尼西亚	拉波塔燃煤发电厂	1140	2021	中国能建
22	越南	海阳燃煤电站项目	1200	2016	中国能建
23	越南	南定燃煤电站项目	1200	2018	中国能建
24	越南	公清燃煤电厂	600	2020	中国能建

根据公开信息整理

表 C-3 · 中国与东南亚国家电网工程项目建设合作

序号	国别	项目名称	签约时间	中方总包企业
1	菲律宾	Pagbilao 500kV EHV变电站	2018	国家电投
2	菲律宾	图伊-达斯马里尼亚斯500kV变电站工程	2018	中国电建
3	菲律宾	Navotas 230kV变电站EPC项目	2019	国家电投
4	菲律宾	宿务-薄荷230kV互连项目	2019	中国电建
5	菲律宾	棉兰老岛—维萨亚斯350kV 直流互联线路项目	2020	中国能建
6	菲律宾	ABUYOU 230kV变电站	2020	国家电投
7	菲律宾	Dumanjug 230kV变电站扩建项目	2020	中国电建
8	菲律宾	Dumanjug 138/69kV扩建工程	2020	中国电建
9	菲律宾	马尼拉-马里劳 230kV线路EPC项目	2021	中国西电
10	菲律宾	菲律宾国家电网公司（NGCP） 230kV GIS变电站EPC项目	2021	中国西电
11	柬埔寨	柬埔寨国家电力公司（EDC） 农村电网扩建1-6期	2010- 2016	中国重机
12	柬埔寨	500kV主网及域网输变电EPC项目	2018	中国重机
13	老挝	万象500/230kV输变电项目	2017	国家电网
14	老挝	老挝南屯-1输变电项目	2017	中国能建
15	老挝	万象115/22千伏输变电项目	2017	特变电工
16	马来西亚	Eastwood 132/33kV GIS变电站	2018	中国西电
17	缅甸	"北电南送"230kV主干网 联通输变电项目	2017	国家电网
18	泰国	曼谷南变电站项目	2017	中国电建
19	泰国	泰国国家电力局（EGAT）500kV 输电线路成套项目	2018	中国西电
20	印度尼西亚	玻雅坑口电站500kV输电线路工程	2019	中国能建

根据公开信息整理

附录 D 东南亚国家展望数据

表 D-1·经济社会发展展望结果

类别	2030	2040
GDP 单位：亿美元 （2010年不变价）	44559	61009
人均GDP 单位：美元/人	6127	7931

表 D-2·转型情景能源需求展望结果

类别	2030	2040
一次能源需求总量 单位：百万吨标油（mtoe）	870	1020
煤	175	123
油	238	218
气	180	275
可再生	277	404
可再生能源占比	32%	40%

表 D-3 · 转型情景电力需求展望结果

类别	2030	2040
电力需求总量 单位：十亿千瓦时（TWh）	1686	2425
电力装机总量 单位：吉瓦（GW）	411	630
煤	85	85
油	17	13
气	130	163
可再生	179	369

01 Overview of Southeast Asia

Overview of
Southeast Asia

Southeast Asia is an important partner of China along Belt and Road. In recent years, the economy of Southeast Asia has developed rapidly and the business environment has been continuously improved. It is an important force for global economic development. With the joint efforts of the two sides, China and Southeast Asian countries have jointly established a series of intergovernmental cooperation mechanisms. The fields of cooperation between the two sides are becoming more and more extensive, the contents of cooperation continue to expand, and the development momentum of bilateral trade and investment cooperation is good.

1 Overview of Southeast Asia

1.1 Brief Introduction of Countries and Regions

Southeast Asia (SEA) is located in the southeast of Asia, consisting of Indochina Peninsula and Malay Archipelago, bordering the Pacific Ocean in the east and the India Ocean in the west, at the crossroads of Asia and Oceania, Pacific Ocean and Indian Ocean, including Brunei, Cambodia, Indonesia, Laos, Malaysia, Myanmar, Philippines, Singapore, Thailand and Vietnam. Southeast Asia has a total area of 4,435,600 square kilometers. The Association of Southeast Asian Nations (ASEAN), founded on August 8, 1967, is an important inter-country political economic and security integration cooperation organization in Southeast Asia. With the summit and ministerial meetings as the main decision-making bodies, ASEAN adheres to the principle of unanimity, the principle of non-interference in internal affairs, the principle of y-x and the principle of consultation. While effectively promoting the integrated development of Southeast Asian countries, it demonstrates the spirit of all countries pursuing equality and mutual respect.

Table 1.1.1 · Basic Information of Major Southeast Asian Countries

Country	Time of Joining ASEAN	Population in 2020 (Unit: 10,000)	Land Area (Unit: 10,000 square kilometers)
Philippines	1967	10811.7	29.97
Cambodia	1999	1671.9	18.10
Laos	1997	727.6	23.68
Malaysia	1967	3236.6	33
Myanmar	1997	5440.9	67.66
Thailand	1967	6962.6	51.3
Brunei	1984	43.3	0.58
Singapore	1967	580.4	0.07
Indonesia	1967	27062.6	190
Vietnam	1995	9646.2	32.9
Total	—	**66072**	**443.56**

Data Source: World Bank, country guide from Ministry of Commerce, research of this report.

In 2020, the total population of Southeast Asian countries is about 660 million, accounting for 8.6% of the total global population. The average annual growth rate in the past five years is 1.1%, basically in line with the global average (1.1%). The population structure in Southeast Asia is relatively young, and the median age of most countries is below 30 years old, which is lower than the global median age (30.9).

Figure 1.1.1 · Median Age of Population in Major Southeast Asian Countries

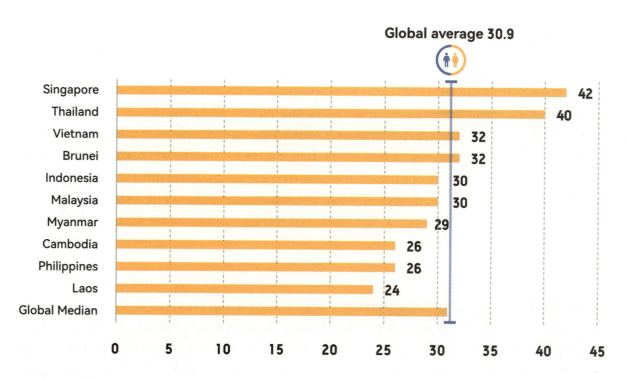

Data Source: Worldometers, research of this report

1.2 Macroeconomic Development

1.2.1 Steady Growth of Total GDP in Major Southeast Asian Countries

In 2020, the total GDP of Southeast Asian countries reached 2.96 trillion US dollars (constant US dollar price in 2010), ranking the 5th largest economy in the world. From 2000 to 2019, the total GDP of major Southeast Asian countries basically maintained steady growth, and the GDP growth rate basically maintained an average annual level of 5%, which was significantly faster than the global average (2.5%). In recent years, the rapid economic development in Southeast Asia is mainly due to the industrial transfer effect of global manufacturing industry. The overall good business environment and demographic dividend of Southeast Asian countries have attracted a large amount of foreign investment.

For a long time, the main countries in Southeast Asia are dominated by export-oriented economy. Southeast Asian countries are highly related to the global economic environment, their economic performance is easily affected by the global macro-economy, and the overall economic resilience still needs to be improved. During the global financial crisis from 2008 to 2009, the contraction of international market demand had a significant negative impact on the manufacturing industry in Southeast Asia. In 2019, with the escalation of trade frictions between China and the United States, the rise of global unilateralism and protectionism, and the tariff game among major powers, the value chain trade of Southeast Asian countries has been impacted to a certain extent.

In 2020, the global COVID-19 epidemic broke out. The economies of Southeast Asian countries fell into a severe recession, and the total amount of GDP in Southeast Asia fell 4.0% year of year. During the epidemic, Southeast Asian countries implemented strict epidemic prevention measures, domestic consumption and investment declined, production and export trade dropped sharply, and the service industry was also hit hard. The industrial chain and supply chain in Southeast Asia were severely affected by the COVID-19 epidemic. Some export-oriented enterprises face serious financial difficulties.

Figure 1.2.1 · Gross GDP and Growth Rate of Major Southeast Asian Countries from 2000 to 2020

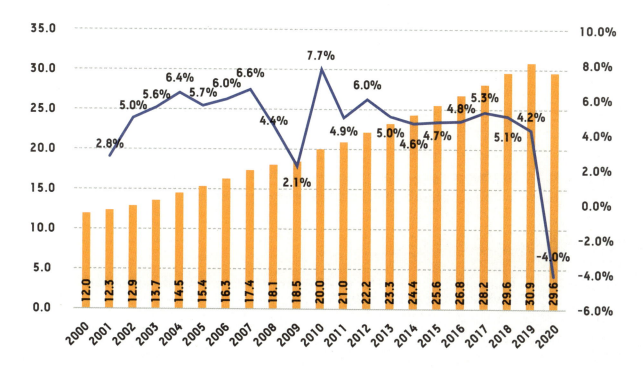

Unit: 100 billion US dollars (constant US dollar price in 2010)
Data Source: World Bank, country guide of Ministry of Commerce, research of this report

Over the past decade, the ASEAN countries with faster economic growth are Laos, Cambodia and Vietnam. Among them, Laos and Cambodia mainly rely on the rapid development of agriculture and natural resources; Vietnam, in addition to agriculture, the manufacturing industry is also developing rapidly, with a trade surplus for several years in a row. The economy of Philippines, Myanmar, Indonesia and Malaysia are growing at a medium-to-high speed, among which the economic growth of the Philippines is mainly driven by domestic infrastructure construction, foreign direct investment, consumer expenditure, overseas labor and business process outsourcing. Myanmar takes agriculture and natural resources as the main driving points of economic development. The economic development structure of Indonesia and Malaysia are dominated by consumer goods, retail, manufacturing and farming. The field of economic development in Thailand is concentrated in consumer goods, retail and manufacturing. Limited by resource endowments and technological factors, the structural adjustment and technological upgrading of Thailand's manufacturing industry are slow. At a time when industrialization has not been completed entirely, it has shown signs of "deindustrialization" to a certain extent. As a highly export-oriented developed country.

Figure 1.2.2 · **Comparison of Cumulative GDP Growth Rate of Southeast Asian Countries from 2010 to 2020**

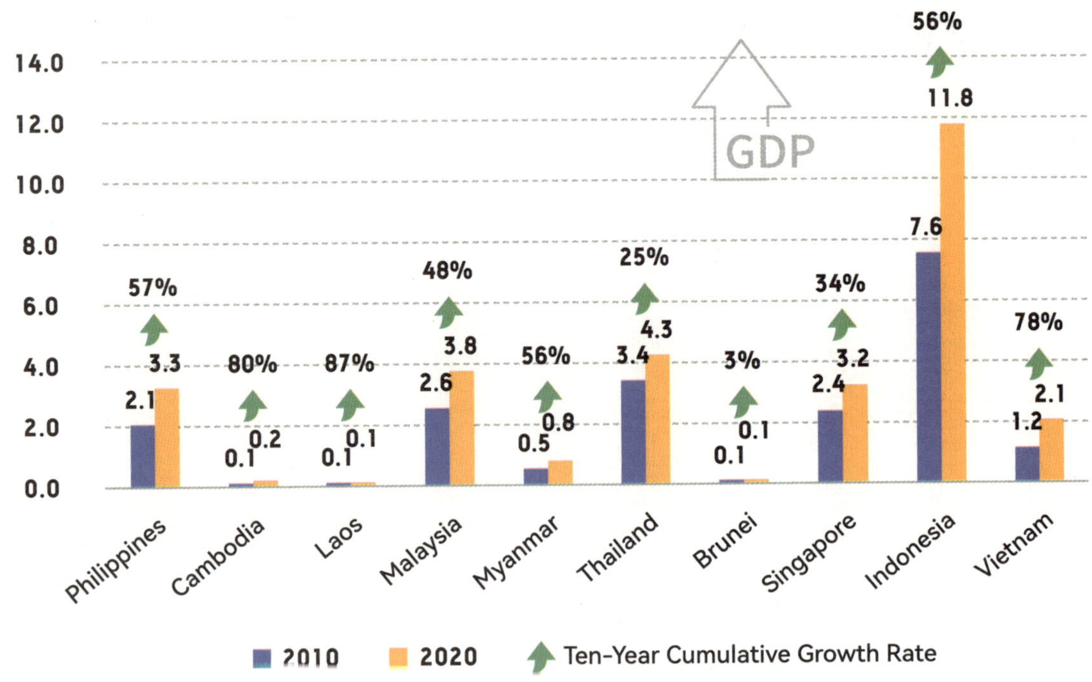

Unit: 100 billion USD (constant USD price in 2010)
Data Source: World Bank, research in this report

The per capita GDP of most countries in Southeast Asia is significantly lower than the global average

In 2020, the per capita GDP of most countries in Southeast Asia is less than US$ 5,000, and the overall per capita GDP of the region is about US$4,485.2, which is significantly lower than the world average (US$10,925.7). Laos, Cambodia, Myanmar and other countries are among the list of least developed countries (LDC) issued by the United Nations Development Policy Committee.

Figure 1.2.3 · Per Capita GDP of Major Southeast Asian Countries in 2020

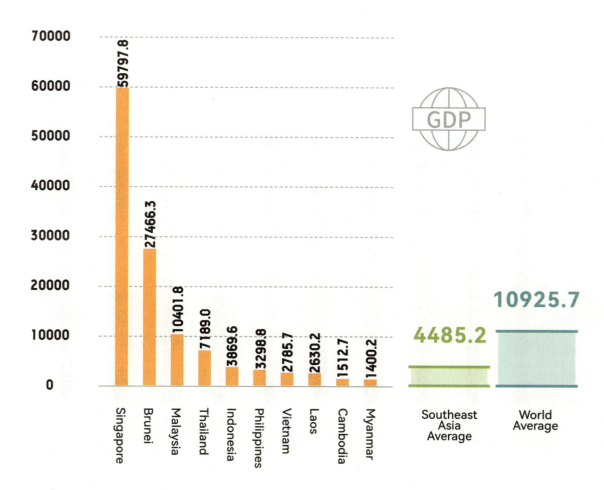

Unit: USD (current exchange rate)
Data Source: World Bank, research in this report

1.2.2 Tertiary sector accounts for more than half of GDP in Southeast Asia

The industrial structure of Southeast Asian countries are quite different, which reflects the differences of national economic development level and development stage to a certain extent. Among them, developed countries such as Singapore and countries with more developed tourism such as Malaysia and Thailand have a relatively high proportion of service industries. Relatively less developed countries or regions have a higher proportion of agriculture and industrial GDP. For example, agriculture accounts for more than 20% in Cambodia and Myanmar, and about 60% in Brunei and Indonesia. Among the developing countries in the world, the tertiary industry accounts for a relatively high proportion in the developing countries in Southeast Asia, among which the consumer goods industry and retail industry are one of the most important economic areas represented by the Philippines, Malaysia and Thailand.

Figure 1.2.4 · Industrial Structure of Southeast Asian Countries in 2020

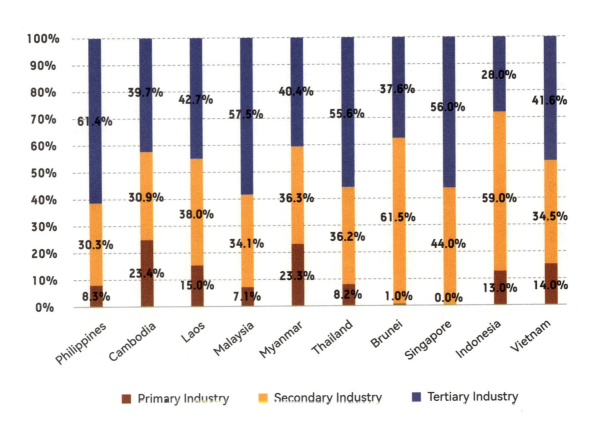

Data Source: World Bank, research in this report

According to the analysis of the evolution of the overall industrial structure of Southeast Asian countries in the past five years, the proportion of primary and secondary industries has declined slowly, the proportion of tertiary industry has gradually increased, and there are signs of "deindustrialization" in some countries. In order to further consolidate the industrial foundation and alleviate the "deindustrialization" process of the industrial structure, Southeast Asian countries have formulated the "Industrial 4.0" development strategy, according to their respective resource endowments, industrial base and market demand, take manufacturing as the core to create key development industries, and promote the upgrading of traditional industries and promote the development of new industries.

The COVID-19 epidemic in 2020 seriously hindered the process of economic transformation and industrial restructuring in Southeast Asian countries, and a considerable number of infrastructure and key projects were forced to stop production. For example, investment in the Eastern Economic Corridor (EEC) project in Thailand's "Industrial 4.0" fell by nearly 50% in the first half of 2020. The secondary and tertiary industries in Southeast Asia as a whole have shrunk greatly, and the proportion of primary industries has rebounded.

Figure 1.2.5 · **Evolution of Overall Industrial Structure in Southeast Asian Countries from 2016 to 2020**

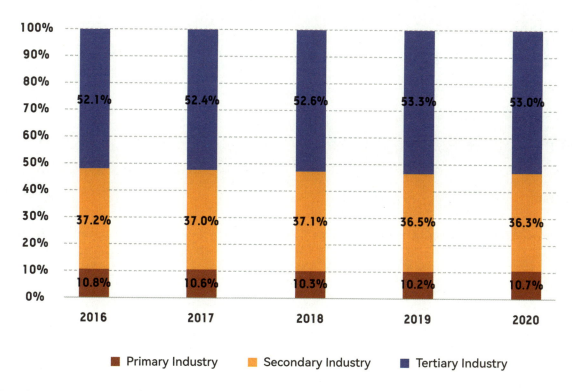

Data Source: World Bank, research of this report

1.2.3 generally good debt situation of Southeast Asian countries

The debt situation of countries in Southeast Asia is generally good, among which Singapore, as a highly export-oriented economy, has a high proportion of national debt and foreign debt. The debt level of other developing countries reflects the economic development speed of each country in the past decade to a certain extent. Taking Vietnam as an example, due to the increase in the scale and frequency of its economic activities, the economic growth rate is relatively fast and the debt ratio is also increasing significantly.

Table 1.2.1 · Debt Level Indicators of Major Southeast Asian Countries

Country	GDP Ratio of National Debt (2019)	GDP Ratio of National Debt (2010)	GDP Ratio of Foreign Debt (2020)	GDP Ratio of Foreign Debt (2010)	Sovereign Credit Rating (2019)
Philippines	39.1%	50.196%	27.2%	36.872%	Baa2
Cambodia	29.57%	—	56.9%	31.983%	B2
Laos	64.13%	—	52.6%	41.040%	—
Malaysia	56.32%	49.56%	67.6%	52.868%	A3
Myanmar	39.19%	—	—	—	—
Thailand	41.47%	26.901%	36.7%	27.1%	Baa1
Brunei	2.63%	—	—	—	—
Singapore	109.37%	101.45%	471.3%	417.015%	AAA
Indonesia	29.29%	26.166%	39.4%	26.796%	Baa2
Vietnam	57.36%	40.7%	47.1%	—	Ba3

Data Source: World Bank, World Population Review, Ceicdata, Country Guide of Ministry of Commerce, research of this report

1.3 Business Environment and National Risks

1.3.1 Business environment of Southeast Asian countries are at a relatively leading level in developing countries

The ranking of business environment convenience can more specifically reflect whether the regulatory environment of the target country or region is conducive to the start-up and operation of local companies. According to the ranking of business environment in 2020 released by the World Bank, the ranking of business environment in Southeast Asian countries is generally good, and most countries rank among the top 100 in the world.

Figure 1.3.1 · Ranking of Business Environment of Southeast Asian Countries by the World Bank in 2020

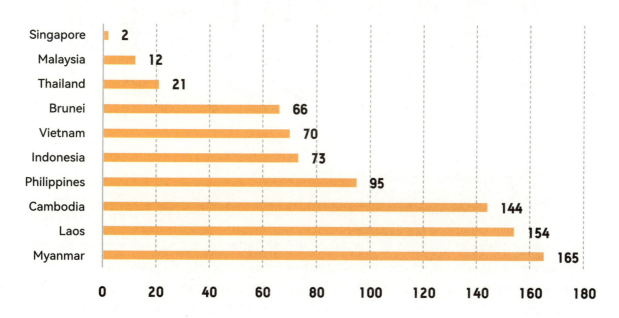

Data Source: World Bank, research of this report

According to the analysis of the business environment scores released by the World Bank in 2010 and 2020, the business environment of Southeast Asian countries as a whole has improved considerably in the past decade. The more prominent countries are Brunei, Indonesia and Vietnam, all with a score increase of more than 10 points.

Figure 1.3.2 · Comparison of Business Environment Scores of Southeast Asian Countries from 2010 to 2020

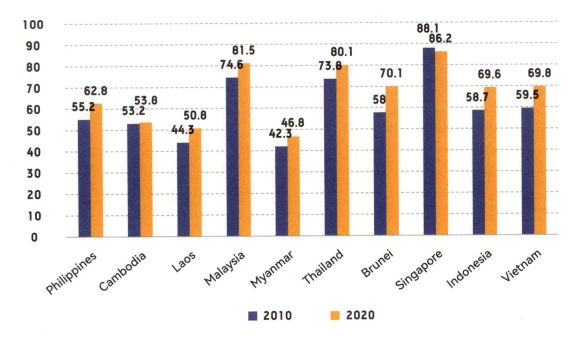

Data Source: World Bank, research of this report

In the face of rapid changes in the economic situation at home and abroad, Southeast Asian countries have actively improved business environment, relaxed market access, adjusted administrative mechanisms and introduced investment facilitation measures. Among them, the Philippines government has promulgated the Act of Business Facilitation and Effective Government Services to improve the efficiency of the government. The Indonesian government has launched a supporting plan to revitalize the economy, in order the improve the existing disadvantages such as trade restrictions, difficulties in land acquisition, and low administrative efficiency. The Vietnamese government has improved its national "one-stop" service mechanism to greatly improve the business environment, the overall performance of countries in the ranking of business environment released by the World Bank in recent years has improved year by year.

1.3.2 The risk rating of Southeast Asian countries are generally good, and the outlook is basically stable

In the national risk ratings issued by OECD and China Export Credit Insurance Corporation, Southeast Asian countries generally have good parity. According to the rating of OECD, most countries are between 0 and 4, which is basically stable compared with previous ratings. According to the national risk rating issued by CITIC insurance, most countries are in the range of 3-5, with moderate to good political and economic conditions, stable business environment but need to be improved, medium to low national risk levels and stable prospects.

Countries with high national risk ratings are mainly Cambodia, Laos and Myanmar. Among them, Cambodia's national risk are mainly reflected in hidden dangers of social stability, low judicial independence and declining competitiveness of pillar industries. Laos' national risks are mainly reflected in the high level of debt risk, the small scale of international reserves, and the potential diplomatic risks of hydropower projects and so on. Myanmar's national risks are mainly reflected in the slow process of national reconciliation, the lack of sustainability of economic growth, and the fact that investment in the mining industry is restricted by environmental protection factors.

Table 1.3.1 · Risk Rating and Prospect of Major Southeast Asian Countries

Country	OECD National Risk Rating		National Risk Rating by China Export Credit Insurance Company	
	Current Rating	Last Rating	Rating Result	Prospect
Brunei	—	—	3	Stable
Cambodia	6	6	7	Stable
Indonesia	3	3	5	Stable
Laos	7	7	6	Stable
Malaysia	2	2	4	Stable
Myanma	6	7	8	Stable
Philippines	3	3	5	Stable
Singapore	0	0	1	Stable
Thailand	3	3	4	Stable
Vietnam	4	4	6	Stable

Data Source: OECD, China Export Credit Insurance Corporation, research in this report

1.4 Overview of Cooperation between China and Southeast Asian Countries

1.4.1 Intergovernmental International Cooperation Mechanism

● **East Asia Cooperation Mechanism (East Asia Summit Energy Ministers Meeting, ASEAN Regional Forum)**

The first East Asia Summit was held in Kuala Lumpur in December 2005, proposing to promote energy security in East Asia. The second East Asia Summit Energy Ministers Meeting established a working group on energy cooperation. The energy ministers' meetings of the subsequent East Asia Summit held consultations on different topics in the field of energy.

Established in 1994, the ASEAN Regional Forum is currently the most influential multilateral dialogue mechanism in the Asia-Pacific region, with 27 member countries including ASEAN, China, the United States, Russia, Japan, South Korea and India. In April 2008, the ASEAN Regional Forum Energy Security Conference was held in Singapore, and member countries fully exchanged relevant experiences.

● **"10+3" Cooperation Mechanism (ASEAN, China, Japan and South Korea Energy Ministers Meeting)**

The first ASEAN, China, Japan and South Korea Energy Ministers Meeting was held in Manila in June 2004, and then an energy ministers meeting was held every year. Under this mechanism, senior energy officials will be responsible for the specific operation of energy cooperation, with five forums on Energy Security, Oil Market, Oil Reserves, Natural Gas, Renewable Energy and Energy Efficiency.

● **Framework of China-ASEAN Free Trade Area**

Thanks to the establishment of the framework of China-ASEAN Free Trade Area, economic and trade cooperation between China and ASEAN countries has developed by leaps and bounds. The construction of free trade zone is divided into three stages, each of which corresponds to different characteristics of economic and trade cooperation.

The first stage, from 2002 to 2010, was the establishment stage of China-ASEAN Free Trade Area, which mainly signed a series of legal documents of the Free Trade Area, such as Goods Trade Agreement, Service Trade Agreement and Investment Agreement. The second stage, from 2011 to 2015, is the completion stage of the free trade zone. During this period, China and ASEAN countries opened up trade and investment markets, promoted commodity circulation, and became each other's largest and third largest trading partners. The third stage, from 2015 to now, is the upgrading stage of the free trade zone, focusing on the all-round improvement of commodity trade and investment efficiency on the basis of the opening of the original market.

Lancang-Mekong Cooperation (LMC) Mechanism

Lancang-Mekong cooperation is a new sub-regional cooperation mechanism initiated by China, Cambodia, Laos, Myanmar, Thailand and Vietnam. Since the First Leaders' Meeting of Lancang-Mekong Cooperation in 2016, the six countries have jointly created a framework of cooperation mechanism, and identified three pillars, namely, Political Security, Economy and Sustainable Development, and Social and Humanities, as well as five priority cooperation directions, namely, Interconnection, Production Capacity, Cross-Border Economy, Water Resources, Agriculture and Poverty Reduction.

In August 2020, Premier Li Keqiang attended the Third Leader's Video Conference of Lancang-Mekong Cooperation, and put forward six initiatives on strengthening Lancang-Mekong Cooperation: pushing water resources cooperation to a new height, expanding trade and interconnection cooperation, deepening sustainable development cooperation, enhancing public health cooperation, strengthening cooperation in people's livelihood, and practicing the concept of openness and tolerance.

Greater Mekong Subregion Cooperation (GMS) Mechanism

The Greater Mekong Subregion includes Cambodia, Vietnam, Laos, Myanmar, Thailand and Yunnan Province of China. Since 2012, GMS has carried out all-round interconnection in the fields of transportation and information and established economic and trade cooperation zones and industrial parks to promote the development of trade facilitation. At the same time, GMS Railway Alliance was established to speed up railway construction and promote the formation of Trans-Asian Railway Network. The Regional Investment Framework Implementation Plan launched in 2014 further increased investment in energy and agriculture.

Regional Comprehensive Economic Partnership (RCEP) Agreement

Regional Comprehensive Economic Partnership (RCEP) was initiated by ASEAN in 2011. On November 15, 2020, the Fourth RCEP Leaders' Meeting was held via videoconferencing. After the meeting, 10 ASEAN countries and 15 Asia-Pacific countries including China, Japan, South Korea, Australia and New Zealand formally signed the Regional Comprehensive Economic Partnership Agreement. The level of openness of trade in services and investment in this RCEP agreement is higher than the respective "10+1" agreements between ASEAN and China, Japan, South Korea and other countries. It includes high-level modernization issues such as intellectual property rights, e-commerce, competition policy, and government procurement. A unified rule has been formed, greatly reducing operating costs, reducing uncertainty, and giving play to the role of an "integrator" of regional economic and trade rules.

At the same time, the RCEP Agreement fully takes into account the national conditions of different countries, gives special and differential treatment to the least developed countries, promotes the inclusive and balanced development of the region, and enables all parties to fully share the RCEP results.

1.4.2 Bilateral Trade

The bilateral trade between China and Southeast Asian countries can be roughly divided into three stages according to the two factors of trade scale and trade balance. The first stage was from 1995 to 2001, during which the bilateral trade between China and Southeast Asian countries started, the scale of import and export increased to a certain extent, and the trade balance between China and Southeast Asian countries showed a slight deficit. The second stage is 2002-2011, which is a stage of rapid development of bilateral trade between China and Southeast Asian countries. During this period, the two sides jointly built the China-ASEAN Free Trade Area, with an average annual growth rate of more than 25%, and the trade deficit between China and Southeast Asian countries increased. The third stage is from 2012 to now. The bilateral trade between China and Southeast Asian countries has slowed down and the overall scale is still increasing. China has gradually entered the trade surplus stage with Southeast Asian countries. The main reason for the formation of the third stage are the impact of the economic slowdown after the financial crisis, and the reduction of the stimulus to trade by measures such as the abolition of tariffs. China and Southeast Asia need to seek opportunities to further deepen bilateral trade relations.

With the rapid development of goods trade between China and Southeast Asian countries, both sides have gradually expanded the trade field to service industry. In 2007, the two sides signed the Agreement of Trade in Services based on the China-ASEAN Free Trade Area to promote the liberalization of bilateral trade in services. Since the signing of the agreement, the scale of import and export of service trade between the two sides has been growing, and the number of mutual visits has reached record highs. At present, ASEAN has become one of China's five largest service trade partners.

1.4.3 Investment Cooperation

In recent years, the investment between China and Southeast Asian countries has made great progress. In 2011, Southeast Asia became the largest overseas investment market for Chinese enterprises. In 2019, China's direct investment flow to Southeast Asia was 13.024 billion US dollars, and the stock at the end of the year was 109.891 billion US dollars. By the end of 2019, China has set up more than 5,600 direct investment enterprises in Southeast Asia, employing nearly 500,000 foreign employees.

In terms of the composition of the industry, the first target industry for China's investment in Southeast Asia is the manufacturing industry, with a direct investment flow of 5.671 billion US dollars in 2019, an increase of 26.1% over the same period last year. The main target countries are Indonesia, Thailand, Vietnam, Malaysia and Singapore. The second target industry is wholesale and retail, with investment flows of 2.269 billion US dollars in 2019, down 34.7% from a year earlier, with Singapore as the main target country. In third place was leasing and business services, totaling 1.189 billion US dollars, mainly to Singapore, Laos and Indonesia. Electricity/heat/gas/water production and supply ranked fourth with 898 million US dollars, with flows to Vietnam, Indonesia, Cambodia and Laos.

Figure 1.4.1 · Major Industries of China's Direct Investment in Southeast Asia in 2019

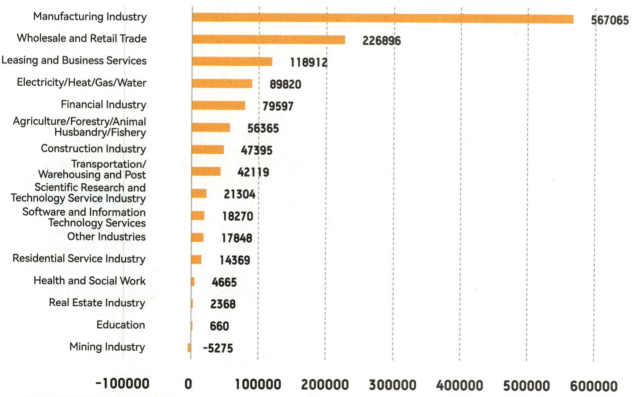

Unit: 10,000 US dollars

Data Source: Statistical Bulletin of China's Foreign Direct Investment in 2019, research of this report

In terms of the country composition of investment flows, Singapore ranked first with 4.826 billion US dollars, down 24.7% from the same period last year, mainly in wholesale and retail, leasing and business services, manufacturing, financial industry, etc. Indonesia and Vietnam ranked second and third with 2.223 billion US dollars (+19.2%) and 1.649 billion US dollars (+43.3%) respectively, mainly in manufacturing and electricity/heat/gas/ water production and supply.

Figure 1.4.2 · Stock of China's Direct Investment in Southeast Asia at the End of 2019

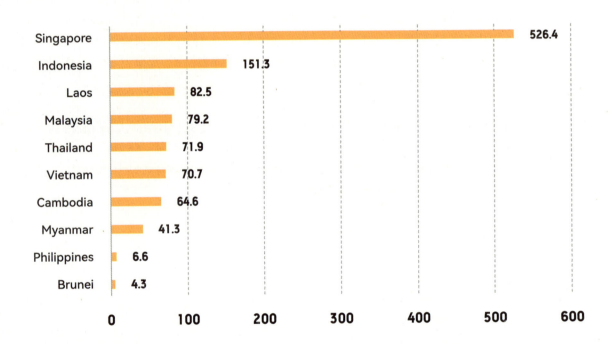

Unit: 100 million US dollars
Data Source: Statistical Bulletin of China's Foreign Direct Investment in 2019, research of this report

The overall investment in China from the Southeast Asian market is also showing a trend of rapid growth. In 2018, ASEAN countries established 1,709 foreign-invested enterprises in China, a year-on-year increase of 35.5%; the actual investment amount reached 5.72 billion US dollars, a year-on-year increase of 12.6%.

Among the Southeast Asian countries, Singapore established 998 foreign-invested enterprises in China in 2018, with an actual investment amount of 5.21 billion US dollars, ranking first in investment scale. Malaysia is second with 454 newly established foreign-invested enterprises with an actual investment of 210 million US dollars. Vietnam and the Philippines achieved substantial growth in investment in China in 2018.

Figure 1.4.3 · **Investment Statistics of Southeast Asian Countries in China in 2018**

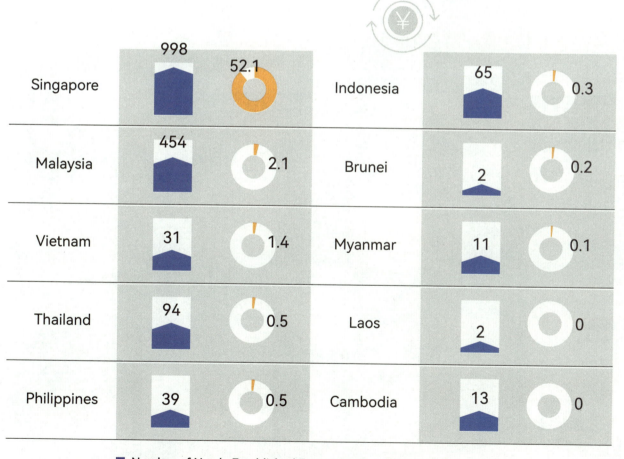

Unit: 100 million US dollars
Data Source: 2019 China Foreign Investment Report, research of this report

02 Energy Industry Development of Southeast Asia

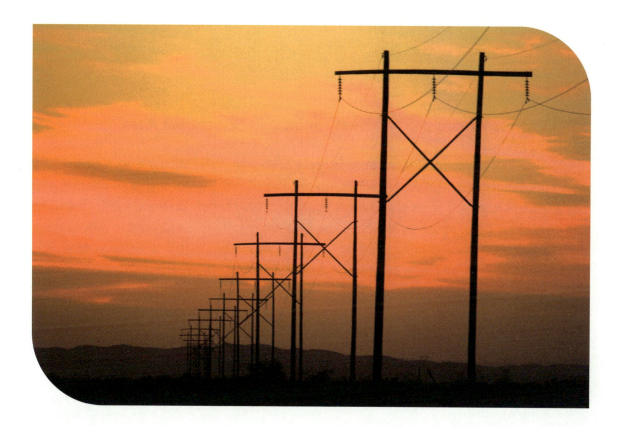

Energy Industry Development
of Southeast Asia

Southeast Asia has certain oil and gas resources and good endowment of renewable energy resources. In recent years, the energy production and consumption in the region are in a period of continuous growth in total and continuous structural adjustment. The energy self-sufficiency rate is relatively high. The power demand maintains a high-speed growth trend and renewable energy grows fast, which is expected to replace gas and electricity as the power source with the largest total installed capacity. The construction of power interconnection has been carried out, but it is still in a relatively early stage, which has great development potential.

2.1   Energy Resources

2.1.1 Fossil Energy

● Coal resources are relatively scarce in Southeast Asia

The coal reserves in Southeast Asia are 42.1 billion tons, accounting for about 9% of the total coal reserves in the Asia-Pacific region and 4% of the total global coal reserves. Coal resources are relatively scarce, and most countries need to rely on imports for their demand for coal resources. Coal resources in Southeast Asia are mainly concentrated in Indonesia, Vietnam, Malaysia, Thailand and other countries, of which Indonesia is the most abundant, accounting for more than 80% of the total coal in Southeast Asia, mainly distributed in Sumatra and Kalimantan.

Figure 2.1.1-1 · Coal Reserves in Southeast Asian Countries

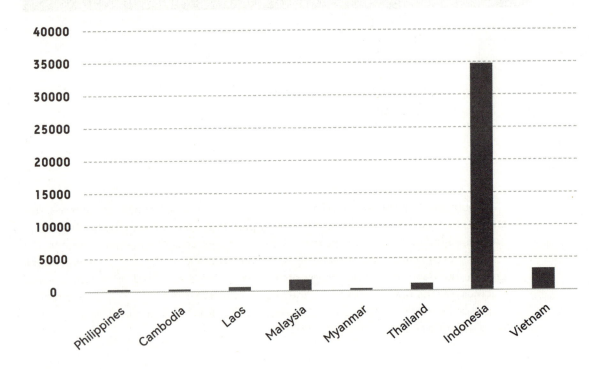

Unit: million tons (mt)
Data Source: International Energy Agency, British Petroleum Company, research of this report

Southeast Asia has certain oil and gas reserves, but its production capacity is shrinking

The oil reserve in Southeast Asia are 1.5 billion tons, accounting for 24% of the total oil reserves in the Asia-Pacific region and 1% of the total oil reserves in the world. The oil resources are abundant but unevenly distributed, mainly in Vietnam, Malaysia, Indonesia, Brunei and other countries. Vietnam has the richest oil reserves, accounting for about 40% of the total oil in Southeast Asia, and is an important oil producer in Southeast Asia, mainly distributed in the Mekong Delta Basin and Nam Con Son Basin and other areas. Malaysia is the second largest oil producer in Southeast Asia, accounting for about 27% of the total oil reserves in Southeast Asia, mainly concentrated on the east coast of Malay Peninsula, Sarawak and Sabah. Indonesia is rich in oil resources, but due to aging oil fields, reduced investment, falling international oil prices and other reasons, Indonesia's oil production is declining year by year. Brunei is rich in oil resources and plays an important role in the Asia-Pacific energy market. More than 95% of the oil produced is exported, and oil export is an important economic pillar of Brunei.

Figure 2.1.1-2 · Oil Reserve in Southeast Asian Countries

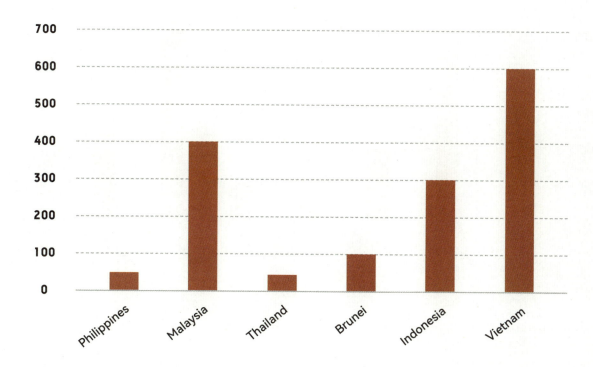

Unit: million tons (mt)
Data Source: International Energy Agency, British Petroleum Company, research of this report

The natural gas reserves in Southeast Asia are 3.6 trillion cubic meters, accounting for about 21% of the total natural gas reserves in the Asia-Pacific region and 2% of the world's total natural gas reserves. Natural gas reserves are rich, but there are great differences in reserves and distribution among countries. Mainly concentrated in Indonesia, Malaysia, Vietnam and other countries. Among them, Indonesia is the most abundant in natural gas reserves, accounting for nearly 40% of the total natural gas in Southeast Asia. However, natural gas production is relatively fluctuating. Due to the impact of unconventional natural gas exploitation in North America, Indonesia's natural gas production has shown a downward trend in the past decade. Malaysia's natural gas reserves are second only to Indonesia, accounting for about 25% of the total in Southeast Asia, mainly distributed in the western and eastern coastal areas. Natural gas production has shown an upward trend in recent years.

Figure 2.1.1-3 · **Natural Gas Reserves in Southeast Asian Countries**

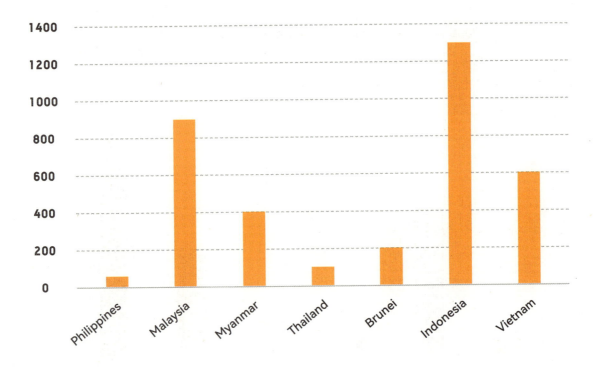

Unit: billion cubic meters (bcm)
Data Source: International Energy Agency, British Petroleum Company, research of this report

2.1.2 Renewable Energy

● **Southeast Asia has a good endowment of hydropower resources**

Fossil energy represented by oil, gas and coal is the main source of power development in Southeast Asia. In addition, Southeast Asia is rich in hydropower resources, and the exploitable amount of hydropower technology is more than 150 GW, which is an important source of clean energy in Southeast Asia, mainly distributed in Myanmar, Indonesia, Vietnam, Laos and other countries. Among them, Myanmar is rich in hydropower resources, with a technological development capacity of more than 46 GW, accounting for about 30% of the total hydropower exploitable capacity in Southeast Asia, mainly concentrated in the Irrawaddy River, Chindwin River and Salween River, and the developed capacity is only about 7% at present. Indonesia has great potential for hydropower development, but due to the scattered resources and high development cost, the current development level is low, and the developed amount of hydropower is less than 10%. In addition, hydropower resources in Vietnam, Laos and other countries also have great development potential.

Figure 2.1.2-1 · Exploitable Capacity of Hydropower Technology in Southeast Asian Countries

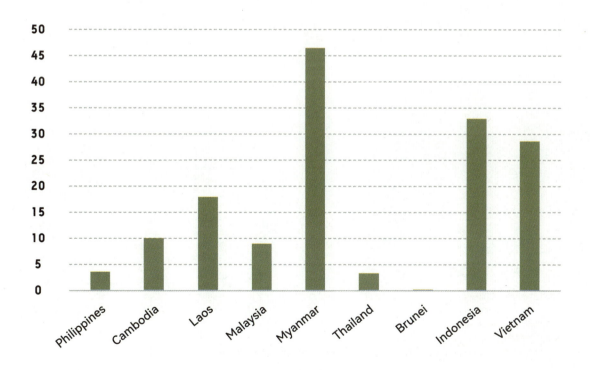

Unit: megawatt (MW)
Data Source: Hydropower & Dams World Atlas 2020, National Planning, research of this report

● Most areas in Southeast Asia are sub-optimal areas of wind energy resources

Southeast Asia has certain wind energy resources, with wind power development potential exceeding 1,000GW, mainly concentrated in Vietnam, Thailand, Laos and other countries in Indochina. Among them, Vietnam has the most abundant wind energy resources, and its wind power development potential accounts for more than half of Southeast Asia. Vietnam's coastline is more than 3,000 kilometers long, and the coastal areas are rich in wind energy resources. The average wind speed of some islands reaches 8m/s. At present, the development and utilization degree is low, and it has great development potential in the future. In addition, the eastern and western regions of Thailand and the central provinces of Laos have certain wind energy potential.

Figure 2.1.2-2 · Potential of Wind Energy Development in Southeast Asian Countries

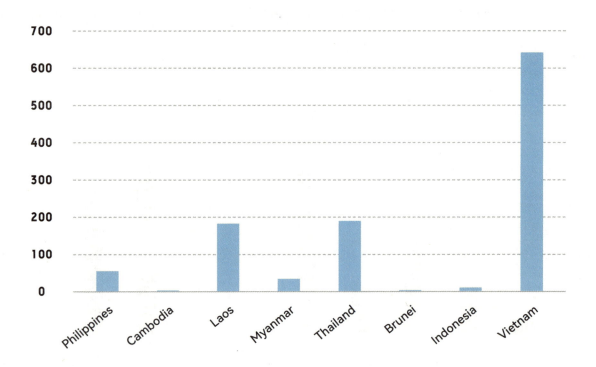

Unit: megawatt (MW)
Data Source: Wind Future in Asia Report, National Planning, research of this report

Photovoltaic development has great potential

Southeast Asia is located near the equator, with abundant solar energy resources, long sunshine hours, annual utilization hours of about 1,400 hours and high radiation intensity. The exploitable amount of photovoltaic technology is close to 10 terawatts, mainly distributed in Myanmar, Cambodia, Thailand, Indonesia, Vietnam and other countries. At present, except Vietnam, which has developed photovoltaic power plants of a certain scale, the development and utilization of photovoltaic resources in other countries is relatively low, which has great development potential in the future.

Figure 2.1.2-3 · **Illumination Hours in Southeast Asian Countries**

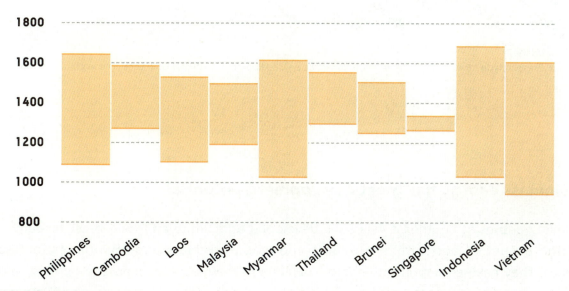

Unit: utilization hours/year
Data Source: SOLARGIS, research of this report

Figure 2.1.2-4 · Exploitable Amount of Photovoltaic Technology in Southeast Asian Countries

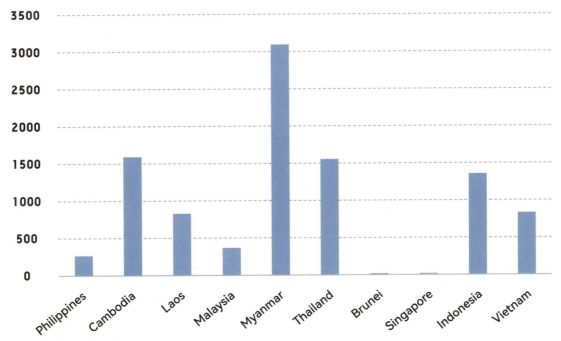

Unit: gigawatt (GW)
Data Source:"Research on Innovation Model of Photovoltaic Scale Development in ASEAN Countries", research of this report

● Biomass energy has great development potential

Most countries in Southeast Asia have developed agriculture and vast forest resources, with high output of agricultural products and wood products and abundant biomass resources. They have an important strategic position in the global biomass energy field, and the theoretical development capacity of biomass exceeds 400GW, among which Vietnam, Indonesia, Malaysia, Thailand, Myanmar and other countries have great development potential. According to statistics, the biomass raw materials from agriculture and forestry departments in Southeast Asia exceed 500 million tons every year, among which the biomass raw material with the greatest potential include rice husk, bagasse, oil palm residue and wood, etc. The biomass residue produced every year exceeds 200 million tons.

2.2   Energy Consumption

2.2.1 Total Energy Consumption

● **The total energy consumption shows a trend of steady growth**

In 2020, energy consumption is Southeast Asia totaled 660 millions tons of standard oil, down 8.5% from the same period last year. From 2000 to 2019, thanks to the demographic dividend of many developing countries in the region, the transfer of global manufacturing and the efforts made by various countries to improve the business environment, the overall economic growth in Southeast Asia was strong and led to an average annual growth rate of 2.9% in total energy consumption. In 2020, affected by the global outbreak of COVID-19, the economy of Southeast Asia experienced a relatively serious recession, and the total energy consumption decreased to a large extent.

**Figure 2.2.1-1 · Total Energy Consumption and Growth Rate in Southeast Asia
from 2000 to 2020**

Unit: million tons of standard oil (mtoe)
Data Source: International Energy Agency, British Petroleum Company, research of this report

The per capita energy consumption is generally low

In 2020, the per capita energy consumption in Southeast Asia is 0.99 tons of standard oil per person, which is lower than the global per capita energy consumption level (1.45 tons of standard oil per person). Due to the differences in economic development level, industrial structure and energy resources endowment of different countries, there are certain differences in per capita energy consumption, among which Brunei and Singapore have higher per capita energy consumption, both exceeding 5 tons of standard oil per person. The per capita energy consumption in Cambodia, Myanmar and the Philippines is relatively low, which is less than 0.5 tons of standard oil per person.

Figure 2.2.1-2 · Total Energy Consumption of Southeast Asian Countries in 2020

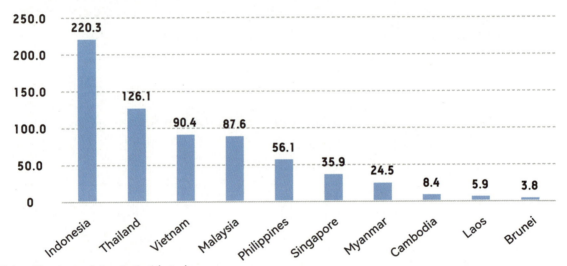

Unit: million tons of standard oil (mtoe)
Data Source: International Energy Agency, British Petroleum Company, research of this report

Figure 2.2.1-3 · Per Capita Energy Consumption of Southeast Asian Countries in 2020

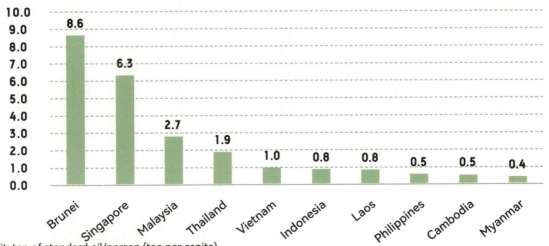

Unit: ton of standard oil/person (toe per capita)
Data Source: International Energy Agency, British Petroleum Company, research of this report

2.2.2 Energy Consumption Structure

● **The consumption of renewable energy exceeds that of coal as the second largest energy consumption category**

In 2020, the total consumption of renewable energy in Southeast Asia will be 200 million tons of standard oil, accounting for 27.9%. Coal consumption is 170 million tons of standard oil, accounting for 24.2%. Oil consumption is 210 million tons of standard oil, accounting for 29.8%. Natural gas consumption is 130 million tons of standard oil, accounting for 18.1%. From 2000 to 2020, the share of coal consumption in Southeast Asia increased by nearly 16 percentage points due to the driving effect of coal-fired power generation; the share of oil decreased significantly by more than 10 percentage points, but is still the largest energy consumer category; before 2018, fossil fuels were the main source of energy consumption growth. But as a result of the large-scale development of wind power and PV after 2018, the proportion of renewable energy consumption is on the rise, and now the proportion of renewable energy consumption has surpassed that of coal, becoming the second largest energy consumption goods.

Figure 2.2.2-1 · **Variety Structure of Energy Consumption in Southeast Asia in 2000-2020**

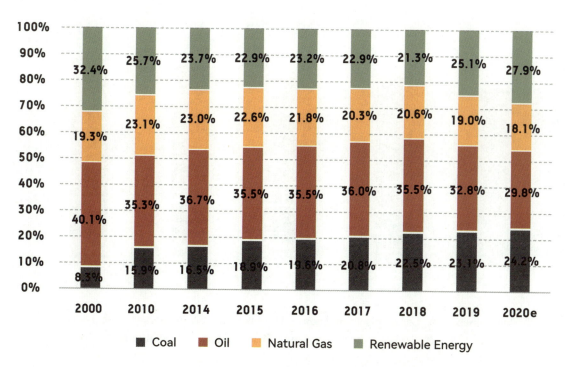

Data Source: International Energy Agency, British Petroleum Company, research of this report

2.2.3 Carbon Emissions

● **Carbon emission is on the rise, but per capita carbon emission is still low**

In 2019, the CO_2 emissions in Southeast Asia are close to 1.7 billion tons, accounting for 8% of the total CO_2 emission in Asia and 5% of the total global CO_2 emissions. From 2015 to 2019, CO_2 emissions in Southeast Asia showed an upward trend, with an average annual growth rate of about 4% and an increase of about 17%. This is because the growth of energy demand in Southeast Asia mainly depends on fossil fuels. Since 2000, 90% of the growth of energy demand comes from coal, oil, natural gas, etc. driven by the growth of fossil energy consumption, CO_2 emissions continue to increase. In terms of countries, Indonesia, Thailand, Malaysia, Vietnam and other countries account for a relatively high proportion in the region, accounting for more than 15% of the total regional emissions; Laos, Cambodia, Vietnam and other countries have grown rapidly with an average annual growth rate of about 10%. Singapore promises to achieve zero net emissions as soon as possible in the second half of this century. In recent years, CO_2 emissions have fallen sharply, with an average annual rate of decline exceeding 10%.

Figure 2.2.3-1 · CO$_2$ Emission from Southeast Asian Countries

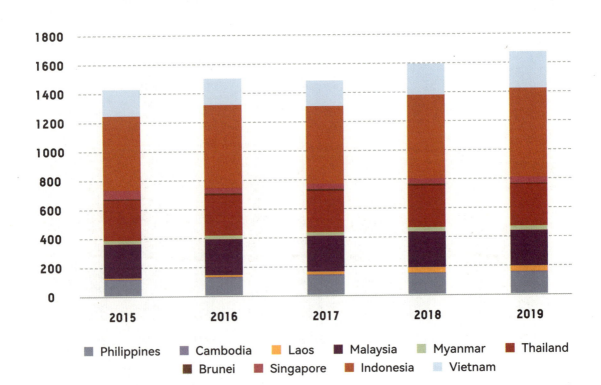

Unit: million tons
Data Source: Our World in Data, research of this report

In 2019, CO_2 emission per capita in Southeast Asia is 2.53 tons / person, which is lower than that in the world, about 57% of Asia and 54% of World. Among them, Brunei has the highest CO_2 emissions per capita, followed by Malaysia and Singapore, and the CO_2 emissions per capita of other countries are less than 5 tons / person, which is closely related to factors such as population, power accessibility, economic development level and industrial structure.

Figure 2.2.3-2 · Per Capita CO_2 Emissions of Southeast Asian Countries in 2019

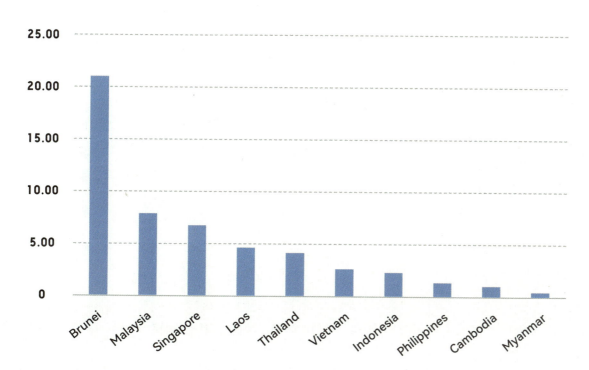

Unit: ton/person
Data Source: Our World in Data, research of this report

In 2019, the carbon emission intensity in Southeast Asia was 2.12 tons/100 US dollars, which was lower than that in the world, accounting for about 72% of the global average carbon emission intensity. From 2000 to 2019, the carbon emission intensity in Southeast Asia showed a trend of first decreasing and then increasing and remained basically unchanged on the whole. From 2000 to 2019, the carbon emission intensity of Laos, Cambodia, Vietnam and Brunei showed an upward trend, while that of other countries declined, which was related to the economic development stage, development characteristics and energy efficiency of various countries.

Figure 2.2.3-3 · Carbon Emission Intensity of Southeast Asian Countries

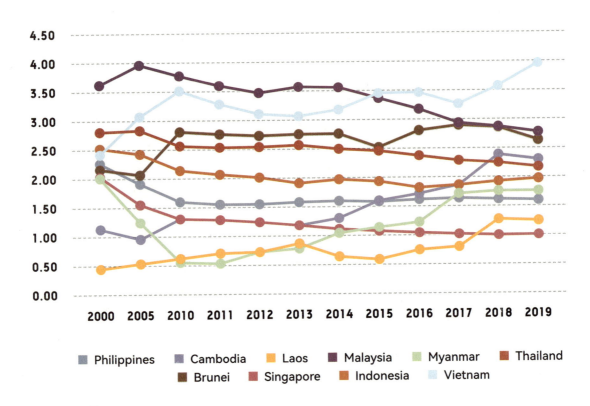

Unit: ton/USD 100
Data Source: knoema, research of this report

2.2.4 Terminal Energy Consumption

● **The industrial and transportation sectors drive the steady growth of terminal energy consumption**

In 2020, the total terminal energy consumption in Southeast Asia will be 450 million tons of standard oil, down 7.8% year-on-year. From 2000 to 2019, the average annual growth rate of total terminal energy consumption was 3.1%. In terms of sub-fields, the terminal energy consumption in the industrial fields is 150 million tons of standard oil, accounting for 33.2%. The terminal energy consumption in the transportation field is 130 million tons of standard oil, accounting for 29.8%. Residents' terminal energy consumption is 70 million tons of standard oil, accounting for 16.5%. The terminal energy consumption of service industry is 30 million tons of standard oil, accounting for 6.1%. Since 2000, the proportion of terminal energy consumption in the transportation sector in Southeast Asia has increased significantly, while the proportion of residential terminal energy consumption has decreased significantly, with a drop of about 17 percentage points.

Figure 2.2.4-1 · Total Amount and Growth Rate of Terminal Energy Consumption in Southeast Asia from 2000 to 2020

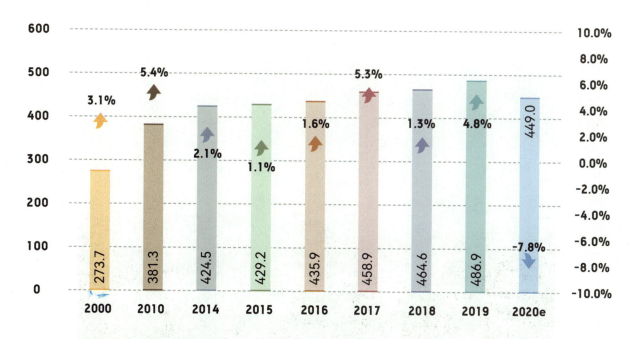

Unit: million tons of standard oil (mtoe)
Data Source: International Energy Agency, International Renewable Energy Agency, research of this report

Figure 2.2.4-2 · Terminal Energy Consumption Structure in Southeast Asia from 2000 to 2020

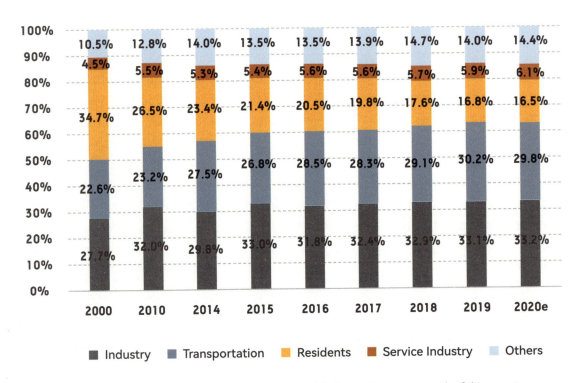

Data Source: International Energy Agency, International Renewable Energy Agency, research of this report

2.2.5 Major Energy Prices

● Sales Price of Petroleum Products

Petroleum products in Southeast Asia are mainly divided into gasoline and diesel, which have their own sales prices, and gasoline prices are higher than diesel prices in most countries. In 2021, the sales price of petroleum products in most countries in Southeast Asia was lower than the global average (the global average gasoline sales price in the same period: USD 1.19/ liter; Sales price of diesel: USD1.06/ liter).

Figure 2.2.5-1 · Prices of Petroleum Products in Southeast Asian Countries in 2021

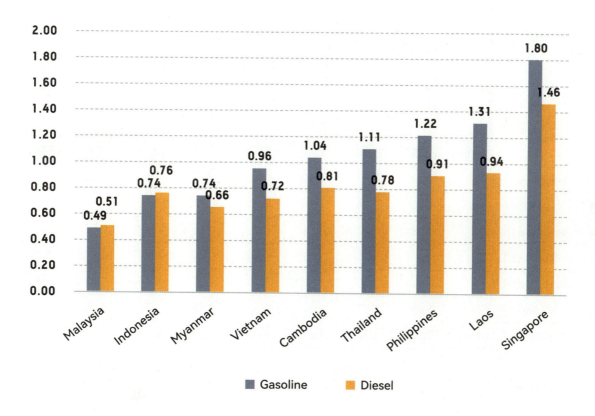

Unit: (US$/L)
Data Source: GlobalPetroPrices, research of this report

In the past 10 years, the prices of petroleum products in most countries in Southeast Asia began to decline gradually after reaching the peak in 2013, and started to show an upward trend again around 2016-2017.

Figure 2.2.5-2 · Gasoline Prices in Southeast Asian Countries from 2011 to 2019

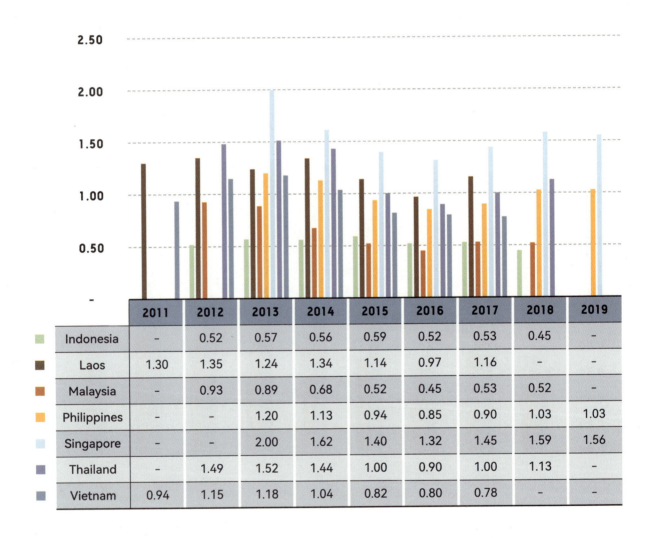

	2011	2012	2013	2014	2015	2016	2017	2018	2019
Indonesia	–	0.52	0.57	0.56	0.59	0.52	0.53	0.45	–
Laos	1.30	1.35	1.24	1.34	1.14	0.97	1.16	–	–
Malaysia	–	0.93	0.89	0.68	0.52	0.45	0.53	0.52	–
Philippines	–	–	1.20	1.13	0.94	0.85	0.90	1.03	1.03
Singapore	–	–	2.00	1.62	1.40	1.32	1.45	1.59	1.56
Thailand	–	1.49	1.52	1.44	1.00	0.90	1.00	1.13	–
Vietnam	0.94	1.15	1.18	1.04	0.82	0.80	0.78	–	–

Unit: (US$/L)
Data Source: Enerdata, research of this report

Figure 2.2.5-3 · Diesel Prices in Southeast Asian Countries from 2011 to 2019

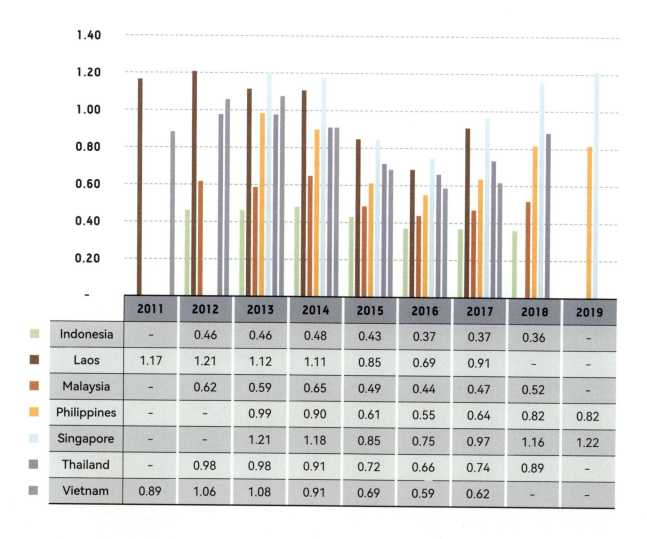

	2011	2012	2013	2014	2015	2016	2017	2018	2019
Indonesia	–	0.46	0.46	0.48	0.43	0.37	0.37	0.36	–
Laos	1.17	1.21	1.12	1.11	0.85	0.69	0.91	–	–
Malaysia	–	0.62	0.59	0.65	0.49	0.44	0.47	0.52	–
Philippines	–	–	0.99	0.90	0.61	0.55	0.64	0.82	0.82
Singapore	–	–	1.21	1.18	0.85	0.75	0.97	1.16	1.22
Thailand	–	0.98	0.98	0.91	0.72	0.66	0.74	0.89	–
Vietnam	0.89	1.06	1.08	0.91	0.69	0.59	0.62	–	–

Unit: (US$/L)
Data Source: Enerdata, research of this report

● **Sales Price of Natural Gas**

The sales price of natural gas in Southeast Asia is mainly divided into two categories: civil and commercial. On the whole, the price of civil natural gas is significantly higher than that of commercial gas. Among the major natural gas consuming countries in Southeast Asia, the domestic gas price of Singapore natural gas sales in 2021 was 13.6 cents/kWh (equivalent calorific value), and the commercial gas price was 12.4 cents/kWh (equivalent calorific value), which were higher than the global average natural gas sales price (4.6 cents/kWh for civil use and 5.3 cents/kWh for commercial use). Since 2013, the price of natural gas in Singapore has increased first and then decreased, with the lowest price in recent years in 2015-2016. On the natural gas sales side in Malaysia, the price of civil gas is 2.0 cents/kWh (equivalent calorific value), and the price of commercial gas is 2.6 cents/kWh (equivalent calorific value), both of which are lower than the global average natural gas sales price.

Figure 2.2.5-4 · Price of Natural Gas in Singapore from 2013-2019

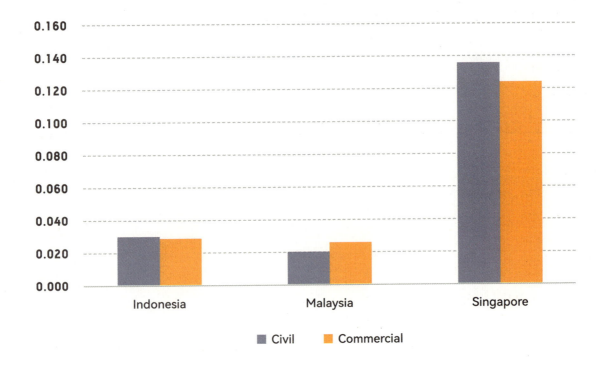

Unit: cents/kWh (US$c /kWh) equivalent calorific value (GCV)
Data Source: Enerdata, research of this report

2.3 Energy Supply

2.3.1 Total Energy Production

● **The total energy production is on the rise**

In 2020, the total energy production in Southeast Asia will be 790 million tons of standard oil, a year-on-year decrease of 3.4%. From 2010 to 2019, the energy production in Southeast Asia showed an overall upward trend. In 2015, affected by the sharp drop in global oil prices, the energy production in this region decreased slightly compared with the previous year, and continued to rise in the following years. In 2020, affected by the global COVID19 epidemic, the total energy production in Southeast Asia declined.

Figure 2.3.1-1 · **Total Energy Production and Growth Rate in Southeast Asia from 2000 to 2020**

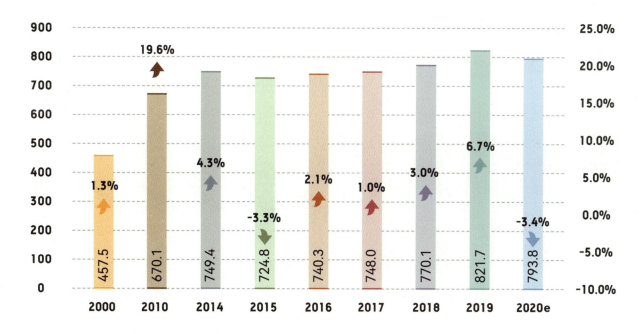

Unit: million tons of standard oil (mtoe)
Data Source: International Energy Agency, International Renewable Energy Agency, research of this report

In terms of countries, Indonesia is a big energy producer in Southeast Asia. In 2020, Indonesia's total energy production will be 450 million tons of standard oil, accounting for more than 1/2 of the total in Southeast Asia. In addition, countries such as Vietnam and Malaysia have higher energy resources, the total energy production in Singapore and other countries is far less than the energy consumption. Generally speaking, due to the different development levels of resources and industries in Southeast Asian countries, the total amount of energy production and structure are quite different.

Figure 2.3.1-2 · Total Energy Production of Southeast Asian Countries in 2020

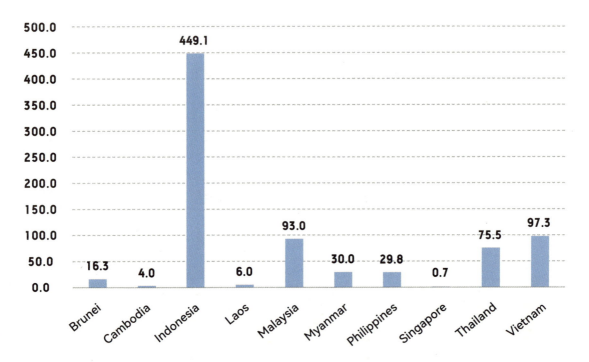

Unit: million tons of standard oil (mtoe)
Data Source: International Energy Agency, International Renewable Energy Agency, research of this report

2.3.2 Energy Production Structure

In 2020, the total renewable energy production in Southeast Asian countries will be 193 million tons of standard oil, accounting for 24.3%. Coal production is 336 million tons of standard oil, accounting for 42.4%. Oil production is 97 millions tons of standard oil, accounting for 12.2%. Natural gas production is 168 million tons, accounting for 21.1%. From 2015 to 2020, the proportion of fossil energy generally showed a downward trend, of which oil decreased by 4.4% and natural gas decreased by 4.4%. The proportion of renewable energy has increased significantly by 4.8%.

Figure 2.3.2-1 · Energy Production Structure in Southeast Asia from 2015 to 2020

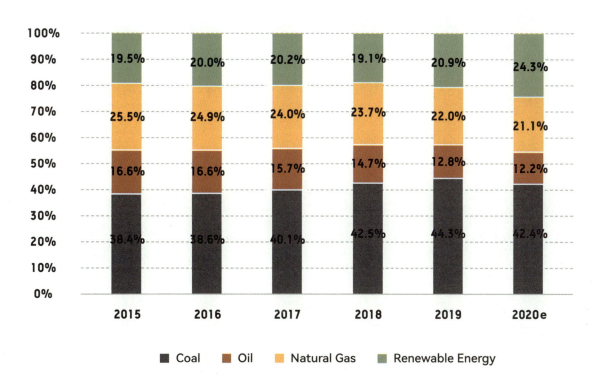

Data Source: International Energy Agency, British Petroleum Company,
International Renewable Energy Agency, research of this report

2.3.3 Energy Self-Sufficiency Rate

● **The energy self-sufficiency rate is relatively high, but oil and gas still have a high level of dependence on foreign supply**

On the whole, the energy self-sufficiency rate in Southeast Asia is relatively high, and the average self-sufficiency rate will reach 120% in 2020. In terms of countries, the energy self-sufficiency rate of Southeast Asian countries is generally good, and the self-sufficiency rate of most countries is higher than 100%. Among them, Brunei and Indonesia have larger energy exports and higher energy self-sufficiency.

Figure 2.3.3-1 · Energy Self-Sufficiency Rate of Southeast Asian Countries in 2020

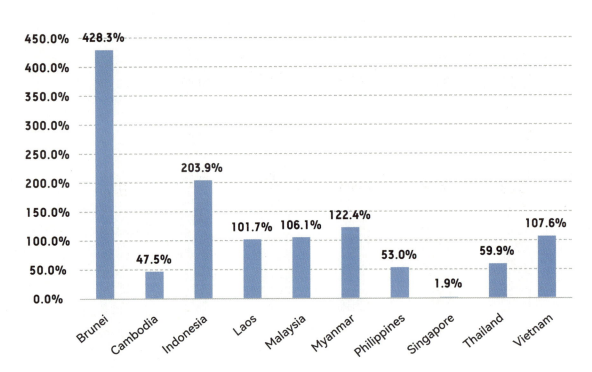

Data Source: International Energy Agency, British Petroleum Company, research of this report

2.4 Electricity Consumption

2.4.1 Electricity consumption is growing faster, but per capita electricity consumption is still very low

Since 2000, with the sustained and stable economic and social development in Southeast Asia, with the improvement of the level of electrification in the region, the demand for electricity has been increasing. Excluding special years, the average annual growth rate of electricity consumption in Southeast Asia has been maintained at more than 5%. The cumulative growth rate of electricity consumption from 2015 to 2020 is about 34.8%, which is significantly higher than the Asian average (24.8%) and the global average (10.1%).

Figure 2.4.1-1 · Total Electricity Consumption and Growth Rate in Southeast Asia from 2000 to 2020

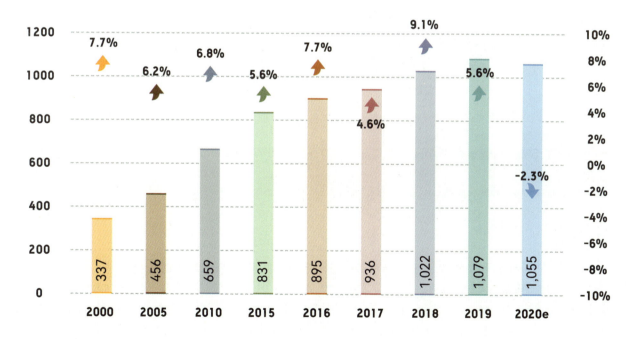

Unit: terawatt hours (TWh)
Data Source: International Energy Agency, Enerdata, research of this report

Because there are still great differences in the level and stage of economic development in Southeast Asian countries, there are also obvious differences in the growth rate of electricity consumption among countries. Between 2015 and 2020, electricity consumption in Cambodia and Vietnam increased by more than 70%, much higher than in other countries in Southeast Asia. From the perspective of cumulative increment of power consumption, Vietnam, Indonesia and Philippines have the largest absolute growth of electricity consumption, reaching 111.4 TWh, 53.9 TWh and 17.1 TWh respectively, which is the main driving force of power growth in Southeast Asia.

Figure 2.4.1-2 · Increase in Electricity Consumption in Southeast Asian Countries from 2015 to 2020

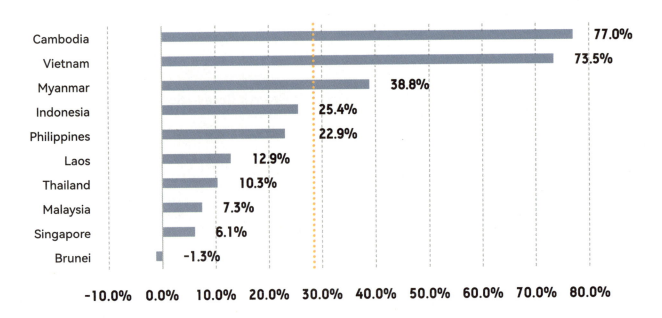

Data Source: International Energy Agency, Enerdata, research of this report

From the perspective of countries, Indonesia and Vietnam are major electricity consumers in Southeast Asia, accounting for 25.2% and 24.9% of the total electricity consumption in 2020 respectively. In addition, Thailand, Malaysia and the Philippines are also countries with high total electricity consumption in Southeast Asia. In terms of per capita electricity consumption, the per capita electricity consumption in Southeast Asia in 2020 is 1581 kWh, which is significantly lower than the Asian average (4300kWh/person). The per capita electricity consumption in Singapore and Brunei is more than 8000 kilowatt hours, Malaysia, Thailand and Vietnam are more than 2500 kilowatt hours, and the per capita electricity consumption in other countries is less than 1000 kilowatt hours.

Figure 2.4.1-3 · Total Electricity Consumption of Southeast Asian Countries in 2020

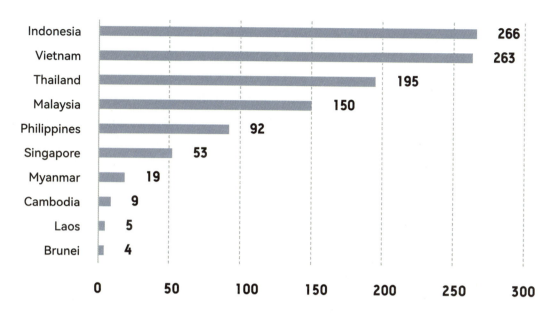

Unit: terawatt hours (TWh)
Data Source: International Energy Agency, Enerdata, CEIC, research of this report

Figure 2.4.1-4 · Per Capita Electricity Consumption in Southeast Asian Countries in 2020

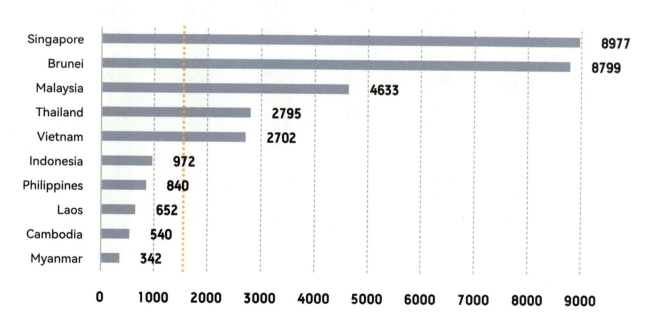

Unit: kilowatt hours (kWh)
Data Source: International Energy Agency, Enerdata, CEIC, research of this report

2.4.2 The proportion of terminal electricity consumption in various industries remains stable

In 2020, the power consumption in the industrial sector in Southeast Asia was 452.5 TWh, accounting for 42.0% of the total terminal electricity consumption. Electricity consumption in residential areas was 332.2 TWh, accounting for 31.5%. Electricity consumption in the service sector was 229.9 TWh, accounting for 21.8%. In recent years, the structure of terminal electricity consumption in various industries in Southeast Asia has remained basically unchanged, and industry is still the main field of terminal electricity consumption. From 2015 to 2020, the proportion of electricity consumption in the industrial sector in Southeast Asia increased slightly, up by 0.5 percentage points. The proportion of electricity consumption in the residential sector remained stable overall. Electricity consumption in the service sector decreased by 1.9 percentage points. With the acceleration of electrification process, the electrification degree of various industries in Southeast Asia is getting higher and higher, and the development of national economy brings great space for the growth of electricity demand, and industry will still be the main driving force for the growth of electricity demand in Southeast Asia.

Figure 2.4.2-1 · Terminal Electricity Consumption Structure in Southeast Asia from 2015 to 2020

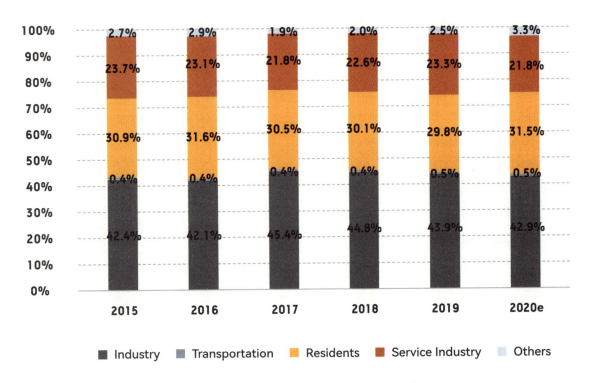

Data Source: International Energy Agency, national energy sector data, research of this report

2.4.3 There are still a large number of people without electricity in some countries

In recent years, the overall power coverage in Southeast Asia has increased. Although the regional power supply rate has reached 96%, there are still nearly 27 million people without electricity, mainly in Myanmar, the Philippines, Indonesia and Cambodia. Among them, Myanmar has the lowest electricity rate in Southeast Asia, with only 68.4%. At present, more than 17 million people still have no access to electricity, mainly in remote rural areas. Power coverage in the Philippines, Indonesia and Cambodia has increased significantly in recent years, but more than 1 million people in remote areas still have no access to electricity. Laos has achieved full power coverage through power grid expansion in recent years.

Figure 2.4.3-1 · Power-on Rate of Southeast Asian Countries in 2019

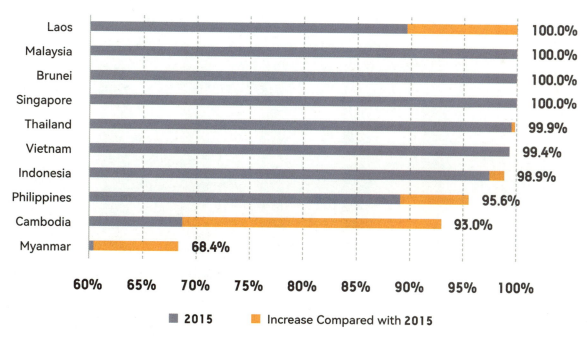

Data Source: World Bank

2.5 Power Supply

2.5.1 Electric power installed capacity grew rapidly, but the per capita installed capacity was still obviously low

In 2020, the total installed power capacity in Southeast Asia was 292 million kilowatts, up by 7.2% compared with the previous year and 50.3% compared with the installed capacity in 2015. The installed power capacity maintained rapid growth. In recent years, the overall industrialization and electrification in Southeast Asia have developed rapidly. In order to meet the increasing demand for electricity, the installed capacity of power in Southeast Asia has expanded rapidly.

Figure 2.5.1-1 · **Total Installed Capacity and Growth Rate of Electricity in Southeast Asia from 2015 to 2020**

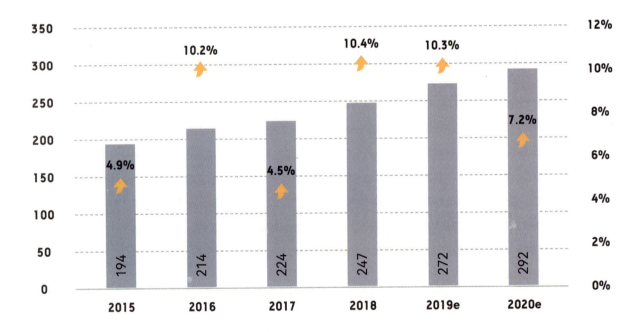

Unit: gigawatt (GW)
Data Source: International Energy Agency, International Renewable Energy Agency, national energy sector data, research of this report

In terms of per capita installed capacity, the per capita installed capacity of power generation in Southeast Asia is only 440 watts, which is less than half of the world's per capita installed capacity (930 watts). Due to the great differences in electrification level and population size in Southeast Asian countries, there is a clear gap in per capita installed capacity among countries. Brunei and Singapore have developed economies and small populations, with per capita installed power exceeding 2 kilowatts. In Indonesia, Philippines, Cambodia and Myanmar, the per capita installed power is less than 300 watts, and the installed power level needs to be improved.

Figure 2.5.1-2 · Per Capita Installed Power Generation Capacity of Southeast Asian Countries in 2020

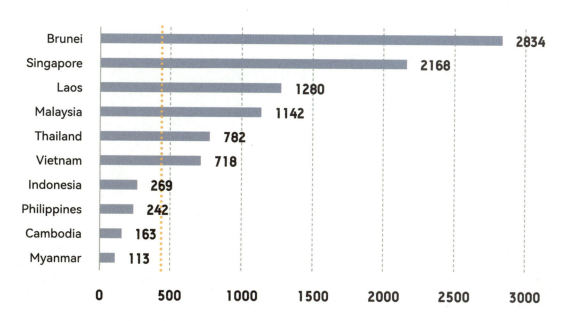

Unit: watt/person (W/person)
Data Source: International Energy Agency, International Renewable Energy Agency, national energy sector data, research of this report

From the perspective of countries, the growth level of power installed capacity in Southeast Asian countries can reflect the recent development of power in various countries. In recent years, Vietnam's power industry has maintained accelerated development, attracting investment vigorously. Within five years, the installed power capacity has increased by 41.3 million kilowatts, and the installed capacity has expanded by 1.5 times, making it the country with the largest cumulative increase and the highest growth rate of power installed capacity in Southeast Asia. In addition, Indonesia (22.4 million kilowatts, 44%) and Thailand (15.8 million kilowatts, 41%) have outstanding power installed capacity growth level.

Figure 2.5.1-3 · Cumulative Increment and Growth Rate of Power Installation in Southeast Asian Countries in 2020

Unit: gigawatt (GW)
Data Source: International Energy Agency, International Renewable Energy Agency, national energy sector data, research of this report

2.5.2 Gas power is still the largest power source in Southeast Asia

In 2020, thermal power is still the main installed power structure in Southeast Asia, of which gas power and coal power account for more than 60% of the total installed power. In recent years, the proportion of coal power has increased, while the proportion of gas power has decreased, but gas power is still the largest type of power installed. The proportion of renewable energy installed has increased steadily, and hydropower is the most important kind of renewable energy, accounting for about 20% of the total installed power.

Figure 2.5.2-1 · **Power Installation Structurein Southeast Asia from 2015 to 2020**

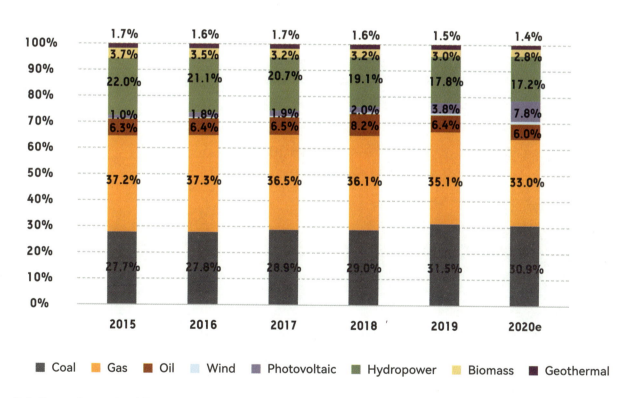

Data Source: International Energy Agency, International Renewable Energy Agency, national energy sector data, research of this report

In 2020, the installed capacity of non-fossil energy in Southeast Asia will reach 30.2%, slightly lower than the global average (33%). From the perspective of countries, the installed capacity of non-fossil energy in Southeast Asian countries is highly correlated with the energy structure, resource endowment and development policies of various countries. Indonesia is rich in hydropower, solar energy and geothermal resources, and encourages the vigorous development of non-fossil energy. It is the country with the highest installed capacity of non-fossil energy in Southeast Asia, with the installed capacity of non-fossil energy exceeding 10.55 million kilowatts, accounting for 22.6% of the total installed capacity of non-fossil energy in the region. In addition, Malaysia, Laos, the Philippines and Vietnam have higher installed capacity of non-fossil energy in the region, accounting for more than 10% of the installed capacity of non-fossil energy in the region, and the installed capacity of non-fossil energy exceeds 500,000 kilowatts.

Figure 2.5.2-2 · Non-Fossil Energy Installed in Southeast Asian Countries in 2020

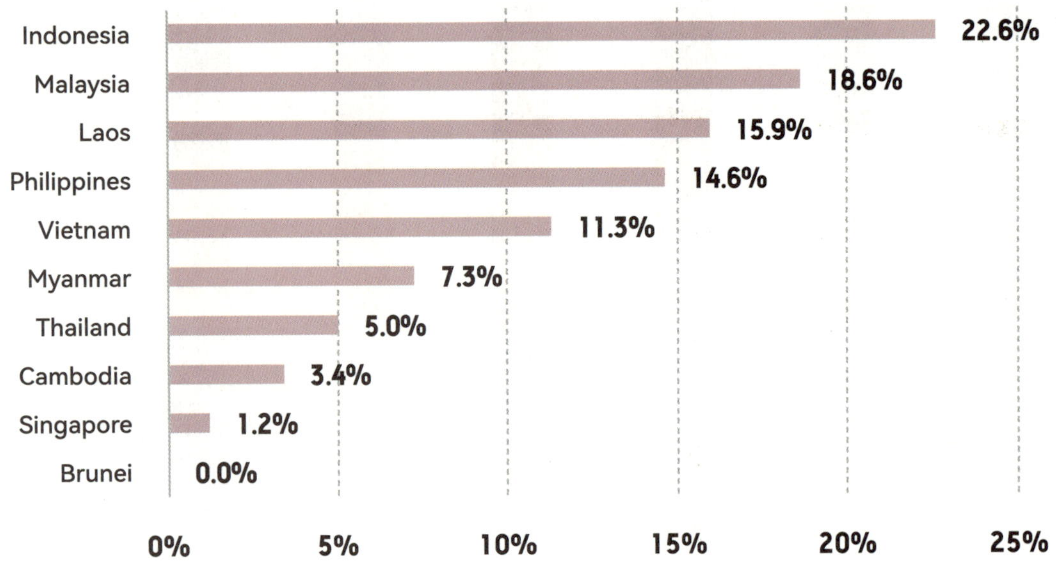

Data Source: International Energy Agency, International Renewable Energy Agency, national energy sector data, research of this report

2.5.3 Most coal power units have been put into operation in the past 10 years

The development of electric power in Southeast Asia started relatively late, and the age of the unit as a whole is relatively young. 57% of the coal power units have been put into operation in the past 10 years, and about 21% of the coal power units are more than 20 years old. Indonesia and Vietnam, as major coal power countries in Southeast Asia, their new units in the past 10 years accounted for 64% and 80% of the total installed coal power respectively. In addition, the coal power units in Laos, Cambodia and Brunei are all newly built within 10 years.

Figure 2.5.3-1 · Age of Coal Power Units in Southeast Asian Countries

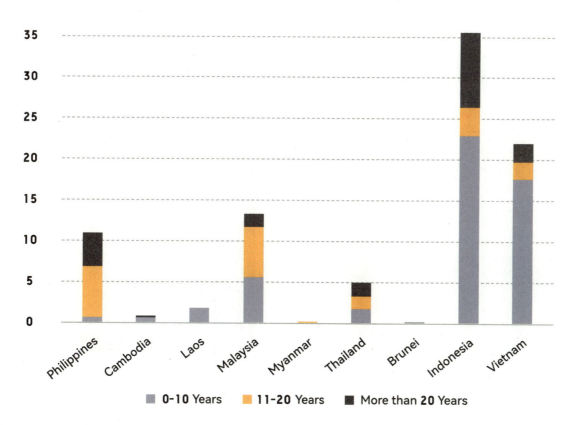

Unit: megawatt (MW)
Data Source: national energy sector data, Enerdata, EndCoal

Gas power is the most important power source in Southeast Asia at present. The age of gas-turbine units in the region is generally small. 34% of gas turbine units have been put into operation in the recent decade, and 30% have been operating for more than 20 years. In the future, the demand form upgrading and renovating some gas turbine units will gradually increase. About 60% of natural gas in Southeast Asia is used for power supply every year. Thailand, Indonesia, Malaysia, and Singapore as major gas power installed countries in the region, all have installed capacity of over 10 million kilowatts. Among them, Indonesia and Malaysia rely on abundant natural gas resources. In recent years, the installed capacity of gas power has been expanded continuously, and gas power will still occupy the main position of their power supply. In addition, Thailand and Singapore have continuously increased their natural gas imports in recent years to support the large-scale development of domestic gas power.

Figure 2.5.3-2 · Age Distribution of Gas Power Units in Southeast Asia

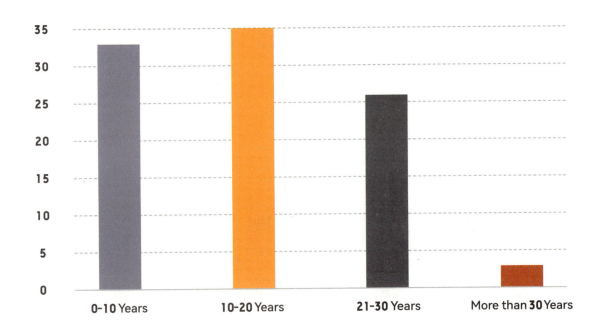

Unit: gigawatt (GW)
Data Source: International Energy Agency

2.6 Power Transmission

2.6.1 The interconnection of power grid is relatively centralized

The power interconnection in Southeast Asia is mainly concentrated in Indochina Peninsula, while cross-border power transactions in Indochina Peninsula are mainly concentrated in Thailand, Laos, Cambodia, Myanmar, Vietnam and China. Due to the large gap in the level of power development among countries, and the difficulty of grid extension in independent island countries such as the Philippines and Indonesia, the cost of power grid interconnection is high, and an integrated power grid system has not yet been formed in the region.

The total length of transmission lines in Southeast Asian countries is about 241,732 kilometers, of which the length of transmission lines of 400 KV and above is 25,805 kilometers, accounting for 11%. The length of 275-220 KV transmission line is 72,113 kilometers, accounting for 30%. The length of 138-115 KV transmission line is 94,796 kilometers, accounting for 39%. The length of 70-22 KV transmission line is 49,283 kilometers, accounting for 20%.

Table 2.6.1-1 · **Grid Length and Voltage Rating of Southeast Asian Countries**

Country	Abbreviation	Line Length Unit: KM	Percentage of 275-220KV (%)	Percentage of 275-220KV (%)	Percentage of 138-115KV (%)	Percentageof 70-22KV (%)
Philippines	PH	20079	–	11	7	82
Cambodia	KH	11301	6	60	34	–
Laos	LA	11595	4	4	89	3
Malaysia	MY	31621	8	42	49	1
Myanmar	MM	13631	–	45	17	38
Thailand	TH	37456	19	42	39	–
Brunei	BN	–	–	–	–	100
Singapore	SG	26458	3	17	–	81
Indonesia	ID	61591	9	6	76	9
Vietnam	VN	28000	31	69	–	–

Data Source: national energy sector data

2.6.2 The level of power interconnection is still low

Transnational power transactions in Southeast Asia are mainly within the region, while electricity is mainly imported from China through the Greater Mekong Subregion Interconnected Power Grid outside the region. In 2019, the total scale of transnational electricity transactions in Southeast Asia exceeded 62 TWh, accounting for about 6% of the total electricity consumption of the whole region in that year. From 2015 to 2018, the import and export power of Southeast Asia maintained a steady growth in general, and showed a slight decline in 2019. Among them, Thailand and Laos are the major power trading countries in Southeast Asia, and their import and export power accounts for 45% and 37% of the total power trading in the whole region respectively.

Figure 2.6.2-1 · Import and Export Electricity of Southeast Asian Countries from 2015 to 2019

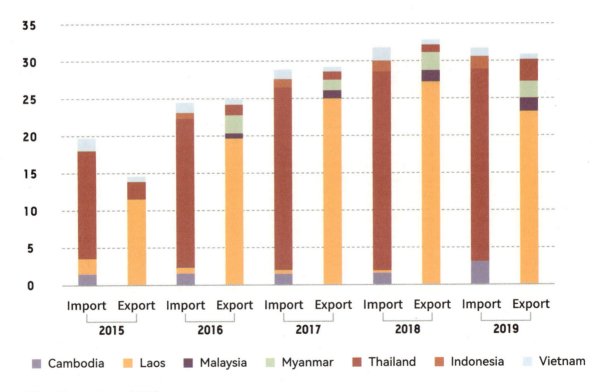

Unit: billion kilowatt hours (TWh)
Data Source: International Energy Agency, national energy sector data

From the perspective of countries, Laos is the largest power exporter in Southeast Asia, mainly delivering power to Thailand, Cambodia, Vietnam and Myanmar, and the total export scale (in terms of currency) accounts for 75% of the region. Thailand is the largest power importer in Southeast Asia, and the total import scale (in terms of currency) accounts for 80% of the region. Cambodia and Indonesia are net importers of electricity in Southeast Asia. In terms of cross-border electricity transactions outside the region, Vietnam and Laos mainly import electricity from China through the Great Mekong Subregion Interconnected Power Grid.

Table 2.6.2-1 · Electricity Import and Export Transactions of Southeast Asian Countries in 2020

	Electricity Transaction Country	Import Value (million dollars)	Export Value (million dollars)	Total Electricity Transaction (million dollars)
Cambodia	Laos	98.3	–	98.3
	Thailand	76.9	–	76.9
	Vietnam	104.1	–	104.1
Laos	China	5.6	–	5.6
	Cambodia	–	35.5	35.5
	Malaysia	–	1.0	1.0
	Myanmar	–	11.6	11.6
	Thailand	75.3	758.4	833.7
	Vietnam	1.1	25.4	26.5
Malaysia	Thailand	1.1	0.2	1.3
	Indonesia	–	122.1	122.1
Thailand	Cambodia	–	107.2	107.2
	Laos	1761.7	93.2	1854.9
	Malaysia	0.2	1.0	1.2
Indonesia	Cambodia	–	13.3	13.3
	Malaysia	120.0	–	120.0
Vietnam	China	107.9	–	107.9
	Cambodia	–	197.5	197.5
	Laos	65.3	2.7	67.9
Total		**2352.2**	**1168.9**	**3521.1**

Data Source: ASEANStats DataPortal

2.7   Electricity Price

2.7.1 Industrial sales electricity price shows an upward trend

The industrial electricity price in Southeast Asian countries ranges from 7 to 17 cents/kWh, which is slightly lower than the global average (12.3 cents/kWh). There are great differences in industrial electricity prices among countries, which are related to the industrial infrastructure, electrification level of industrial fields and electricity price policies. Among them, the industrial electricity prices in Singapore and Cambodia are relatively high, and in 2020, the industrial electricity prices will exceed 14 cents/kWh. In recent years, the industrial electricity price in Southeast Asia has shown an overall upward trend.

Figure 2.7.1-1 · Industrial Sales Electricity Prices of Southeast Asian Countries from 2015 to 2020

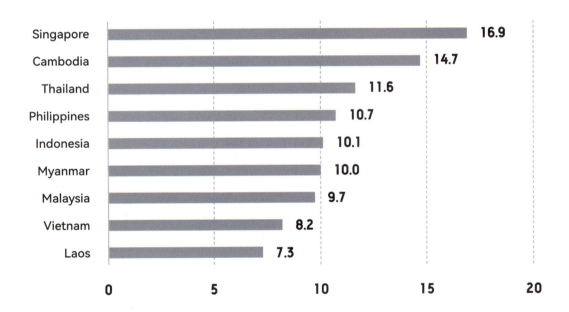

Unit: cents/kWh (US$c/kWh)
Data Source: GlobalPetrolPrices, Enerdata

Table 2.7.1-1 · Industrial Sales Electricity Prices of Southeast Asian Countries from 2015 to 2020

Country	Abbreviation	2015	2016	2017	2018	2019	2020
Philippines	PH	-	-	-	11.7	-	10.7
Cambodia	KH	-	-	-	-	14.7	14.7
Laos	LA	7.7	7.9	7.9	-	-	7.3
Malaysia	MY	7.8	7.4	7.8	8.6	-	9.7
Myanmar	MM	-	-	-	-	-	10.0
Thailand	TH	9.7	8.8	9.1	9.8	-	11.6
Brunei	BN	-	-	-	-	-	-
Singapore	SG	15.2	12.1	13.7	16.0	16.4	16.9
Indonesia	ID	8.6	7.9	8.2	7.8	-	10.1
Vietnam	VN	6.6	6.5	6.5	7.8	-	8.2

Unit: cents/kWh (US$c/kWh)

Data Source: GlobalPetrolPrices, Enerdata

*Brunei electricity price data is not available at present

2.7.2 Residential electricity prices are generally lower than industrial electricity prices

Residential electricity price in Southeast Asia is generally lower than the industrial electricity price due to cross-tariff subsidies and tariff bundling, with the household electricity price in most countries is lower than the global average (13.8 cents/kWh). The residential electricity prices in different countries vary greatly, among which the residential electricity prices in the Philippines and Cambodia are relatively high, exceeding 15 cents per kilowatt-hour in 2020, and less than 8 cents per kilowatt hour in Vietnam, Indonesia, Malaysia, Laos and Myanmar. In recent years, the residential electricity price in Southeast Asia has shown an overall downward trend, which is closely related to the level of power development.

Figure 2.7.2-1 · Residential Sales Electricity Price in Southeast Asian Countries in 2020

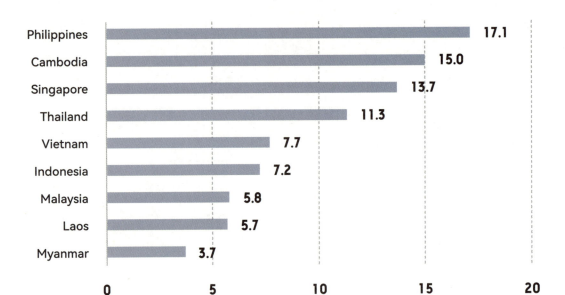

Unit: cents/kWh (US$c/kWh)
Data Source: GlobalPetrolPrices, Enerdata
*Brunei electricity price data is not available at present

Table 2.7.2-1 · Residential Sales Electricity Price in Southeast Asian Countries from 2015 to 2020

Country	Abbreviation	2015	2016	2017	2018	2019	2020
Philippines	PH	20.3	17.6	16.8	16.7	15.7	17.1
Cambodia	KH	-	-	-	-	-	15.0
Laos	LA	7.1	7.2	7.2	-	-	5.7
Malaysia	MY	7.7	7.3	6.8	7.4	-	5.8
Myanmar	MM	-	-	-	-	-	3.7
Thailand	TH	12.0	10.9	11.2	11.0	-	11.3
Brunei	BN	-	-	-	-	-	-
Singapore	SG	16.9	14.6	16.0	18.1	18.5	13.7
Indonesia	ID	6.3	6.4	7.9	10.3	-	7.2
Vietnam	VN	8.2	7.5	7.6	-	-	7.7

Unit: cents/kWh (US$c/kWh)

Data Source: GlobalPetrolPrices, Enerdata

*Brunei electricity price data are not available at present

2.8 Renewable Energy Power

2.8.1 Renewable Energy maintains the trend of rapid development

In recent years, the installed capacity of renewable energy in Southeast Asia has been expanding continuously. In 2020, the total installed capacity of renewable energy reached 87.97 million kilowatts, an increase of 31.9 million kilowatts compared with 2015, with a cumulative growth rate of 56.9%. Southeast Asia is rich in hydropower resources, with increasing demand for electricity and better investment and development mode, which makes hydropower one of the most attractive clean energy resources. Hydropower is still the most important renewable power in the region. In recent years, photovoltaic installed capacity has grown rapidly, and has gradually become the main driving force for the growth of renewable energy installed capacity in Southeast Asia. In addition, Southeast Asia is rich in biomass energy, which is an important renewable energy resource. At the same time, the Philippines and Indonesia are rich in geothermal resources and have great potential for geothermal power generation.

Figure 2.8.1-1 · Installation Structure of Renewable Energy in Southeast Asia from 2015 to 2020

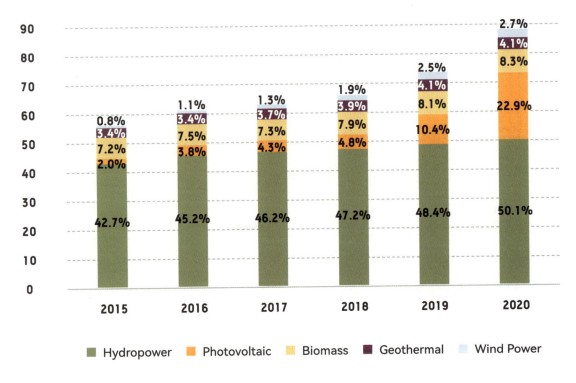

Unit: Gigawatt (GW)
Data Source: International Renewable Energy Agency

2.8.2 Installed capacity of photovoltaic and wind power show a trend of accelerated growth

In recent years, the installed capacity of photovoltaic and wind power in Southeast Asia has shown a trend of accelerated growth, with an average annual growth rate of over 60% and 25% respectively. In 2020, the installed capacity of photovoltaic and wind power will account for 26% and 3% of the total installed capacity of regional renewable energy respectively. Among them, the installed capacity of photovoltaics has increased rapidly in the recent three years, reaching 22.85 million kilowatts in 2020, which is 1.2 times larger than that of the previous year. At the same time, the installed capacity of wind power has been expanding in recent years, with the installed capacity exceeding 2.7 million kilowatts in 2020, which is 2.4 times larger than that in 2015.

Figure 2.8.2-1 · Total Installed PV Capacity & Yearly Growth Rate in Southeast Asia from 2015 to 2020

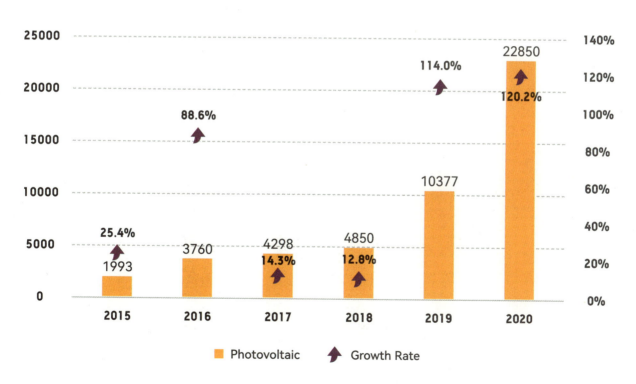

Figure 2.8.2-2 · Total Installed Wind Power Capacity & Yearly Growth Rate in Southeast Asia from 2015 to 2020

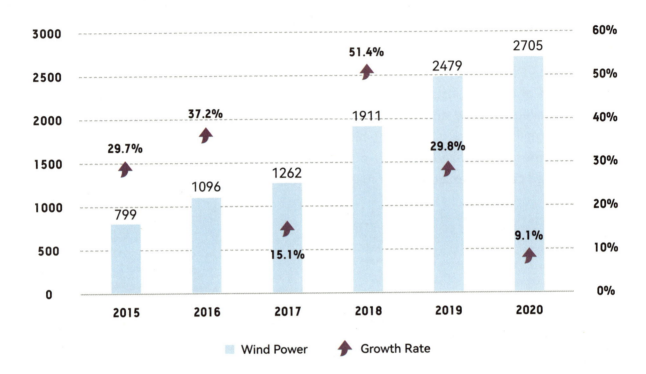

Unit: megawatt (MW)

Data Source: International Renewable Energy Agency, research of this report

2.8.3 Photovoltaic and wind power installations are relatively concentrated

From the perspective of countries, the installed capacity of photovoltaics and wind power in Southeast Asia is relatively concentrated, of which photovoltaics are mainly concentrated in Vietnam (72%), Thailand (13%), Malaysia (7%) and the Philippines (5%); Wind power is mainly distributed in Thailand (56%), Vietnam (22%), Indonesia (16%) and the Philippines (6%). From 2015 to 2020, the country with the largest increase in photovoltaic installed capacity in Southeast Asia is Vietnam (16,499MW), and Thailand (1,563MW), Malaysia (1,264MW) and the Philippines (875MW) are also prominent. The largest increase in wind power installed capacity is in Thailand (1,273MW), and the installed capacity growth in Vietnam (464MW) and Indonesia (153MW) is also obvious.

Figure 2.8.3-1 · Installation Increment of Photovoltaic and Wind Power in Southeast Asian Countries from 2015 to 2020

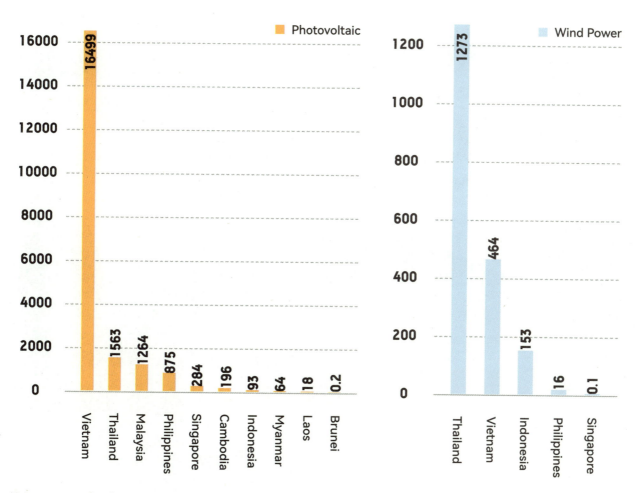

Unit: megawatt (MW)

Data Source: International Renewable Energy Agency, research of this report

03 Current Situation of Energy Cooperation between China and Southeast Asian Countries

Current Situation of Energy Cooperation between China and Southeast Asian Countries

Southeast Asia is an important region for China's energy and power enterprises to "go out", and the two countries have achieved fruitful results in energy cooperation. Trade in oil, natural gas and coal between the two sides is very active, ensuring the energy security of each country effectively. Enterprises from both sides have carried out a large number of projects in the fields of hydropower, new energy, thermal power and power grids, including investment, project design and project engineering services, improving local power supply and enhancing the well-being of local people.

3.1 Energy Trade Cooperation

3.1.1 The oil trade between China and Southeast Asian countries remains general growth

China has maintained close oil trade cooperation with Southeast Asian countries for a long time. From 2015 to 2019, the oil trade volume between China and Southeast Asia showed an overall growth trend, with an average annual growth rate of 3.2%. In 2020, affected by the COVID-19 epidemic, international oil prices continued to fall, and the oil trade between China and Southeast Asian countries decreased by 33.8% compared with 2019, with a total trade volume of only 15.4 billion US dollars, accounting for 7.1% (216.2 billion US dollars) of the total oil trade between China and the world, and 8.7% (177.6 billion US dollars) of the total oil trade between Southeast Asia and the world.

Figure 3.1.1-1 · Total Oil Trade between China and Southeast Asian Countries from 2015 to 2020

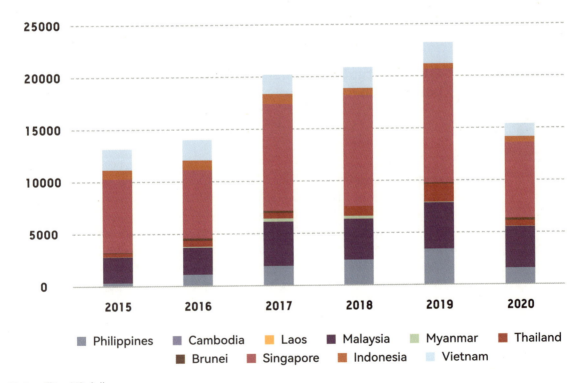

Unit: million US dollars
Data Source: ASEAN Stats Data Portal

From the perspective of countries, Singapore and Malaysia have larger oil trade volume with China. Among them, Singapore is an important oil refining center and oil trade hub in the world. On the other hand, CAO and PetroChina acquired 20.6% and 45.5% shares of Singapore Petroleum Company in 2004 and 2009 respectively. The above factors have accumulated favorable conditions for China and Singapore to carry out oil trade cooperation, and the oil trade volume between China and Singapore has maintained a relatively high level all year round, reaching 7.5 billion US dollars in 2020. As the second largest oil producer in Southeast Asia, Malaysia has long exported crude oil to China. In recent years, China's exports of refined oil products to Malaysia are also increasing, and the oil import and export trade between China and Malaysia is gradually becoming balanced. In addition, China and Myanmar have maintained a high oil trade activity through the China-Myanmar oil and gas pipeline for a long time. By May 2020, Myanmar has delivered 30 million tons of crude oil to China through the China-Myanmar oil and gas pipeline. The Myanmar-China oil and gas pipeline is a milestone in China's diversification of oil transportation channels, which effectively alleviates China's dependence on the Straits of Malacca and further enhances oil supply security.

Figure 3.1.1-2 · Oil Import and Export Trade Volume between China and Southeast Asian Countries in 2020

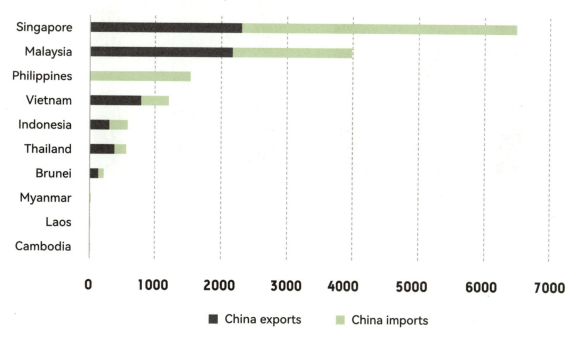

Unit: million US dollars
Data Source: ASEAN Stats Data Portal

3.1.2 China's natural gas imports from Southeast Asian countries continue to rise

Southeast Asia is one of the main regions of China's natural gas imports, and the natural gas trade volume between China and Southeast Asian countries has fluctuated in recent years. In 2020, affected by the COVID-19 epidemic, natural gas trade between China and Southeast Asian countries decreased by 25.5% compared with 2019, and the total trade volume was only 5.3 billion US dollars, accounting for 15.2% of China's total natural gas trade with the world (34.9 billion US dollars) and 16.4%of total natural gas trade between Southeast Asia and the world (32.4 billion US dollars).

Figure 3.1.2-1 · Total Natural Gas Trade between China and Southeast Asian Countries in 2015-2020

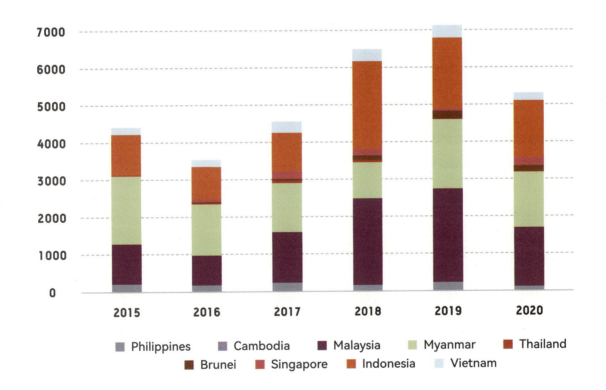

Unit: million US dollars
Data Source: ASEAN Stats Data Portal

From the perspective of countries, natural gas imports come from Malaysia, Indonesia and Myanmar. Among them, Malaysia and Indonesia export liquefied natural gas to China, while Myanmar exports natural gas to China through China-Myanmar oil and gas pipeline.

In recent years, China's natural gas imports from Malaysia, Indonesia and Myanmar have shown an overall upward trend, with an average annual growth rate of 9.4% from 2015 to 2020. In 2020, China imported 14.18million tons of natural gas from the above three countries, mainly imported liquefied natural gas, accounting for 78.6% of the total imports.

Figure 3.1.2-2 · China's Natural Gas Imports in Southeast Asia from 2015-2020

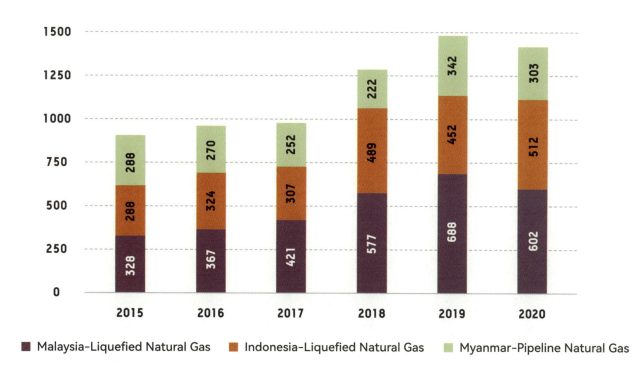

Unit: 10,000 tons
Data Source: China Customs

3.1.3 Southeast Asia is the most important area of coal import for China

The coal trade between China and Southeast Asia is dominated by China's imports from Southeast Asia. In 2020, the coal trade between China and Southeast Asian countries is about 7.8 billion US dollars. According to the General Administration of Customs of China, nearly half of China's coal imports come from Southeast Asian countries.

From the perspective of countries, Indonesia is the main source of China's coal imports, and China's annual coal imports from Indonesia account for more than 70% of China's total coal imports from Southeast Asia.

Figure 3.1.3-1 · Total Coal Trade between China and Southeast Asian Countries from 2015 to 2020

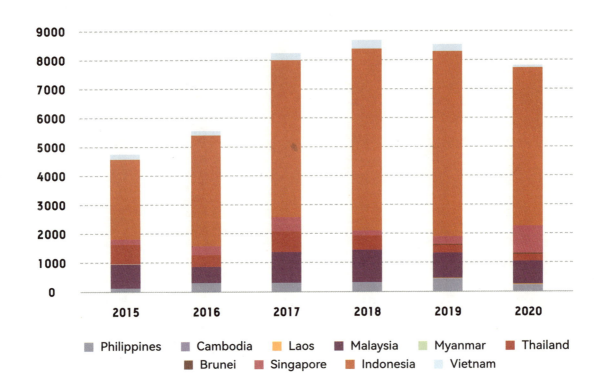

Unit: million US dollars
Data Source: ASEAN Stats Data Portal

Figure 3.1.3-2 · Coal Import and Export Trade Volume between China and Southeast Asian Countries in 2020

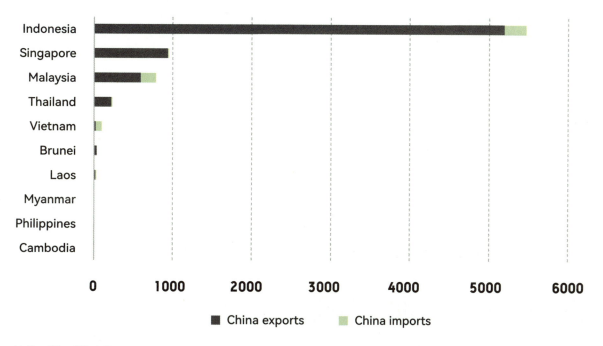

Unit: million US dollars
Data Source: ASEAN Stats Data Portal

3.2 Investment Cooperation in the Field of Electric Power

3.2.1 Hydropower is the major form of renewable energy investment cooperation

China's renewable energy investment cooperation in Southeast Asian Countries mainly focuses on hydropower, involving a few solar energy and biomass power generation projects. From the perspective of countries, investment in renewable energy projects is mainly distributed in Cambodia, Laos, Malaysia, Myanmar, Thailand, Indonesia and Vietnam.

Table 3.2.1 · Major Renewable Energy Investment Cooperation Projects between China and Southeast Asian Countries

Serial Number	Country	Project Name	Installed Capacity (MW)	Chinese Investment Enterprise	Investment Model
1	Cambodia	Kamchay Hydropower Station	193.2	China Power Construction	BOT
2	Cambodia	Stung Atay Hydropower Project	120	Datang Group	BOT
3	Cambodia	Stung Russei Chrum Downstream Hydropower Station	338	China Huadian	BOT
4	Cambodia	Level 2 Hydropower Station	400	China Huaneng	BOT
5	Cambodia	Upper Tatay Hydropower Station	150	China Heavy Machinery	BOT
6	Laos	Nam Ngum No.5 Hydropower Station	120	China Power Construction	BOT
7	Laos	Namtha River No. 1 Hydropower Station	168	China Southern Power Grid	BOT
8	Laos	Nam Ou River Cascade Hydropower Station	1272	China Power Construction	BOT
9	Laos	Meikong River Pak Beng Hydropower Project	912	Datang Group	BOT
10	Laos	Meikong River Sanakham Hydropower Station Project	660	Datang Group	BOT
11	Laos	Salalong 1 Hydropower Station Project	70	Yunnan Energy Investment	BOT
12	Laos	Nam Ngum No.1 Surface Floating Photovoltaic Power Generation Project	1200	Hangzhou Safefound Technology	—
13	Malaysia	Kedah Solar Power Station	50	China General Nuclear Power Group	—
14	Myanmar	Shweli Level 1 Hydropower Station	600	China Huaneng	BOT
15	Myanmar	Chipwi Nge Hydropower Plant	99	State Power Investment	BOT
16	Myanmar	Song Thai Binh Hydropower Project	240	Datang Group	BOT
17	Indonesia	Batang Toru Hydropower Station Project	510	Zhefu Holdings	Equity Merger and Acquisition
18	Vietnam	Seo Chong Ho Hydropower Station	220	Southern Power Grid	BOT
19	Vietnam	Hanoi Waste Incineration Power Generation Project	75	China Tianying	—

Organized according to Public Information

When investing in the construction of hydropower projects in Southeast Asia, the main mode adopted by Chinese enterprises is greenfield investment, and the installed scale of hydropower projects is mostly more than 100,000 kilowatts. From a national point of view, China has more hydropower investment in Cambodia, Laos, Myanmar and other countries.

In the development of non-water renewable energy projects in Southeast Asia, the number of projects in which China participates in investment and construction is still small. However, the trend of energy low-carbon transformation and development in Southeast Asian countries is strong, and it has become the consensus of all countries to adopt clean, low-carbon, intelligent and efficient energy supply methods to solve the problem of energy accessibility. Southeast Asian countries have successively formulated development plans for non-water renewable energy and promulgated a series of policies for energy transformation. The future market of non-water renewable energy in Southeast Asia is promising, which will provide a lot of opportunities for China to carry out deeper cooperation in renewable energy with Southeast Asian countries.

3.2.2 Investment in thermal power is mainly based on coal power with large capacity and high parameters

The thermal power projects invested by China in Southeast Asian countries are mainly coal-fired power with large capacity and high parameters. From the perspective of investment model, the coal-fired power projects invested and cooperated by China and Southeast Asian countries are mainly greenfield investment, involving minority equity mergers and acquisitions. From the perspective of countries, the investment in thermal power projects is mainly distributed in Cambodia, Indonesia, Vietnam and other countries.

In recent years, the cumulative installed capacity of coal-fired power projects invested by Chinese-funded enterprises in Southeast Asian countries is nearly 10 million kilowatts, accounting for about 10% of the total installed capacity of coal-fired power in Southeast Asia. These include gigawatt-level coal-fired power plants such as the No.7 Coal-Fired Power Plant in Java, Indonesia, Boya Pithead Coal-Fired Power Plant in Indonesia and Hai Duong Coal-Fired Power Plant in Vietnam. Most of the thermal power units invested by Chinese-funded enterprises have adopted advanced and environment-friendly clean coal-fired power technology, and the annual utilization hours are generally high, which has made an important contribution to further improving the safety and stability of the local power system.

Table 3.2.2 · Thermal Power Investment Cooperation Projects between China and Southeast Asian Countries

No.	Country	Project Name	Installed Capacity (MW)	Chinese Investment Enterprises	Investment Pattern
1	Cambodia	Sihanoukville Coal-Fired Power Station	700	China Huadian	BOT
2	Indonesia	Batam Coal-Fired Power Station	130	China Huadian	BOT
3	Indonesia	South Sumatra Muaraenim Coal-Fired Power Station	300	National Energy Group	BOO
4	Indonesia	Boya Pithead Coal-Fired Power Station	1320	China Huadian	BOOT
5	Indonesia	Bali Coal-Fired Power Station	426	China Huadian	BOOT
6	Indonesia	South Sumatra No.1 Independent Coal-Fired Power Plant	700	National Energy Group	BOO
7	Indonesia	Java No.7 Coal-Fired Power Plant	2100	National Energy Group	BOO
8	Indonesia	Bengkulu Coal-Fired Power Station Project	200	China Electric Power Construction	BOOT
9	Indonesia	Banten Thermal Power Project	670	SDIC Group	Equity Merger and Acquisition
10	Indonesia	Meulaboh Coal-Fired Power Generation Project	450	Datang Group	BOOT
11	Indonesia	Jambi No.2 Supercritical Coal-Fired Unit	700	China Huadian	—
12	Vietnam	Hai Duong Coal-Fired Power Station	1200	CEEC	BOT
13	Vietnam	Vinh Tan Coal-Fired Power Plant Phase I	620	Southern Power Grid China Power International	BOT
14	Vietnam	Coastal Coal-Fired Power Station Project Phase II	1320	China Huadian	BOT

Organized According to Public Information

3.2.3 Power grid investment has increased, and equity acquisition projects have increased

In recent years, China has increased its investment in power grids in Southeast Asian countries. From the perspective of investment model, the main power grid projects invested and cooperated by China and Southeast Asian countries are acquisitions. From the perspectives of countries, investment in power grid projects is mainly distributed in the Philippines, Cambodia, Laos, Malaysia, Singapore and Indonesia.

Table 3.2.3 · Power Grid Investment Cooperation Projects between China and Southeast Asian Countries

No.	Country	Project Name	Chinese Investment Enterprises	Investment Pattern
1	Philippines	Franchise Right of Philippine National Grid (NGCP)	National Power Grid	Equity Merger and Acquisition
2	Cambodia	Phnom Penh–Battambang 294km 230KV Transmission and Transformation Project	Datang Group	BOT
3	Laos	Establishment of Laos National Transmission Network Company EDL-T)	Southern Power Grid	—
4	Indonesia	275KV Substation and Transmission Project	Datang Group	BOT
5	Indonesia	Jambi No.2 Coal Power Joint Venture Project 118KM 500KV Transmission Line	China Huadian	—

Organized According to Public Information

3.3 Cooperation in construction of electric power projects

3.3.1 The planning and design consulting work achieved remarkable results

In recent years, the cooperation between China and Southeast Asian countries in energy planning and design consultation has achieved remarkable results.

In terms of planning consultation, China has carried out research on energy and power cooperation planning for Vietnam, the Philippines, Laos, Myanmar and other countries, which not only effectively promoted the orderly and healthy development of the energy and power industry in the host country, but also laid a good foundation for the two sides to jointly carry out practical project cooperation. Among them, "Laos Electric Power Planning Research" is the first time that the Chinese government has assisted "Belt and Road Initiative" countries in preparing national electric power plans, which has been highly praised by the Laos government. The preparation of the plans has promote the signing of the Memorandum of Understanding of Establishing Strategic Partnership for Electric Power Cooperation, which is of milestone significance.

In terms of project design consultation, Chinese design units give full play to the advantages of the whole industrial chain, and provide a series of services such as assessment and review, survey and design, project construction and management, operation and maintenance, investment and operation, technical services, equipment manufacturing and building materials for a large number of thermal power, hydropower, new energy and power grid projects in Southeast Asian countries, effectively driving China's technology, standards, equipment and services to "go global".

Table 3.3.1 · China–Southeast Asia National Electric Power Planning and Design Consulting Projects

No.	Country	Project Name	Responsible Unit	Time
1	Myanmar	China-Myanmar Electric Power Cooperation Planning	China Renewable Energy Engineering Institut	2015
2	Vietnam	Study on Sino-Vietnamese Energy Cooperation Planning	China Electric Power Planning & Engineering Institute	2016
3	Philippines	Research on Sino-Philippines Energy Cooperation Planning	China Electric Power Planning & Engineering Institute	2017
4	Laos	Research on Laos Electric Power Planning	China Electric Power Planning & Engineering Institute	2018
5	Myanmar	General Planning of Water Resources for Sustainable Hydropower Development in Myanmar	China Renewable Energy Engineering Institut	2019

Organized According to Public Information

3.3.2 Southeast Asia is the main market for the construction of China's overseas power projects

In recent years, Southeast Asia has gradually grown into a major market for Chinese-funded enterprises to provide overseas energy project construction services.

In terms of power project engineering services, up to now, the installed capacity of power project engineering services provided by Chinese-funded enterprises in Southeast Asian countries is nearly 30 GW, among which renewable energy projects exceed 13GW. The power project construction services provided by Chinese-funded enterprises are mainly concentrated in Indonesia, Vietnam, the Philippines, Laos and other countries.

Figure 3.3.2-1 · Engineering Construction Cooperation between China and Southeast Asian Countries from 2016 to the First Half of 2021

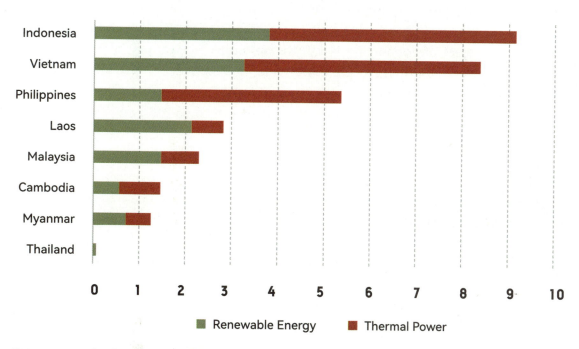

Unit: megawatt (MW)
Data Source: Based on public information of the government and enterprise

In terms of renewable energy project engineering services, the renewable energy project engineering services of Chinese-funded enterprises in Southeast Asian countries have expanded from the early hydropower projects to new energy fields such as photovoltaic, wind power and biomass power generation. In recent years, Chinese-funded enterprises have participated in the construction of new energy projects in Southeast Asia with more than 5,000 MW, creating a number of large-scale demonstration projects of new energy power generation for partner countries. Among them, Vietnam is the largest market for China's cooperation in photovoltaic and wind power projects in Southeast Asia. The 500MVp photovoltaic power generation project undertaken by China Power Construction Corporation in Dau Tieng, Vietnam is the largest single photovoltaic power station in Southeast Asia at present, and the largest semi-submerged photovoltaic project in the world.

In term of engineering services for thermal power projects, besides coal-fired power projects, Chinese-funded enterprises have also undertaken a number of large-scale gas-fired power projects in Southeast Asia. In terms of power grid project engineering services, Chinese-funded enterprises have undertaken a number of power grid infrastructure and transmission line construction projects in Indochina countries, the Philippines and Malaysia, which have effectively improved the power transmission capacity of Southeast Asian countries and further improved the local power grid security and stability. For example, the transmission and transformation project of connecting North Kachin State of Myanmar with the 230 KV backbone network, undertaken by the State Power Grid, has an annual transmission capacity of 300,000 kilowatts, which meets the electricity demand of 5 million households in Myanmar, helps Myanmar to set up the "transmitting power from north to south" power channel, and further accelerates the pace of infrastructure interconnection between China and Myanmar and its neighboring countries. The expansion project of rural power grid in Cambodia, undertaken by China National Heavy Machinery, covers rural power grids in 13 provinces of Cambodia, effectively solves the problem of rural power consumption, and significantly improves the coverage rate of power grid in Cambodia.

3.4 Power Interconnection Cooperation

3.4.1 China has achieved power interconnection with some Southeast Asian countries

In recent years, the economies of Southeast Asian countries have developed rapidly, and the power market demand in various countries is strong. Countries are increasingly willing to optimize the allocation of resources and ensure reliable power supply by strengthening power interconnection, which provides an important opportunity window for speeding up the power interconnection between China and Southeast Asian countries. Up to now, China has achieved power interconnection with Myanmar, Vietnam and Laos through 14 circuits of 110KV and above transmission lines, which has further enhanced the power supply guarantee capacity of the three countries and effectively solved the power consumption problem of people without electricity in some remote areas.

Table 3.4.1 · Power Interconnection betweenChina and Southeast Asian Countries

Country	Networking Line
China-Myanmar	1-Loop 500KV Line
	2-Loop 220KV Line
	3-Loop 110 KV Line
	8-Loop 35KV Line
	36-Loop 10KV Line
China-Vietnam	3-Loop 220KV Line
	4-Loop 110KV Line
China-Laos	1-Loop 115KV Line
	3-Loop 35KV Line

Data Source: <China Electric Power Development Report 2020>, General Electric Power Planning and Design Institute

In 2004, the first power grid interconnection project between China and Vietnam, the 110KV interconnection project from Hekou, Yunnan Province to Lao Cai, Vietnam, was put into operation, marking the beginning of China's first large-scale power transmission abroad. Up to now, China and Vietnam are mainly interconnected through 3-loop 220KV lines, and China exports electricity to Vietnam.

In 2001, China and Laos realized the interconnection of power grids, and successively supplied power from Yunnan to northern Laos through 10KV, 35KV and 115KV lines, which enabled rural and remote areas in northern Laos to realize power interconnection. In November 2017, President Xi Jinping and Laos President Boungnang witnessed the signing of the Memorandum of Understanding on Establishing Strategic Partnership for Power Cooperation. In August 2018, China Southern Power Grid Corporation and Laos Ministry of Planning and Investment signed the Memorandum of Understanding on Feasibility Study of Developing and Constructing Laos National Transmission Network Company (EDL-T), which was jointly funded by China Southern Power Grid Corporation and Laos National Power Company, formally signed a franchised agreement with the Laos government, which marked a substantial step in the mutually beneficial and win-win cooperation between China and Laos in the field of transmission. Up to now, Southern Power Grid Company has completed the preparation of the feasibility study of China-Laos networking and is seeking the opinions of Laos.

At the end of 2014, Myanmar first proposed to build a 500KV transmission line from Yunnan, China to send electricity to Yangon, Myanmar. In 2017, the Chinese working group of this project, composed of China Southern Power Grid Corporation and State Grid Corporation was formally established. In January 2020, witnessed by the leaders of China and Myanmar, China Southern Power Grid Corporation and Myanmar Ministry of Electricity and Energy signed the Memorandum on Feasibility Study of China-Myanmar Networking Project, and Myanmar authorized the Chinese working group to be responsible for the feasibility study of China-Myanmar Networking Project. After the completion of the China-Myanmar interconnection project, it will help alleviate the power shortage in Myanmar, improve people's livelihood and help Myanmar's social and economic development.

3.4.2 The scale of electricity trade is still small

China has carried out power trade cooperation with Vietnam, Laos and Myanmar through interconnection lines. At present, the scale of power trade is generally small, with annual trading capacity generally maintained at around 4 TWh and the annual transaction volume maintained at around 100 million US dollars. In 2020, China will export 1.94 TWh, 544 GWh and 90 GWh of electricity to Vietnam, Myanmar and Laos respectively, and import 1.539 TWh of electricity from Myanmar, with an annual turnover of 114 million US dollars.

Table 3.4.2 · Electricity Import and Export between China and Southeast Asia Countries in 2020

Country	Electricity Imported from China(GWh)	Electricity Exported to China(GWh)
Myanmar	544	1539
Vietnam	1940	—
Laos	90	—

Data Source: <China Electric Power Development Report 2020>, China Electric Power Planning & Engineering Institute

3.5 International Exchanges and Cooperation

3.5.1 Actively carry out international exchanges and cooperation relying on multilateral and bilateral cooperation platforms in the energy field

Relying on international conferences and forums under various multilateral and bilateral institutional frameworks and cooperation mechanisms, China and Southeast Asian countries have maintained close and friendly international exchanges and cooperation in the energy field for a long time.

Table 3.5.1 · Main International Exchange Platforms between China and Southeast Asian Countries

	Communication Platform
Multilateral	China-ASEAN (10+1) Leaders Meeting
	Lancang-Mekong River (LMC) Cooperation Leaders Meeting
	Greater Mekong Subregion (GMS) Economic Cooperation Leaders Meeting
	East Asia Summit Energy Ministers Meeting
	ASEAN and China, Japan and Korea (10+3) Energy Ministers Meeting
	ASEAN and China, Japan and Korea (10+3) Round Table Dialogue on Clean Energy
	East Asia Summit Clean Energy Forum
	East Asia Summit New Energy Forum
	China-ASEAN Power Cooperation and Development Forum
	Meeting of Asia-Pacific Economic Cooperation (APEC) Energy Working Group
Bilateral	Meeting of China-Laos Energy Cooperation Working Group
	Meeting of China-Thailand Energy Cooperation Working Group
	China-Myanmar Electric Power Cooperation Committee Meeting
	Meeting of the Intergovernmental Joint Steering Committee on Sino-Philippine Oil and Gas Cooperation

Energy cooperation is an important topic in high-level meetings of heads of state and government, such as China-ASEAN (10+1) Leader's Meeting, Lancang-Mekong Cooperation (LMC) Leaders' Meeting, Greater Mekong Subregion (GMS) Economic Cooperation Leaders' Meeting. In November 2020, Premier Li Keqiang pointed out at the 23rd China-ASEAN Leader's Meeting: Chine welcomes all parties to sign the Regional Comprehensive Economic Partnership Agreement, implement the China-ASEAN Free Trade Agreement and upgrade the Protocol, continue to deepen the docking of the "Belt and Road Initiative" with the ASEAN development plan, support the construction of major projects in ASEAN infrastructure, energy resources and other fields, and provide support for regional economic and trade exchanges.

In terms of multilateral energy cooperation

High-end dialogue platforms such as the Energy Ministers Meeting of East Asia Summit, the Energy Ministers Meeting of ASEAN and China, Japan and Korea (10+3), and the Round Table Dialogue on Clean Energy between ASEAN and China, Japan and Korea have established important international cooperation channels for energy cooperation between China and Southeast Asian countries. At the same time, international forums and conferences such as the Clean Energy Forum of the East Asia Summit, the New Energy Forum of the East Asia Summit, the China-ASEAN Power Cooperation and Development Forum, and the Asia-Pacific Economic Cooperation (APEC) Energy Working Group Meeting have also set up efficient interactive platform for information exchange as well as exchanges and cooperation between China and Southeast Asian countries in the field of energy and power. In September 2021, the China-ASEAN Power Cooperation and Development Forum was held in Nanning, Guangxi. Zhang Jianhua, director of China National Energy Administration, said that power, as the core of energy technology, is an important area of cooperation between China and ASEAN countries.

In terms of bilateral energy cooperation

A series of bilateral meetings, such as the China-Laos Energy Cooperation Working Group Meeting, the China-Thailand Energy Working Group Meeting, the China-Myanmar Power Cooperation Committee Meeting, and the China-Philippines Inter-governmental Joint Steering Committee Meeting on Oil and Gas Cooperation, have created a good platform for in-depth exchanges between the two sides in the field of energy and power. In October 2017, China National Energy Administration and Laos Ministry of Energy and Minerals co-chaired the first meeting of the China-Laos Energy Cooperation Working Group in Guangzhou. China and Laos had in-depth exchanges and reached broad consensus on China's assistance to Laos in formulating power plans, strengthening China-Laos networking and sending power to third countries, cooperation between enterprises of the two countries in the investment, construction and operation of Laos transmission network, and mutual power transmission between the two countries.

3.5.2 Capacity building is an important way for China to assist Southeast Asian countries in strengthening energy soft power construction

Capacity building is an important way for China to assist Southeast Asian countries in strengthening their soft power construction. Through a large number of capacity-building activities such as personnel training, project investigation, exchange seminars and sharing of best practices. China and Southeast Asian countries have extensive communication on energy and power cooperation and exchange, which provides an effective platform for Southeast Asian countries to train and build a professional and localized energy talent team, and also lays a solid foundation for broader and deeper energy cooperation between China and Southeast Asia.

In 2019, China Electric Power Planning and Design Institute was entrusted by China National Energy Administration to organize the Lancang-Mekong Power Interconnection Cooperation Project and held three training courses and two seminars in China. Representatives from the energy and power authorities, power enterprises and international organizations from the six countries of Lancang and Mekong River region participated in the training, investigation and discussion activities, conducted in-depth discussion on the technologies, standards, policies and related laws of power interconnection, and conducted in-depth exchanges around the practical experience and achievements of power industries in various countries, as well as the realization path and cutting edge technologies of regional power interconnection. The project has trained more than 100 power professionals in Lancang-Mekong countries, which has made positive contributions to improving the power technology management level, promoting the construction of regional power interconnection facilities and driving the sustainable development of power in the Lancang-Mekong region.

In 2017, China Hydropower Planning and Design Institute and ASEAN Energy Center Launched the flagship project of China-ASEAN clean energy cooperation: China-ASEAN clean energy capacity building plan. In 2018 and 2019, the project held two trainings around the fields of "multi-energy complementation" and "pumped storage". In 2020, the project focused on "enhancing the proportion of photovoltaic applications in ASEAN". The application of advanced photovoltaic applications such as water-photovoltaic complementarity and waterborne photovoltaic in ASEAN region is warmed-up and discussed. In July 2021, the project held a warm-up meeting around the theme of "promoting large scale development of wind power in ASEAN" and looked forward to the potential of wind power development in ASEAN countries. The project aims to promote the sustainable development of regional clean energy, share experiences in clean energy development policy planning and technology application, and promote the exchange and construction of core talents in related fields, aiming at the five thematic areas of pumped storage, wind power, solar power, nuclear power and traditional hydropower, it is planned to train 100 policy and technical backbone personnel for ASEAN countries in ten years.

04 Energy Development Outlook in Southeast Asia

Energy Development Outlook in Southeast Asia

Energy consumption in Southeast Asia is expected to continue to grow at a fast pace, and energy transition will accelerate significantly. Renewable energy is expected to become the largest energy consumer in Southeast Asia by 2030, and the share of installed renewable energy will hit 50% by 2030, with PV and wind power in most regions becoming more affordable by 2030. Under the trend of global carbon neutralizing, the fossil energy mix in Southeast Asia will also undergo significant adjustments, with coal and oil consumption expected to peak between 2025 and 2030. There will still be a slight increase in installed coal capacity, but gas power will be the main contributor to the increase in thermal power capacity. Natural gas consumption will maintain a steady growth trend driven by the development of gas power.

4.1 Scene setting

By taking a holistic approach to population growth, economic development, policy improvement and technological progress, this study designed three scenarios for 2040, namely, continuation scenario, transformation scenario and accelerated transformation scenario. Among them, the continuation scenario is the predicted future energy development situation based on the fact that the current policies and measures remain largely unchanged and the technological innovation advances steadily. The transformation scenario is a predicted future energy development situation based on the realization of the United Nations Sustainable Development Goals and relevant energy and climate change targets in the Paris Agreement, the implementation of energy transformation policies and the acceleration of technological innovation. The accelerated transformation scenario is a predicted future energy development situation based on the goal of realizing the UN Sustainable Development Goals and the Paris Agreement as soon as possible, drastically adjusting the existing energy policies of various countries, and applying a large number of innovative technologies on a large scale.

4.2 Prospects for energy development in Southeast Asia

4.2.1 Sustained and rapid momentum of economic growth

Southeast Asia is one of the most active regions in global economic growth. With the gradual economic recovery after the epidemic, the domestic demand in this region will continue to grow, the infrastructure construction will be accelerated, and the industrialization level and urbanization rate will gradually go up. It is expected that the economy will maintain a rapid growth momentum in the future, which is one of the important engines of global economic growth. By 2030, the total GDP of Southeast Asia will be close to 4.5 trillion US dollars, and the average annual growth rate will exceed 4% from 2021 to 2030. By 2040, the total GDP of Southeast Asia will exceed 6 trillion US dollars, and the average annual growth rate will exceed 3% from 2030 to 2040.

Figure 4.2.1-1 · Total GDP of Southeast Asia from 2000 to 2040

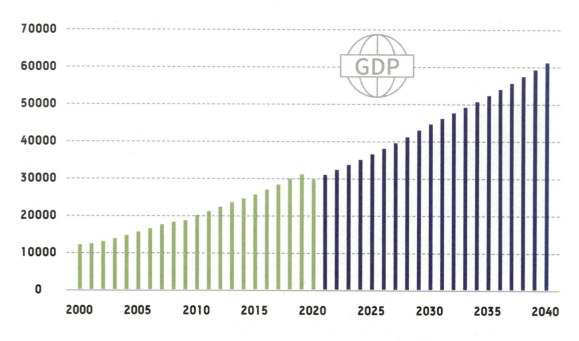

Unit: 100 million USD

Data source: World Bank, International Monetary Fund, and the research of this report

From the perspective of per capita GDP, by 2030, this indicator in Southeast Asia has been significantly improved, and is expected to reach more than 6000 USD/person, which is nearly 40% higher than that in 2020, but still far below the current global average level (about 11,000 USD/person). There is great potential for economic development and much room for improvement in the future. By 2040, the per capita GDP in Southeast Asia will be close to 8,000 USD/person, which is nearly 80% higher than that in 2020.

Figure 4.2.1-2 · Per capita GDP in Southeast Asia from 2020 to 2040

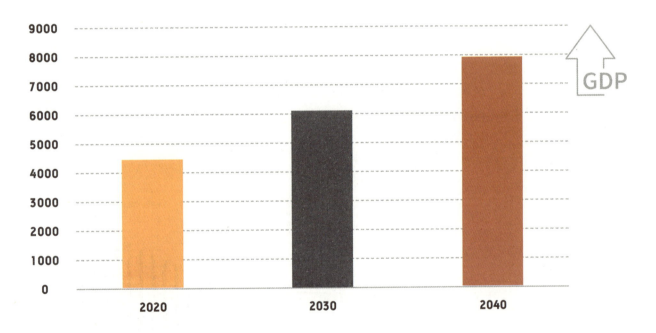

Unit: USD/person
Data source: United Nations Population Division, International Monetary Fund, and the research of this report

4.2.2 Energy demand will increase steadily

Influenced by many factors such as rapid economic development, accelerated industrialization and upward urbanization rate, the energy demand in Southeast Asia will show a steady growth trend in the future and become an important driver for the growth of global energy demand. Under the continuation scenario, the energy demand in Southeast Asia is growing rapidly. In 2030, the total energy demand exceeds 900 million tons of standard oil, an increase of more than 30% compared with 2020, the average annual growth rate is close to 3% from 2021 to 2030, and the total energy demand in 2040 exceeds 1.1 billion tons of standard oil. Under the transformation scenario, energy utilization efficiency continues to improve, energy conservation and emission reduction efforts are intensified, technological innovation capacity is enhanced, the potential of energy transformation is unleashed, and the growth of energy demand slows down. The total energy demand in 2030 is close to 900 million tons of standard oil, an increase of more than 25% compared with that in 2020, the average annual growth rate in 2021-2030 exceeds 2%, and the total energy demand in 2040 exceeds 1 billion tons of standard oil. Under the accelerated transformation scenario, the energy utilization efficiency has been further improved, the electrification level has been continuously improved, emerging technologies have been widely used, and the energy consumption has shown a slow growth. In 2030, the total energy demand exceeded 800 million tons of standard oil, an increase of about 16% compared with 2020, and the average annual growth rate from 2021 to 2030 was about 1.5%. In 2040, the total energy demand exceeded 900 million tons of standard oil.

Figure 4.2.2-1 · Forecast of Energy Demand in Southeast Asia from 2000 to 2040

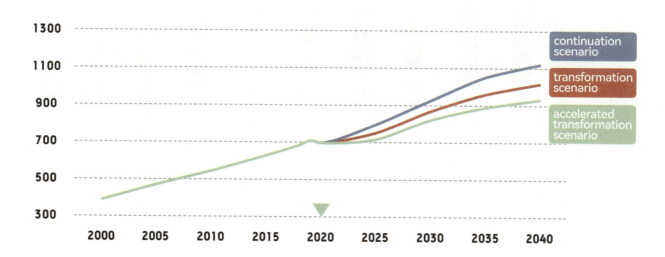

Unit: million tons of standard oil
Data source: International Energy Agency, BP, research of this report

From the perspective of energy consumption mix, under the transformation scenario, the proportion of coal consumption in Southeast Asia has been declining since 2020, and is expected to drop to 20% in 2030 and 14% in 2040. With improving transportation electrification, the proportion of oil consumption has shown a downward trend since 2015, falling to 27% in 2030 and 21% in 2040. The proportion of natural gas consumption is increasing then declining, with 19% in 2030 and 17% in 2040. The proportion of renewable energy consumption is rising rapidly, and reaches 34% in 2030 and 48% in 2040, which becomes one of the main sources of energy consumption in Southeast Asia.

Figure 4.2.2-3 · Energy consumption structure in Southeast Asia from 2000 to 2040

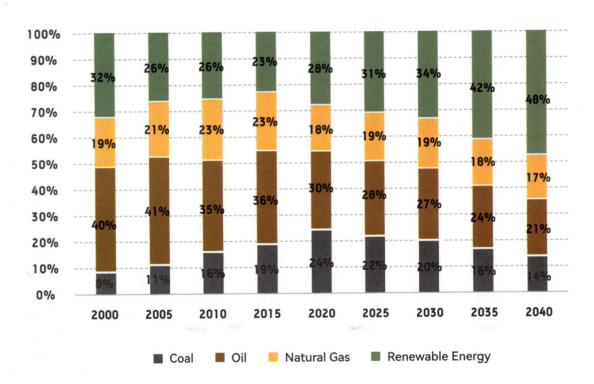

Data source: International Energy Agency, research of this report

4.2.3 Demand for coal is expected to peak in 2025

Southeast Asia is one of the regions with the fastest growth in power demand in the world. With limited economic development, many countries tend to choose low-cost coal power when developing power. By 2020, nearly 20 GW of coal power is still under construction, most of which are located in countries like Indonesia, Vietnam and the Philippines.

With transforming global energy, many Southeast Asian countries, such as the Philippines, have announced that they will stop building new coal power. Affected by coal power stock and economic development, coal will remain dominant in energy consumption in Southeast Asia in the short term, while coal demand will continue to decline in the long term. Under the transformation scenario, it is predicted that the coal consumption in Southeast Asia will peak around 2025, nearly 200 million tons of standard oil, and the proportion of coal consumption will decrease to 20% in 2030, which is about 4 percentage points lower than that in 2020. In 2040, coal consumption will drop to about 140 million tons of standard oil.

Figure 4.2.3-1 · Forecast of coal demand in Southeast Asia from 2000 to 2040

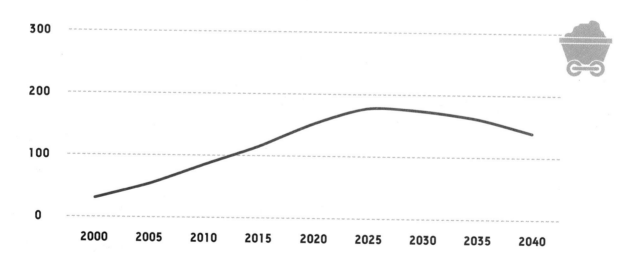

Unit: million tons of standard oil
Data source: International Energy Agency, BP, research of this report

4.2.4 The proportion of oil consumption continues to decline, and the demand for natural gas increases rapidly

Southeast Asia is rich in oil and gas resources, which is an important source of energy consumption in countries of this region. In recent years, due to the aging of oil fields, the reduction of investment, the decline of international oil prices and other factors, the oil production has shown a downward trend. At present, the oil self-sufficiency rate is only 50%, which is mainly imported from the Middle East, and the dependence on imported oil will continue to increase in the future. Under the transformation scenario, the oil demand in Southeast Asia shows a momentum of slow growth, and it is estimated that the oil consumption will peak around 2030, about 240 million tons of standard oil, and will decline slowly after reaching the peak. In 2040, the total oil demand will drop to about 220 million tons of standard oil. The improvement of fuel efficiency and the transportation electrification are the main factors affecting oil consumption in this region.

Figure 4.2.4-1 · Oil Demand Forecast in Southeast Asia from 2000 to 2040

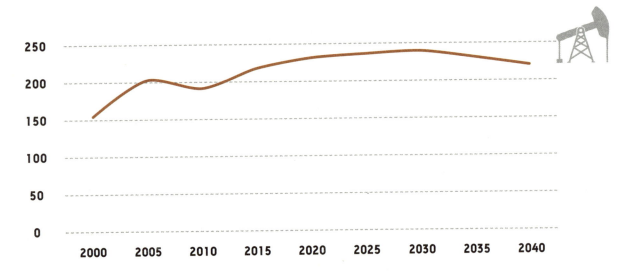

Unit: million tons of standard oil
Data source: International Energy Agency, BP, research of this report

Southeast Asia is rich in natural gas resources, with a self-sufficiency rate of over 120%, mainly exporting. In recent years, the output of natural gas in Southeast Asia has been volatile. In addition, due to the impact of unconventional natural gas exploitation in North America, the supply of natural gas has shown a downward trend. In the future, Southeast Asia will transition from a net exporter of natural gas to a net importer, especially the dependence on imported liquefied natural gas will continue to increase.

Under the transformation scenario, as the proportion of coal consumption decreases, the demand for natural gas will continue to increase, and the natural gas consumption in the power sector will increase rapidly to make up for the power gap caused by the suspension of construction of coal-fired power units. In 2030, the natural gas demand in Southeast Asia will reach about 170 million tons of standard oil. In 2040, the natural gas demand in Southeast Asia will near 180 million tons of standard oil.

Figure 4.2.4-2 · Forecast of Natural Gas Demand in Southeast Asia from 2000 to 2040

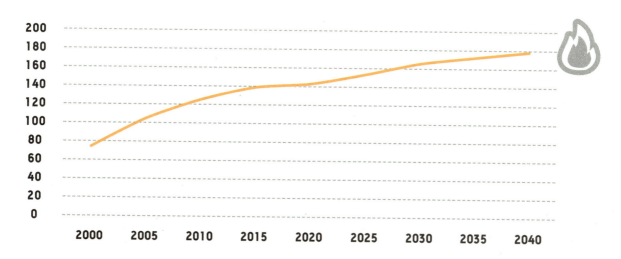

Unit: million tons of standard oil
Data source: International Energy Agency, BP, research of this report

Natural gas is an important option for energy transformation in Southeast Asia, and Southeast Asia will be increasingly dependent on imported natural gas in the future. China is a big natural gas importer in the region. Based on the overall interests of natural gas consumers, China can explore and build a regional natural gas cooperation mechanism with Southeast Asia, strengthen the cooperation of regional oil and gas trade centers, promote the interconnection of regional oil and gas pipelines, and facilitate the diversification of natural gas imports and trade.

In order to improve oil and gas interconnection and transmission efficiency, infrastructure fields such as oil and gas development and pipeline network construction are the development priorities of many countries in Southeast Asia. China leads oil and gas exploitation and pipeline network construction, and has mastered the world's advanced ultra-deep well drilling technology. Logging while drilling (LWD) technology is remarkably applied, and the oil and gas storage and transportation construction technology has leapt forward. Thus, China may cooperate with Southeast Asian countries in the field of oil and gas infrastructure construction.

4.2.5 The demand for renewable energy will aggressively increase

Southeast Asia is rich in renewable energy resources such as hydropower, solar energy and biomass energy. Against the backdrop of global energy transformation, countries will vigorously develop renewable energy, and most countries have implemented policies and measures such as on-grid tariff and project auction to encourage the development of renewable energies. Based on the renewable energy development goals of various countries, under the transformation scenario, it is estimated that the total demand for renewable energy in Southeast Asia will approach 290 million tons of standard oil in 2030, an increase of more than 40% compared with that in 2020, and the average annual growth rate from 2021 to 2030 will approach 4%. Among them, the increasing demand of renewable energy such as water energy and solar energy is mainly used for power generation, while biomass fuel will be mainly used for activities such as biomass gasification, heating and cooking. After 2030, the demand for renewable energy will increase rapidly. It is estimated that the total demand for renewable energy in Southeast Asia will be close to 500 million tons of standard oil in 2040, and the average annual growth rate will be close to 5% from 2030 to 2040.

Figure 4.2.5-1 · Forecast of Renewable Energy Demand in Southeast Asia from 2000 to 2040

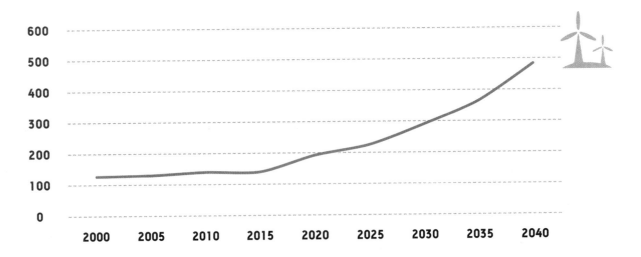

Unit: million tons of standard oil
Data source: International Energy Agency, BP, research of this report

4.3   Prospects of Power Development in Southeast Asia

4.3.1   Power demand is surging

With the economic recovery and the improvement of electrification rate after the epidemic, the power consumption in Southeast Asia will remain growing rapidly, and the growth rate will still be high in the world. Under the continuation scenario, the total power demand will reach 1800 TWh in 2030, the average annual growth rate will exceed 5% from 2021 to 2030, and the total power demand will exceed 2700 TWh in 2040. Under the transformation scenario, the total power demand will approximate 1700 TWh in 2030, the average annual growth rate will be close to 5% from 2021 to 2030, and the total power demand will reach 2400 TWh in 2040. Under the accelerated transformation scenario, the total power demand will reach about 1600 TWh in 2030, the average annual growth rate will exceed 4% from 2021 to 2030, and the total power demand will reach about 2200 TWh in 2040.

Figure 4.3.1-1 · Power Demand in Southeast Asia from 2000 to 2040

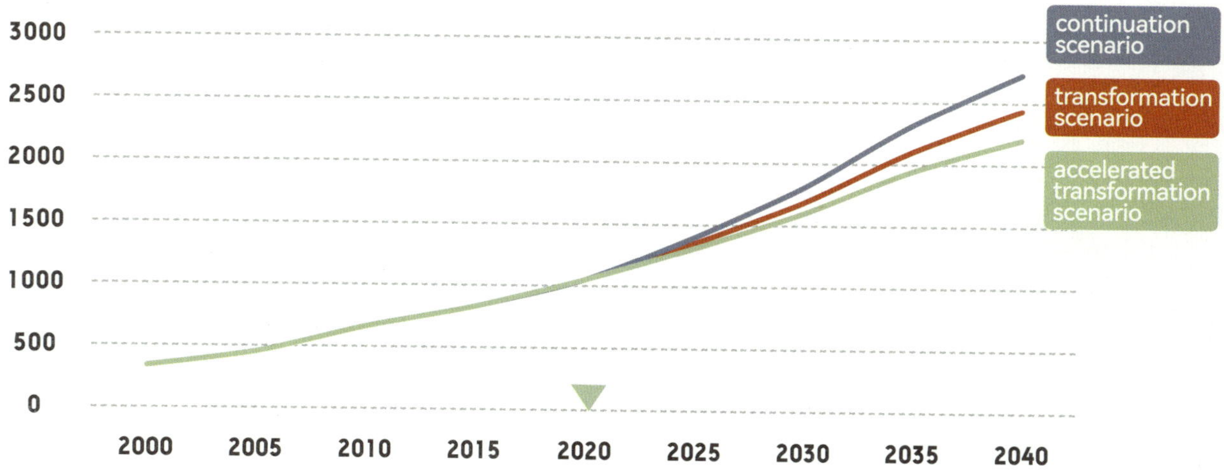

Unit: one billion kilowatt-hours (TWh)
Data source: research in this report

In terms of countries, Vietnam and Indonesia are the countries with the highest absolute power demand growth in the region from 2021 to 2040, reaching 541.2 TWh and 452.7 TWh respectively, which have become important sources of power demand growth in the region. In addition, Thailand, countries such as the Philippines and Malaysia have a large increase in power demand, reaching more than 68 TWh. The improvement of economic development and industrialization is the main engine for power demand growth in Southeast Asia.

Figure 4.3.1-2 · Power Demand Increment of Southeast Asian Countries from 2021 to 2040

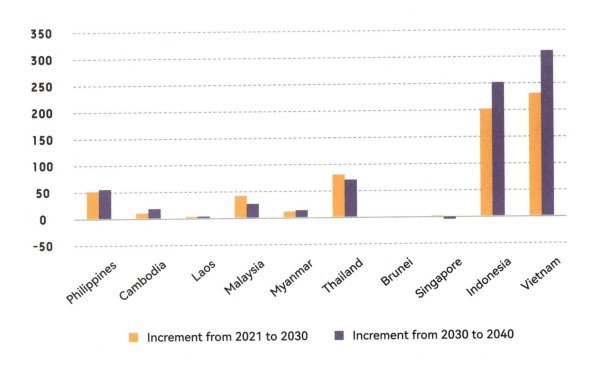

Unit: one billion kilowatt-hours (TWh)
Data source: research in this report

4.3.2 There is great potential for power infrastructure construction

With the increase of power load in Southeast Asian countries, the demand for power infrastructure construction in this region is huge in the future. Under the continuation scenario, the total installed capacity in Southeast Asia will approximate 400 GW in 2030, with an average annual growth rate of 3% from 2021 to 2030. It is estimated that the total installed capacity will exceed 560 GW in 2040. Under the transformation scenario, the total installed capacity will exceed 460 GW in 2030, with an average annual growth rate of 5% from 2021 to 2030, and surpass 640 GW in 2040. Under the accelerated transformation scenario, the total installed power will approach 550 GW in 2030, with an average annual growth rate of 6% from 2021 to 2030, and exceed 700 GW in 2040.

Figure 4.3.2-1 · Total installed capacity in Southeast Asia from 2010 to 2040

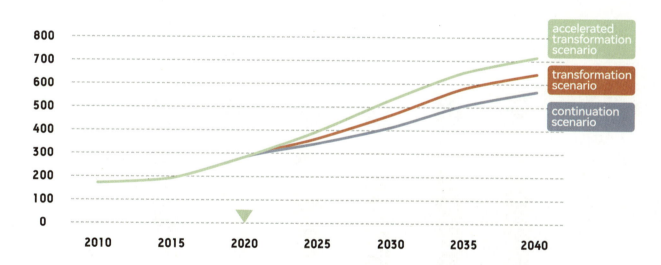

Unit: GW

Data source: International Energy Agency, research in this report

4.3.3 The power supply structure is gradually clean and low-carbonized

With advancing carbon neutralization, the newly-built coal-fired power in Southeast Asia will be significantly reduced. In the short term, gas-fired power will be rapidly developed to partially replace coal-fired power units. In the long term, installed capacity of renewable energy will be developed in a large scale and become the most important installed capacity in Southeast Asia. Under the transformation scenario, due to the high pollutants and CO_2 emission, the installed capacity of coal-fired power will be transformed on a large scale, and the installed capacity of coal-fired power will remain generally unchanged in 2030, and its share will drop to 19%. The installed capacity of oil-fired power is declining, and its proportion will drop to about 4% in 2030. The installed capacity of gas-fired power will increase steadily, and its proportion drop to about 29% in 2030. The installed capacity of renewable energy, mainly wind power, photovoltaic, hydropower and biomass develops rapidly, and its installed capacity has increased to over 49% in 2030, making it the most important type installed capacity for power generation in Southeast Asia.

Figure 4.3.3-1 · Installed capacity mix in Southeast Asia from 2010 to 2040

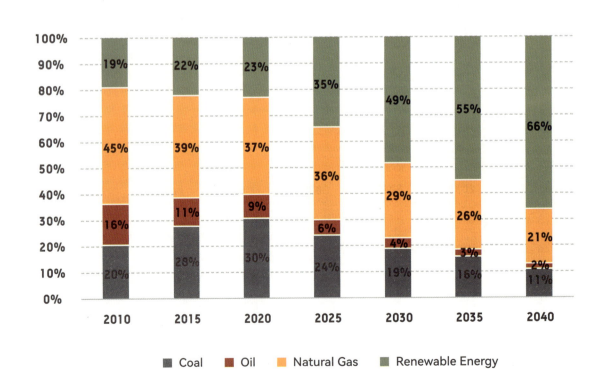

Data source: International Energy Agency, research of this report

Coal power

At present, installed capacity in Southeast Asia is still mainly fossil fuel-fired. Under the transformation scenario, with the drastic reduction of newly built coal power, coal-fired installed capacity in Southeast Asia will increase slightly in 2030 from the present level, and the newly added part is mainly the coal power projects currently under construction. In 2040, the installed capacity of coal-fired power plants will gradually decrease, and the existing installed capacity of coal-fired power plants will be transformed towards higher efficiency and flexibility on a large scale. Meanwhile, the existing coal-fired power plants will be used for biomass co-combustion to reduce the carbon emissions of coal-fired power units.

Figure 4.3.3-2 · **Installed capacity of coal-fired power in Southeast Asia from 2020 to 2040**

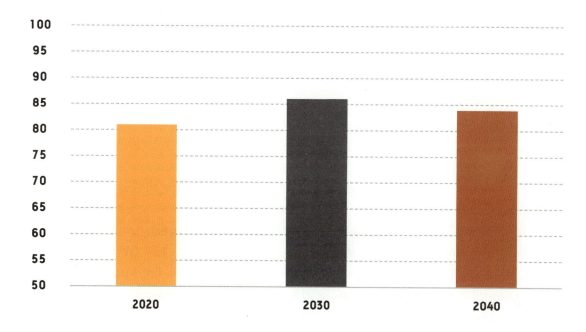

Unit: GW
Data Source: Research in this report

By 2030, fossil energy generating units will still account for more than half of the total installed capacity in Southeast Asia, and thermal power generating units in operation need to be clean and energy-saving to reduce pollutant emissions and improve energy utilization efficiency. At the same time, the thermal power units in Southeast Asia need to be more flexible to meet the needs of system regulation and adapt to large-scale renewable energy access to the power system.

China has built the world's largest clean and efficient coal-fired power system, with a total of 950GW of ultra-low emission units, leading the world in emission standards. Chinese enterprises have accumulated rich experience in ultra-low emission and energy-saving renovation of coal-fired power units, and can participate in the upgrading and renovation of thermal power units in Southeast Asia. In addition, China has comprehensive technical advantages in improving the flexibility of thermal power units, and has accumulated a lot of practical experience in promoting the integration of thermal power units and renewable energy, and may strengthen cooperation with power generation enterprises in Southeast Asia.

● Gas-fired Power

Natural gas is one of the important approaches to energy transformation in Southeast Asia. In order to reduce the emission of CO_2 and pollutants, and make up for the power gap caused by the suspension of construction of coal-fired power, Southeast Asia will continue to increase the installed capacity of gas-fired power and it will become the biggest fossil energy source in the region. By 2030, gas-fired installed capacity will reach about 130 GW, an increase of about 35% compared with 2020. By 2040, the installed capacity of gas-fired power will exceed 160 GW, an increase of more than 60% compared with 2020. Gas-fired power will become the only fossil power source that will continue to grow before 2040. At the same time, the role of this power will gradually change from base load power source to flexible peak-shaving power source. In the future, it will be mainly used as a regulating power source to help build a power system with a high proportion of renewable energy.

Figure 4.3.3-3 · Installed capacity of gas fired power in Southeast Asia from 2020 to 2040

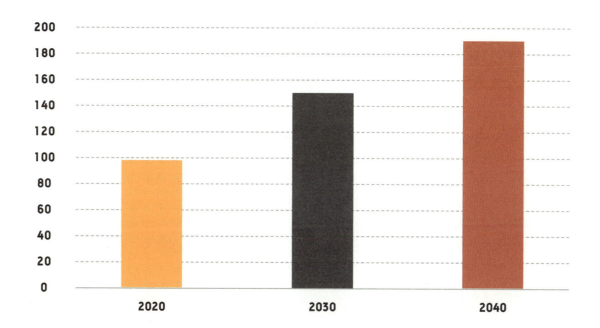

Unit: GW
Data Source: Research in this report

As a relatively clean fossil fuel, natural gas will be an alternative in certain phases of energy transformation in Southeast Asia. Natural gas power generation has the advantages such as environmental friendliness, optimization of energy mix, ensuring the security and stability of power grid, and will become one of the hot areas in Southeast Asia in the future. At present, the proposed new gas-fired capacity has exceeded 90 GW. At the same time, natural gas-fired power stations will play a more flexible role in peak shaving, realizing the coordinated development with renewable energy.

At present, China's installed capacity of gas-fired power has exceeded 100 GW, which has well supported the development of China's power industry. China has strengths in technologies and experience in aspects like gas-fired power project construction, gas turbine equipment, and flexible transformation, and has achieved breakthroughs in many key technologies of gas turbines. In the future, China can cooperate with Southeast Asian countries in investment, construction, technology research and development, flexible transformation and other fields of natural gas power generation projects, and vigorously promote the development of gas-fired power projects in Southeast Asia.

● **Photovoltaic Power Station**

The Levelized Cost of Energy (LCOE) is the power generation cost calculated after leveling the cost and power generation in the life cycle of a project, that is, the present value of cost in the life cycle/the present value of power generation in the life cycle. The time value of capital, depreciation of fixed assets, tax and other factors are considered when the cost is calculated.

Southeast Asia is rich in photovoltaic resources. With the development of technologies, the cost advantage of photovoltaic power generation will gradually become evident. According to the calculation, the photovoltaic power cost in Southeast Asia will be around 9 cents/kWh in 2020, and in some areas with sound light resources, the photovoltaic power cost will be about 7 cents/kWh. It is estimated that by 2030, the cost of photovoltaic power generation in Southeast Asia will be reduced to about 5 cents/kWh, and in some areas with sound light resources, the cost of photovoltaic power generation will be reduced to less than 4 cents/kWh, and the price of photovoltaic power generation will be more competitive.

Figure 4.3.3-4 · The Levelized Cost of Energy in Southeast Asian countries in 2020

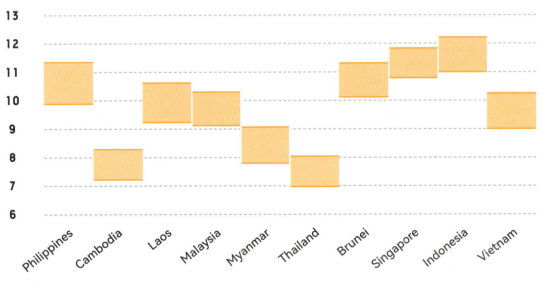

Unit: cents/kwh
Data source: the research in this study

Figure 4.3.3-5 · The Levelized Cost of Energy in Southeast Asian countries in 2030

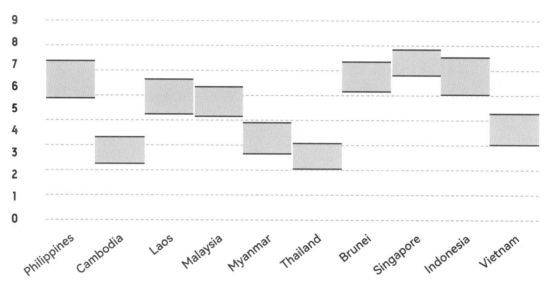

Unit: cents/kwh
Data source: Research in this study

By taking an integrated approach to factors such as photovoltaic resource endowment, economic development phases, power demand and power price competitiveness in Southeast Asia, it is estimated that by 2030, the installed photovoltaic capacity in Southeast Asia will approximate 70 GW, and the total installed photovoltaic capacity in 2030 will exceed 90 GW. From 2030 to 2040, about 160 GW of photovoltaic installed capacity will be added, and in 2040, the total installed photovoltaic capacity will exceed 230 GW. Among them, countries such as Indonesia, Vietnam, Thailand, and the Philippines have a larger increase in installed photovoltaic capacity.

Figure 4.3.3-6 · Forecast of installed capacity of photovoltaic power generation in Southeast Asian countries from 2021 to 2040

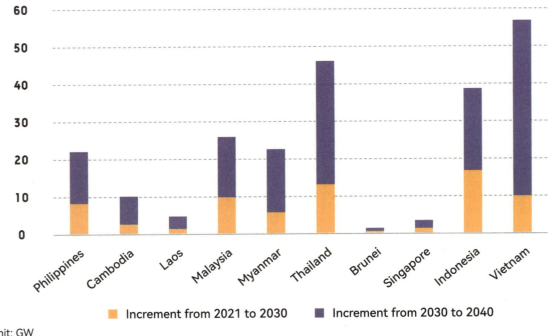

Unit: GW
Data source: Research in this report

Southeast Asia is rich in photovoltaic resources and has great potential for developing photovoltaic power plants. With cost-effectiveness of photovoltaic power generation becoming increasingly apparent, photovoltaic development in Southeast Asia will be promising in the future. China is the country with the largest investment in photovoltaic power plants in the world, and may participate in the investment and construction of photovoltaic power generation projects in Southeast Asia, providing financial and technical support for the development and utilization of photovoltaic resources in the region. In the meantime, China is also an important photovoltaic equipment production base in the world, with advanced technology and equipment advantages in centralized and distributed photovoltaic power plants, thus can provide equipment and technical services for photovoltaic development in Southeast Asia. For countries with rapid development of photovoltaic power, Chinese photovoltaic manufacturers can also invest and build factories in the local areas to serve them and increase their presence in peripheral regions at the same time.

Wind power

Southeast Asia has certain wind energy resources. According to the calculation, in 2020, wind LCOE Southeast Asia will approach 12 cents/kWh, and in Indo-China Peninsula where wind energy resources are abundant, LCOE of wind can reach about 10 cents/kWh. It is estimated that by 2030, the wind LCOE will be reduced to about 7 cents/kWh in Southeast Asia and 5 cents/kWh in Indo-China Peninsula.

Figure 4.3.3-7 · Wind LCOE in Southeast Asian countries in 2020

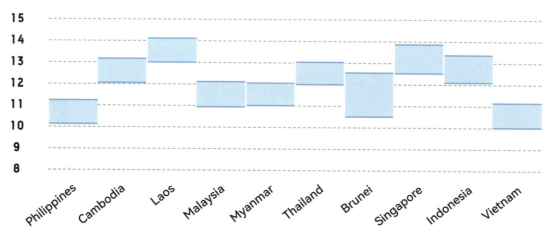

Unit: cents/kwh
Data source: the research in this study

Figure 4.3.3-8 · Wind LCOE in Southeast Asian countries in 2030

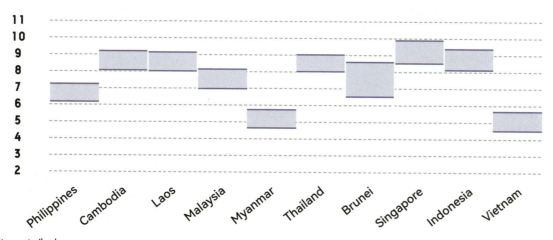

Unit: cents/kwh
Data source: Research in this study

By taking a holistic approach to factors such as wind energy resource endowment, economic development phases, power demand and electricity price competitiveness in Southeast Asia, it is estimated that by 2030, the newly installed wind power capacity in Southeast Asia will approach 40 GW, and the total installed capacity of wind power in 2030 will approximate 43 GW. From 2030 to 2040, the installed capacity of wind power will reach 80 GW, and the total installed capacity of wind power in 2040 will exceed 120 GW. Among them, countries such as Vietnam, Thailand, and the Philippines have increased more of their installed capacity of wind power.

Figure 4.3.3-9 · Forecast of installed hydropower capacity in Southeast Asian countries from 2021 to 2040

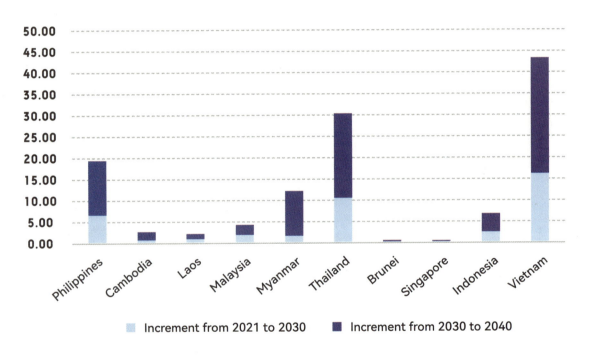

Unit: GW
Data source: Research in this report

Southeast Asia has some wind energy resources, the vast majority of which are low wind speed resources, which is similar to the low wind speed regions in eastern and central China, and has a certain development potential of low-speed wind power stations. China has advanced technology and rich experience in the development of low-speed wind power, and has established a full-fledged low wind speed equipment production line. Chinese enterprises may cooperate with Southeast Asia in the fields of investment, construction and equipment manufacturing of onshore low-speed wind farms.

Hydropower

Hydropower is the largest renewable energy source for power generation in Southeast Asia. At present, while hydropower resources to be developed are abundant, mainly concentrated in countries like Myanmar, Indonesia, Vietnam, and Laos. It is estimated that by 2030, the installed capacity of hydropower in Southeast Asia will be close to 40 GW, and the total installed capacity of hydropower in 2030 will approach 90 GW. From 2030 to 2040, the newly installed hydropower capacity will stand at about 45 GW, and the total installed hydropower capacity in 2040 will approximate 135 GW.

Figure 4.3.3-10 · Forecast of installed hydropower capacity in Southeast Asian countries from 2021 to 2040

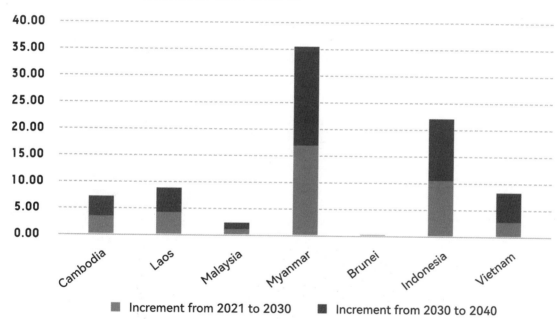

Unit: GW

Data Source: Research in this report

Hydropower is biggest renewable energy source for power generation with the largest installed capacity in Southeast Asia, which is endowed with sound hydropower resources and is promising for the development in the future. China has significant advantages in the construction of large-scale hydropower projects and the management and operation of hydropower in river basins. Meanwhile, China has been increasingly better geared in manufacturing complete sets of equipment and innovating its technologies. Its management of survey, design, construction and operation of hydropower industry ranks among the top in the world. China has accumulated rich experience in coordinating hydropower development, ecological environment protection and reservoir resettlement, and may cooperate with Southeast Asian countries in fields like hydropower project development, engineering construction and equipment manufacturing.

● **Pumped storage power station**

Southeast Asia is rich in hydropower resources and has great potential to develop pumped storage power stations. As a clean regulated power source with the most fledged technology, the highest cost-effectiveness and the largest development scale, pumped storage power station may effectively complement wind power, solar power and thermal power. In the context of large-scale development of renewable energy, pumped storage will play an important role in Southeast Asia. At present, the Philippines and Thailand already have pumped storage power stations of a certain scale, with a total installed capacity close to 2 GW. In the future, the planned and announced installed capacity of pumped storage power stations in Southeast Asia will approach 7 GW, mainly distributed in countries like Vietnam, Indonesia, and Laos.

Figure 4.3.3-11 · Forecast of installed capacity of pumped storage stations in Southeast Asian countries from 2021 to 2040

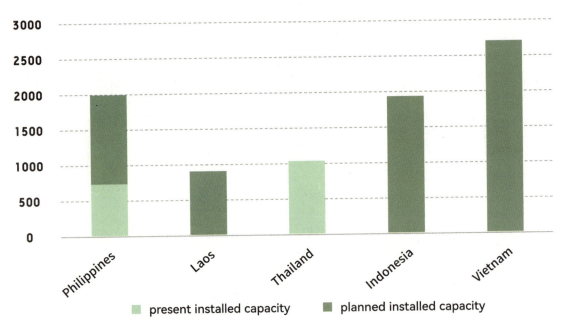

Unit: GW
Data source: International hydropower association, research in this report

At present, pumped storage power station is still the most fledged and economical large-scale energy storage mode in the world, and will have a good development prospect in Southeast Asia in the future. China is the country with the largest installed capacity of pumped storage power stations, and has advanced technical advantages and rich practical experience in this field. Both sides can actively carry out planning and research of pumped storage power station, and promote cooperation in project development and construction as needed.

● Power storage

Energy storage is an important equipment foundation and key supporting technology to realize the green and low-carbon transformation of energy. At present, the interconnection degree of power grids in Southeast Asia is low. With the continuous growth of the market share of intermittent renewable energy power, energy storage will play an important role in ensuring the stability of power system. The Philippines and Indonesia have a large number of islands, scattered populations, frequent typhoons and other natural disasters, which lead to the difficulty of power supply in remote islands and can not be connected to the main network of power companies. It has great potential to deploy energy storage devices. The distribution of load centers and resource centers in Thailand and Vietnam is inconsistent, and the power grid connection between load centers and resource centers is relatively weak. The existing power grid and supporting energy storage devices for new energy power generation will help to realize the large-scale development and utilization of new energy. The deployment of new electric energy storage devices can effectively improve the power support level in Southeast Asia and reduce the impact of intermittency and fluctuation of new energy on the power system. It is estimated that by 2030, the new electric energy storage capacity in Southeast Asia will exceed 10 GW, and the new electric energy storage capacity will be about 20 GW from 2030 to 2040. Among them, Indonesia, the Philippines, Malaysia and other island countries have great potential for power storage development to meet the power demand of remote islands; At the same time, Vietnam's power grid structure is relatively narrow, and the deployment of energy storage devices can effectively avoid the system stability problem caused by large-scale power flow transfer.

Figure 4.3.3-12 · Power storage capacity in Southeast Asia from 2021 to 2040

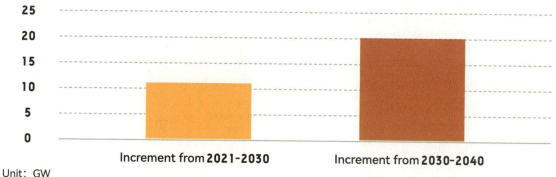

Unit: GW
Data Source: Research in this report

China has strong technical strength in the field of new energy storage, and has significant advantages in the whole industrial chain from material preparation to system integration, and will continue to vigorously promote the high-quality and large-scale development of energy storage in the future. Chinese enterprises can participate in the investment and construction of energy storage projects in Southeast Asia, and carry out in-depth cooperation with relevant countries in Southeast Asia in the upstream and downstream of the energy storage industry chain.

4.3.4 There is a large space for power grid infrastructure construction

● **Backbone grid**

Southeast Asia's power grid infrastructure is weak, and equipment aging is serious. At present, some countries have not yet established complete backbone grids, and there are still a lot of rural areas without access to the grid. The number of people without access to power exceeds 40 million, and the power accessibility level needs to be improved urgently. In addition, the distribution of energy resources in Southeast Asian countries is uneven, and power production is distant from load centers. Strengthening regional power interconnection and coordinating regional energy and power resources facilitate optimal allocation of resources in the region. At present, the power connectivity in Southeast Asia is mainly realized in the Indochina Peninsula. Due to the difficulty of power grid extension in independent island countries such as the Philippines and Indonesia, this region's power needs to be more interconnected.

Southeast Asia has formulated the development plan of ASEAN Common Power Grid (APG), which connects the independent power systems of each country through the transmission network between neighboring countries, and gradually expands to the sub-regions, finally realizing the integrated Southeast Asia power grid system. The specific implementation plan is to promote the construction of 16 bilateral power interconnection projects, 45 grids in total. Under the transformation scenario, by 2030, the new cross-border connected power capacity in Southeast Asia will approach 20 GW.

New energy is characterized by volatility, randomness and intermittence, which is significantly different from traditional power sources such as thermal power and hydropower. The large-scale development of new energy is bound to reshape the power system in all dimensions. With the large-scale development of new energy sources in Southeast Asia, the safe and stable operation of power system is facing new risks and uncertainties, which greatly increases the difficulty of ensuring power supply, and the regulation ability and flexibility of power system need to be improved.

China has advanced technological advantages in the construction and operation of power system with high share of new energy. It has accumulated rich experience in the field of large-scale new energy access to power system and gained a whole set of knowledge on the transformation path of power system, and jointly promotes the development of green power from the generation side, power grid side and power consumption side. Chinese enterprises may cooperate with Southeast Asia in power systems with high share of new energy, and jointly promote technology research and development, project development and construction, equipment manufacturing and capacity building with Southeast Asian countries.

● Smart grid

There is a big gap in the development level of power grid infrastructure among countries in Southeast Asia, and the power grid operation in most countries is backward, and the demand for power grid infrastructure transformation and upgrading is strong. Singapore and Malaysia power grids are more intelligent, among which Singapore power grid is one of the most stable national grids in the world. Since the smart energy system project was initiated in 2009, the intelligence of Singapore power grid has been upgraded again. With smart grid technology as the core, Malaysia has built a low-carbon and intelligent power system, and realized the modern energy transformation of the city.

In the future, with the large-scale development of renewable energy, a high proportion of renewable energy will be connected to the power system in Southeast Asia, which requires the supporting power grid to have higher degree of automation in regulation and stronger capacity to operate steadily. The rapid development of distributed energy also needs more efficient distribution grid technology, so as to build a distributed smart grid for distributed generation and interactive power supply. In this context, smart grid technology has a sound application prospect in Southeast Asia, which will become one of the most promising investment areas in the emerging markets of smart grid. By 2030, the investment in smart grid infrastructure in Southeast Asia will reach about 10 billion US dollars, among which Indonesia, Malaysia, Thailand, Singapore, the Philippines and Vietnam have great development potential.

05 Suggestions on energy cooperation between China and Southeast Asian countries

Suggestions on energy cooperation between China and Southeast Asian countries

Southeast Asia has rapidly grown into the world's most important energy consumption market and production base, and the future energy development prospects are very broad. In order to further maintain and expand the energy cooperation between China and Southeast Asia, it is recommended that in-depth pragmatic cooperation should be pursued in the fields of common concern like power system with high share of renewable energy, green energy industrial chain, power interconnection, natural gas demand side, energy technology innovation and mutual recognition of standards, personnel communication and technology exchanges, to jointly build a clean, low carbon, safe and efficient energy system.

5.1 Strengthen multilateral and bilateral pragmatic cooperation in power system with high share of renewable energy

With the continuous acceleration of the global energy low-carbon transformation, Southeast Asian countries have also formulated ambitious renewable energy development plans, and renewable energies such as wind and photovoltaic power usher in a window of opportunity. Large-scale connection of the renewable energy to the grid will exert far-reaching influence to their power system. The safety and stability of the power system, balance of supply and demand, and efficient operation face new challenges. Some countries have already experienced problems such as wind and light power abandonment.

Thus, it is suggested that all parties promote the in-depth alignment of energy transformation paths, coordinate and optimize the power system in all aspects such as technology standards, market mechanisms, and operation mode, initiate specific joint work group under the bilateral and multilateral mechanisms; foster cooperation in the fields such as the improving the flexibility of power system and safety and stability of the grid; and improve capacity of the power system to consume renewable energy and facilitate these countries to realize high-quality transformation and development of their power industry.

5.2　Develop green energy industrial chain cooperation

In the post-epidemic era, many Southeast Asian countries have taken green energy development as an important driving force for economic recovery, but most countries lack experience in green energy development and the green energy industry chain is still not full-fledged.

It is suggested that both sides strengthen all-round cooperation in upstream and downstream of green energy industrial chain, such as investment in green energy projects, capacity cooperation and engineering construction, so as to enhance the basic capacity of green energy development; give full play to the leading role of green energy in upstream and downstream industries, and promote the industrialization and economic development of various countries; strengthen the development and utilization of green energy to improve energy accessibility, promote the realization of affordable, reliable and sustainable modern energy services for all, and foster green energy to play a greater role in eliminating poverty, increasing employment and improving people's well-being.

5.3   Vigorously promote regional power connectivity

With the global energy low-carbon transformation and development becoming the consensus of all countries, Southeast Asian countries rich in clean energy resources are accelerating the development of renewable energy such as hydropower, wind power and solar power according to local conditions, which provides a natural driving force for power connectivity. At the same time, the signing of Regional Comprehensive Economic Partnership Agreement (RCEP) accelerates the development of regional economic integration, which also provides strong support for regional power integration.

It is suggested that under the RCEP Joint Committee, Expert Working Group on Energy Connectivity of United Nations Economic and Social Commission for Asia and the Pacific (UNESCAP), the Regional Power Trade Coordination Committee under the Greater Mekong Subregion (GMS) mechanism or their affiliated bodies, and the Lancang-Mekong Cooperation (LMC) mechanism, the two sides strengthen the discussion on related issues of power connectivity, jointly formulate action roadmap, promote the construction of power interconnection grid, drive more projects to be delivered, and realize the coordinated development of the whole power industry chain. At the same time, it is suggested that the two sides foster the research on cross-border power trade mechanism, cross-border power trading center construction scheme, cross-border power dispatching and trading mode to promote the regional power integration.

5.4 Comprehensively strengthen regional natural gas demand side cooperation

The development of coal-fired power in the world is further restricted, and Southeast Asian countries are facing multiple choices in energy transformation. How to select and utilize natural gas has a great influence on the specific delivery path of energy transformation in Southeast Asian countries.

It is suggested that both sides should base themselves on the overall interests of natural gas consuming countries, launch a joint initiative together to boost the cooperation on the demand side of natural gas in the international arena, explore the establishment of a ministerial mechanism for regional natural gas cooperation, strengthen the cooperation of regional oil and gas trade centers, promote the joint efforts of both sides in natural gas cooperation, and continuously improve the discourse power on natural gas pricing.

5.5 Foster energy technology innovation cooperation and outcome transformation

The rapid development and large-scale application of new green energy technologies and information technologies have laid a solid foundation for more diverse and flexible green energy cooperation.

It is suggested that the two sides continue to deepen cooperation in green energy technology innovation, continuously drive down the cost of green energy technology, and comprehensively enhance the competitiveness of regional green energy online; jointly set up joint laboratories and research centers to conduct cooperative research on new energy technologies such as hydrogen energy, energy storage, integrated energy and smart energy, and foster new drivers for energy cooperation between the two sides; attach importance to the transnational transformation and application of energy innovation technologies, and advance a group of leading technological innovation demonstration projects, so that the dividends of green energy technology progress can benefit more countries.

5.6 Promote mutual trust in technical standard alignment and equipment certification

There are some differences in the standard systems between Southeast Asian countries and China, which lead to problems such as higher project construction costs and more difficult quality control, and bring some challenges to more efficient and convenient energy cooperation between the two sides.

It is suggested that the two sides hold standardization exchange seminars to sort out the common problems and absence of standards in national standards systems, strengthen mutual understanding of energy project construction and equipment manufacturing standards, promote exchanges and cooperation in international certification of power product quality and technology, and promote serious mutual trust between the two sides in equipment; jointly establish China–Southeast Asian countries standardization alliance, promote the development of regional standardization cooperation, explore cooperation in the preparation of local technical standards, and jointly participate in the update and formulation of international standards.

5.7 Strengthen personnel communication and technical assistance

Efficient personnel communication and technical assistance are the important foundation for both sides to carry out sustainable and high-quality energy cooperation.

It is suggested that the two sides rely on Ministerial Seminar or BRI Energy Cooperation, Leading Talents Training Program, China-ASEAN Clean Energy Training Program, and the Lanmei Power Connectivity Capacity Building Program to strengthen personnel training and exchanges, promote mutual learning among countries, and propel the all-round reserve of talents in the field of green energy; at the same time, according to the needs of various countries, organize technical assistance in the field of green energy, including assisting in plan compilation, dispatching experts, providing technical services and specific consultation, so as to provide technical support for the rapid development of green energy in various countries.

06 Appendix

Appendix

Appendix A Basic Energy Data of Southeast Asian Countries

Table A-1 · Total energy consumption by category in South East Asia from 2000 to 2020

	2000	2010	2014	2015	2016	2017	2018	2019	2020e
Coal	31.9	85.7	100.1	116.1	124.4	136.5	153.7	165.4	159.5
Oil	153.8	190.1	222.2	217.9	225.9	237.0	242.8	234.6	196.2
Natural Gas	74.0	124.6	139.3	138.5	138.5	133.4	140.9	135.7	119.6
Renewable Energy	124.3	138.8	143.7	140.5	147.5	150.7	145.7	179.8	183.8

Unit: Mtoe
Data Source: International Energy Agency, British Petroleum Company, and research by this report

Table A-2 · Total final consumption by sector in South East Asia from 2000 to 2020

	2000	2010	2014	2015	2016	2017	2018	2019	2020e
Industry	75.8	122.0	126.4	141.5	138.4	148.7	152.9	161.2	149.1
Transport	61.7	88.5	116.9	114.8	124.4	129.7	135.3	147.0	133.8
Resident	95.0	101.1	99.5	91.9	89.6	91.0	81.7	81.8	74.1
Service Industry	12.4	20.8	22.4	23.1	24.6	25.8	26.5	28.7	27.4
Others	28.7	49.0	59.3	58.0	58.9	63.7	68.3	68.2	64.7

Unit: Mtoe
Data Source: International Energy Agency, International Renewable Energy Agency, and research of this report

Table A-3 · Total energy production by category in South East Asia from 2000 to 2020

	2015	2016	2017	2018	2019	2020e
Coal	278.0	285.5	299.9	327.2	364.3	336.2
Oil	120.6	122.6	117.6	113.2	105.4	96.7
Natural Gas	185.0	184.2	179.2	182.4	180.5	167.7
Renewable Energy	141.2	148.0	151.3	147.3	171.6	193.2

Unit: Mtoe

Data Source: International Energy Agency, British Petroleum Company, International Renewable Energy Agency, and research by this report

Table A-4 · CO_2 Emission from Southeast Asian Countries

	2015	2016	2017	2018	2019
Philippines	112.1	122.2	134.5	138.9	144.3
Cambodia	8.5	9.7	11.2	15.5	16.0
Laos	8.8	14.3	17.9	32.3	32.8
Malaysia	233.3	246.7	248.9	249.1	250.1
Myanmar	22.1	25.5	23.7	26.1	26.2
Thailand	283.3	281.7	286.3	292.5	288.3
Brunei	7.0	7.5	9.6	9.6	9.1
Singapore	62.1	40.3	39 .1	38.3	38.9
Indonesia	507.0	568.2	531.0	576.6	617.5
Vietnam	184.4	185.4	182.6	211.8	247.7

Unit: Mt
Data Source: Our World in Data, research by this report

Table A-5 · Carbon Emission Intensity of Southeast Asian Countries

	2000	2005	2010	2011	2012	2013	2014	2015	2016	2017	2018	2019
Philippines	2.2	1.9	1.6	1.5	1.5	1.5	1.5	1.6	1.6	1.6	1.6	1.6
Cambodia	1.1	1.0	1.3	1.3	1.2	1.2	1.3	1.6	1.7	1.8	2.4	2.3
Laos	0.4	0.5	0.6	0.7	0.7	0.8	0.6	0.6	0.7	0.8	1.2	1.2
Malaysia	3.6	3.9	3.7	3.6	3.4	3.5	3.5	3.4	3.2	2.9	2.9	2.8
Myanmar	2.0	1.2	0.5	0.5	0.7	0.8	1.0	1.1	1.2	1.7	1.7	1.7
Thailand	2.8	2.8	2.5	2.5	2.5	2.6	2.5	2.5	2.4	2.3	2.2	2.1
Brunei	2.1	2.0	2.8	2.8	2.7	2.7	2.7	2.5	2.8	2.9	2.8	2.6
Singapore	2.0	1.5	1.3	1.3	1.2	1.2	1.1	1.0	1.0	1.0	1.0	1.0
Indonesia	2.5	2.4	2.1	2.0	2.0	1.9	1.9	1.9	1.8	1.8	1.9	2.0
Vietnam	2.4	3.0	3.5	3.3	3.1	3.1	3.2	3.4	3.5	3.2	3.6	3.9

Unit: ton/USD 100
Data Source: knoema, research by this report

Appendix B Basic Power Data of Southeast Asian Countries

Table B-1 · Total Power Consumption of Southeast Asian Countries from 2015 to 2020

Country	Abbreviation	2015	2016	2017	2018	2019e	2020e
Philippines	PH	74.9	82.5	86.1	90.2	95.9	92.0
Cambodia	KH	5.1	6.2	7.2	8.7	9.1	9.0
Laos	LA	4.2	5.0	4.4	5.0	5.0	4.7
Malaysia	MY	139.8	145.2	152.0	157.2	160.0	149.9
Myanmar	MM	13.4	13.1	18.2	18.8	19.5	18.6
Thailand	TH	176.9	193.8	193.1	195.1	201.3	195.1
Brunei	BN	3.9	3.0	3.7	3.8	3.9	3.8
Singapore	SG	49.5	50.7	51.7	52.6	53.8	52.5
Indonesia	ID	211.9	225.9	234.5	263.3	275.2	265.8
Vietnam	VN	151.6	169.6	185.4	227.2	255.4	263.0
Total	-	895.0	936.3	1021.9	1079.2	1054.7	659.3

Unit: terawatt hours (TWh)
Data Source: International Energy Agency, Enerdata, CEIC, research of this report

Table B-2 · Total Installed Power of Southeast Asian Countries from 2015 to 2020

Country	Abbreviation	2015	2016	2017	2018	2019e	2020e
Philippines	PH	18726	21474	22809	23918	25630	26182
Cambodia	KH	1682	1712	1919	2228	2458	2729
Laos	LA	6276	6735	6946	7196	8023	9316
Malaysia	MY	31069	33668	34182	34389	36310	36962
Myanmar	MM	5036	5242	5778	5787	6097	6165
Thailand	TH	38648	44996	45807	53037	54326	54460
Brunei	BN	922	922	922	922	1227	1227
Singapore	SG	13395	13445	13618	13653	12563	12582
Indonesia	ID	50400	55000	58400	62700	69600	72800
Vietnam	VN	27982	30744	33156	42965	55940	69300
Total	–	**194136**	**213939**	**223536**	**246794**	**272174**	**291724**

Unit: megawatt (MW)
Data Source: International Energy Agency, International Renewable Energy Agency, national energy sector data, research of this report

Table B-3 · Installed Capacity of Coal Power in Southeast Asian Countries From 2015 to 2020

Country	Abbreviation	2015	2016	2017	2018	2019e	2020e
Philippines	PH	5893	7419	8049	8844	10417	10944
Cambodia	KH	403	429	564	551	709	859
Laos	LA	1878	1878	1878	1878	1878	1878
Malaysia	MY	8546	9546	10546	10546	13284	13284
Myanmar	MM	120	120	160	160	160	160
Thailand	TH	6710	6980	6980	4216	5021	5021
Brunei	BN	0	0	0	0	220	220
Singapore	SG	0	0	0	0	0	0
Indonesia	ID	26775	28259	29943	30723	33764	35605
Vietnam	VN	3415	4899	6583	14725	20250	22091
Total	-	53740	59530	64703	71644	85703	90062

Unit megawatt(MW)
Data Source: International Energy Agency, national energy sector data, EndCoal, research of this report

Table B-4 · Installed Capacity of Gas Power in Southeast Asian Countries from 2015 to 2020

Country	Abbreviation	2015	2016	2017	2018	2019e	2020e
Philippines	PH	2862	3431	3447	3453	3453	3453
Cambodia	KH	0	0	0	0	0	0
Laos	LA	0	0	0	0	0	0
Malaysia	MY	13506	14075	14897	14897	14403	14403
Myanmar	MM	1695	1824	2175	2178	2448	2496
Thailand	TH	22941	27678	27678	33201	33201	33201
Brunei	BN	909	909	909	909	994	994
Singapore	SG	10587	10582	10736	10719	10708	10670
Indonesia	ID	12545	14156	14495	16302	20537	21600
Vietnam	VN	7144	7144	7144	7363	9803	9395
Total	-	72188	79799	81480	89022	95547	96212

Unit: megawatt (MW)
Data Source: International Energy Agency, national energy sector data, research of this report

Table B-5 · Photovoltaic Installation in Southeast Asian Countries from 2015 to 2020

Country	Abbreviation	2015	2016	2017	2018	2019e	2020e
Philippines	PH	173	784	908	914	973	1048
Cambodia	KH	12	18	29	29	99	208
Laos	LA	3	4	22	22	22	22
Malaysia	MY	229	279	370	536	882	1493
Myanmar	MM	21	32	44	48	88	84
Thailand	TH	1425	2451	2702	2967	2988	2988
Brunei	BN	1	1	1	1	1	1
Singapore	SG	46	97	116	160	272	329
Indonesia	ID	79	88	98	69	155	172
Vietnam	VN	5	5	8	105	4898	16504
Total	-	1993	3760	4298	4850	10377	22850

Unit: megawatt (MW)
Data Source: International Renewable Energy Agency, research of this report

Table B-6 · Wind Power Installation in Southeast Asian Countries from 2015 to 2020

Country	Abbreviation	2015	2016	2017	2018	2019e	2020e
Philippines	PH	427	427	427	427	443	443
Cambodia	KH	0	0	0	0	0	0
Laos	LA	0	0	0	0	0	0
Malaysia	MY	0	0	0	0	0	0
Myanmar	MM	0	0	0	0	0	0
Thailand	TH	234	507	628	1103	1507	1507
Brunei	BN	0	0	0	0	0	0
Singapore	SG	0	0	0	0	0	0
Indonesia	ID	1	1	1	144	154	154
Vietnam	VN	136	160	205	237	375	600
Total	-	799	1096	1262	1911	2479	2705

Unit: megawatt (MW)
Data Source: International Renewable Energy Agency, research of this report

Table B-7 · Hydropower Installation in Southeast Asian Countries from 2015 to 2020

Country	Abbreviation	2015	2016	2017	2018	2019e	2020e
Philippines	PH	3613	3623	3632	3719	3761	3761
Cambodia	KH	930	930	980	1330	1330	1330
Laos	LA	4355	4813	5006	5256	6083	7376
Malaysia	MY	5742	6121	6145	6165	6245	6275
Myanmar	MM	3198	3264	3304	3304	3304	3304
Thailand	TH	3639	3649	3649	3667	3667	3667
Brunei	BN	0	0	0	0	0	0
Singapore	SG	0	0	0	0	0	0
Indonesia	ID	5322	5666	5703	5772	5976	6210
Vietnam	VN	15905	17131	17809	17989	18069	18165
Total	-	42703	45197	46228	47203	48436	50088

Unit: megawatt (MW)
Data Source: International Renewable Energy Agency, research of this report

Table B-8 · Biomass Installed Capacity in Southeast Asian Countries from 2015 to 2020

Country	Abbreviation	2015	2016	2017	2018	2019e	2020e
Philippines	PH	233	259	276	341	393	368
Cambodia	KH	32	30	50	51	51	51
Laos	LA	40	40	40	40	40	40
Malaysia	MY	1580	1558	818	839	919	931
Myanmar	MM	2	2	5	5	5	5
Thailand	TH	3231	3395	3824	4196	4255	4389
Brunei	BN	0	0	0	0	0	0
Singapore	SG	205	210	211	219	219	219
Indonesia	ID	1734	1775	1849	1875	1884	1887
Vietnam	VN	161	188	192	380	380	380
Total	-	7218	7456	7264	7946	8145	8270

Unit: megawatt (MW)
Data Source: International Renewable Energy Agency, research of this report

Appendix C Southeast Asian Countries Outlook Data

Table C-1 · Projections for economic and social development

Category	2030	2040
GDP (100 mln USD) (in 2010 prices)	44559	61009
GDP per capita (USD per capita)	6127	7931

Table C-2 · Projections for energy demand under transition scenario

Category	2030	2040
Total primary energy demand (Mtoe)	870	1020
Coal	175	123
Oil	238	218
Natural gas	180	275
Renewable	277	404
Proportion of renewable energy	32%	40%

Table C-3 · Projections for power demand under transition scenario

Category	2030	2040
Total power demand (TWh)	1686	2425
Total installed capacity (MW)	411	630
Coal	85	85
Oil	17	13
Natural gas	130	163
Renewable	179	369

电力规划设计总院简介

　　电力规划设计总院（以下简称"电规总院"）是一所具有近70年发展历程的国家级高端咨询机构，是中央编办登记管理的事业单位，主要面向政府部门、金融机构、能源及电力企业，提供产业政策、发展战略、发展规划、新技术研究以及工程项目的评审、咨询和技术服务，组织开展科研标准化、信息化、国际交流与合作等工作。

　　经国家能源局批准，电规总院设有国家电力规划研究中心、全国电力规划实施监测预警中心、全国新能源消纳监测预警中心、国家能源科技资源中心、电力规划设计标准化管理中心、电力工程造价发布牵头单位、国家能源局研究咨询基地等机构。

　　结合服务于政府、行业的定位和长远发展需要，电规总院提出了"能源智囊、国家智库"的发展愿景和建设"世界一流的能源智库和国际咨询公司"的战略目标。近年来先后完成国家"十三五"、"十四五"能源发展规划、电力发展规划、能源国际合作专项研究和雄安新区能源发展规划等重大规划研究，参与国家与地方能源电力体制改革等重要政策研究，承担能源电力监管的支持性任务，组织落实行业重大系统性工程，深度参与能源国际合作，为建设绿色低碳、安全高效的现代能源体系提供了高质量的智库研究支持。先后入选中国社会科学院"中国核心智库"、中央企业智库联盟、"一带一路"智库合作联盟和中国智库索引来源智库，在上海社科院《中国智库报告》等权威排名中位列前茅。

　　2020年以来，电规总院为响应国家"碳中和、碳达峰"战略目标，服务国家能源主管部门，先后开展了一系列支撑能源绿色低碳转型发展的研究课题，提出2030年、2060年我国能源消费、碳排放的刚性约束和发展目标，提出加快构建以新能源为主体的新型电力系统的发展路径，推行电力系统各环节的数字化升级改造和智慧化调控体系建设。目前，相关研究成果已经被政府有关部门采纳。

　　电规总院是中国电力规划设计行业的"国家队"，拥有一支以全国工程勘察设计大师为学术带头人的高素质专家队伍。近三年，受能源及电力企业、金融机构等的委托，开展了一百多项企业发展规划、大型流域输电规划、节能环保规划等规划研究，承担了多项国家电力示范工程、重点工程的牵头设计工作，完成能源电力工程评审、评估、咨询项目1700余项，发电容量超过5.8亿千瓦，220千伏及以上线路长度超过7.4万公里，变电容量超过4.4亿千伏安，累计节约投资超过300亿元。

　　电规总院与国际能源署、能源宪章、联合国亚太经社会、亚太经合组织等国际组织建立起了良好的合作关系，先后合作设立了国际能源署中国联络办公室、联合国亚太经社会（ESCAP）能源互联互通专家工作组中方秘书处、中国参与APEC能源合作伙伴网络新能源和可再生能源专家组国内对口单位、中国-中东欧国家能源项目对话与合作中心中方秘书处、中欧能源技术创新合作办公室等机构，承担相关工作。先后加入国际能源署洁净煤中心、中日联合委员会，是能源宪章工业咨询委员会亚太地区主席单位。

　　未来，电规总院将以智慧为核心，以创新为动力，努力打造成为世界一流的能源智库和国际咨询公司，与各界同仁携手努力，共同推进全球能源向清洁低碳可持续发展转型。

地　址：北京市西城区安德路 65 号

邮　编：100120

网　址：www.eppei.com

Introduction of China Electric Power Planning and Engineering Institute

The history of the China Electric Power Planning and Engineering Institute (hereinafter referred to as "EPPEI") can be traced back to the Design Management Bureau of the Electric Power Management Administration. Founded in 1954, it was a public institution registered and managed by the State Commission Office of Public Sectors Reform. Since 2011, the EPPEI has been directly managed by China Energy Engineering Group Co., Ltd. In May 2014, China Electric Power Planning & Engineering Institute Co., Ltd. was established, which is the same institution as EPPEI, but with two names.

Orientated towards serving the government, the industry and the needs of long-term development, EPPEI put forward the development vision of "energy think-tank, national think-tank", and started a new journey of building "world-class energy think tank and international consulting company". At the 2020 annual work conference, EPPEI put forward the preliminary idea of accelerating transformation and development in all directions, focusing on four major businesses: planning and research, whole-process engineering consulting, big data and internationalization, and optimized and adjusted the production organization. Planning and research will focus more on the development of the industry, including leading researches in three areas of the 14th Five-Year Plan: energy, power and science and technology. Engineering consulting will strive to transform into whole-process engineering consulting. A big data center has been set up based on the existing platform, and will further provide big data consulting services for the industry. At the same time, EPPEI will actively explore overseas markets to expand international business.

As the "national team" of China's electric power planning and engineering industry, EPPEI has strong technical strengths, comprehensive professional facilities and a team of highly skilled experts. There are a total of 312 employees, including five national engineering survey and design masters, six experts who enjoy special government allowances, 93 professor-level senior engineers and 132 senior engineers. There are 145 doctors and postdocs (almost all of them are Project 985 university graduates), and 112 masters. There are 241 employees in Luosida Company, a subsidiary of EPPEI, including 49 senior engineers or higher-level engineers. There are 31 employees in Nengzhixin Company, another subsidiary of EPPEI, including 14 senior engineers or higher-level engineers.

With the approval of the National Energy Administration, there are a few permanent institutions within EPPEI, such as the National Electric Power Planning and Research Center, the National Electric Power Planning Implementation Monitoring and Early Warning Center, the Electric Power Planning and Engineering Standard Management Center, and the Leading Company of Power Engineering Cost Release. At the same time, there are five secretariats or offices of international energy cooperation organizations established in EPPEI, including the International Energy Agency-China Liaison Office, China-Finland Energy Cooperation Platform, the Chinese Secretariat of China-CEEC Center for Dialogue and Cooperation on Energy Projects, the Chinese Secretariat of the Expert Working Group on Interconnection of UNESCAP Energy Committee, and the "Belt and Road initiative" Energy Partnership Secretariat of the National Energy Administration.

Driven by innovation, EPPEI will focus on intelligent development, strive to become a world-class energy think tank and international consulting company. EPPEI will work together with all circles at home and abroad to jointly promote global energy transition towards clean, low-carbon and sustainable development, and promote the sustainable development of mankind.

Address: No.65 Ande Road, Xicheng District, Beijing

Zip code: 100120

Website: www.eppei.com